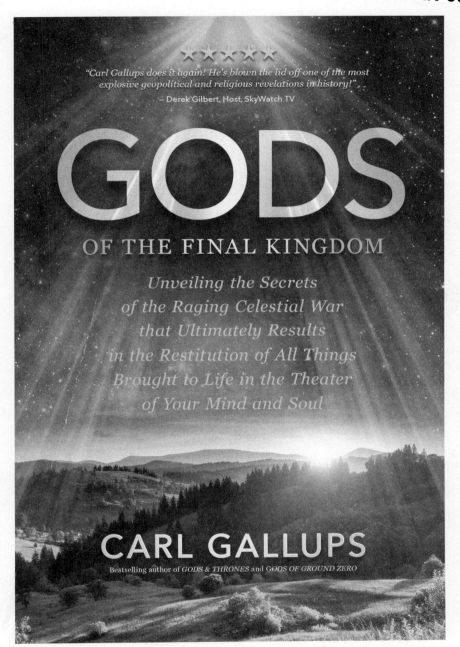

★★★★★

"Carl Gallups does it again! He's blown the lid off one of the most explosive geopolitical and religious revelations in history!"
— Derek Gilbert, Host, SkyWatch TV

GODS
OF THE FINAL KINGDOM

*Unveiling the Secrets
of the Raging Celestial War
that Ultimately Results
in the Restitution of All Things
Brought to Life in the Theater
of Your Mind and Soul*

CARL GALLUPS
Bestselling author of *GODS & THRONES* and *GODS OF GROUND ZERO*

DEFENDER

CRANE, MO

Gods of the Final Kingdom: Unveiling the Secrets of the Raging Celestial War that Ultimately Results in the Restitution of All Things Brought to Life in the Theater of Your Mind and Soul
By Carl Gallups

Defender Crane, MO 65633 ©2016 Defender Publishing
All rights reserved.
Published 2016. Printed in the United States of America.

ISBN: 9781948014250

A CIP catalog record of this book is available from the Library of Congress.

Cover illustration and design by Jeffrey Mardis.

FOR PARKER AND SHELBY

Pam and I pray that your lives, marriage, and ministry will be blessed of the Lord in every imaginable way. Seeing the two of you joined together as husband and wife is an unspeakable joy to our souls.

ACKNOWLEDGMENTS

I want to thank the amazing ministry, editorial, marketing, shipping, and publishing team at Defender Publishing. Because of you, writing has once again become a joy for me. May the Lord bless you for that gift.

I also want to acknowledge my three main research assistants: my amazingly insightful son, Pastor Brandon Gallups, dear friend and ministry partner Messianic Rabbi Zev Porat, and my vitally important Internet and conference ministry partner since 2008, Mike Shoesmith. You men are absolutely invaluable to my life and ministry endeavors. Thank you for your input in helping to shape the final message of this book as well as others.

As always, I am deeply indebted to my precious wife, best friend, and God-ordained chief ministry partner. Without Pam in my life, I could do nothing truly worthwhile and successful. Obviously, the Lord knew that from the beginning—to him goes the final and ultimate glory.

To Randy and Teresa Tinker, Phil and Suzie Carey, Beth Gallups, Paul Gallups, and Dennis and Brenda Walburn—thank you for your love and patience through the many years of our doing life together. I love you.

AUTHOR'S NOTE

This is the third in the "Gods" trilogy. The first two are *Gods and Thrones* and *Gods of Ground Zero*. Each of these books was written so as to not require reading in a specific order. However, if one eventually reads all three, I am convinced that an entirely new world of biblical illumination will be opened to the student of God's Word.

Cited within these books are several scholarly resources, including original language studies, biblical language dictionaries, biblical encyclopedias, biblical historical works, and the commentaries of respected modern scholars. However, readers will also find a healthy dose of commentary that is offered by the classical scholars—those from the 1700s–early 1900s.

I use these classical resources to accomplish a very distinct purpose. I want readers to see for themselves that so many of the gems of biblical truth they're getting ready to discover have been noted for centuries by reputable and still often-quoted biblical experts. I want readers to ask, "If so many others have seen these vital truths for so long, why is it that we rarely, if ever, hear them taught in our modern pulpits, classrooms, Bible colleges, and seminaries?"

I've long been concerned that much of the heart of the Bible's intended communication has been purposely obfuscated down through the ages. And, I am convinced that a great deal of that message-clouding was originally orchestrated at the deepest realms of spiritual darkness. After you've read this book, I believe you'll understand exactly why this is so.

Now…with the turn of the next page, we'll pull back the veil. The contextual revelations of what you will soon discover may surprise you. But, you'll be much richer for having made these discoveries. I promise. I'm honored that you have chosen to take this journey with me. Let's get started!

CONTENTS

There is the kingdom of God and the kingdom of the evil one, and man cannot find or make a third domain; if he is not in the one he is in the other.

—HENRY DONALD MAURICE SPENCE-JONES[1]

PART ONE

The Parting

For in [Jesus Christ] all things were created:
things in heaven and on earth, visible and invisible,
whether thrones or powers or rulers or authorities;
all things have been created through him and for him.
—COLOSSIANS 1:16

1

ENTERTAINING ANGELS

Do not forget to show hospitality to strangers,
for by so doing some people have shown hospitality
to angels without knowing it.
—Hebrews 13:2

I'm going to let you in on a very personal matter.

Over two decades ago—about five years after I had begun my pastoral responsibilities in what was then a small church in the rural Florida panhandle—I had an angelic encounter. It's a true story, but one that I've never before shared outside my church family.

As of this writing, I've not had another "visitation" like it. I didn't ask the Lord to do such a thing for me in the first place, nor will I ask Him to do so in the future. If I understand Scripture correctly, there can be great spiritual vulnerability involved in actively seeking such "appearances" from the unseen realm.[2]

But I am convinced that this particular angelic appearance was genuine. And it came at just the right time in my life. After that encounter, it took me a couple of days to understand the significance of what had actually transpired. When the full force of the moment's reality hit me, it dramatically altered my life and ministry perspective. To this day I still draw tremendous strength from the experience.

This is how the story unfolded…

During the earliest years of the 1990s, our church family had been forced—through no fault of our own—to endure an extremely tough time. The disclosure of the situation eventually exploded throughout the local community. Every imaginable twist and version of the story began to spring forth, like a blooming field of daisies on a spring morning.

Because of everything that had transpired, I faced several important decisions that ultimately resulted in the biblical removal of a person from our church membership. If that had been the only matter we had to deal with, the ordeal would have been much simpler. But, as it turned out, the person's removal was just the tip of the iceberg. I will not unfurl all the sordid details of the matter here, but suffice it to say that it eventually escalated into a gut-wrenching experience, enveloping the lives of many innocent people along the way as well.

As the specifics of the saga became clearer to me, I realized that the future of my fledgling ministry hung in the balance. But I was determined to do the right thing—*the biblical thing*—regardless. I would not "sweep under the carpet" anything about this situation, as I literally had been ordered to do by a key church leader that was behind the fueling of the disruption. When the issue was finally brought before the membership, one man was voted out of the church and another one had already left, in shocking disgrace, of his own accord. However, both had been assured by our church leadership that upon the offer of their genuine repentance, they would be welcomed back into the church with open arms. Neither came back, and neither tried to make amends.

Within days of that vote, the extended families of the two men had departed our fellowship as well. I had hoped it wouldn't come to that, but our leadership fully expected it would. Our church was not very large. The exit of so many people was devastating. But we pressed on. We had followed a godly course—seeking a redemptive, biblical solution.

The community in which our church was located was still very small at the time of the ordeal. In those days, we were living in one of those areas where everyone knew everyone else's business—or at least they wanted to believe they did. So they told their stories accordingly, as if they knew all the intimate details firsthand. Which they didn't. Not even close.

Consequently, the broadcast of "those problems out at *that* church," primarily fueled by the ones who had left in anger, soon flooded the local church society's gossip circles. From there, the "news" spilled over into the rumor mills of several prominent business establishments and even reverberated through the halls of the local courthouse. As the story continued to take on its own grotesque life, the ludicrous chatter only grew worse.

The wave of public defamation began to build like a great tsunami, and it was headed straight for us. It seemed our community had never before seen a local congregation actually remove someone from membership because of abject, unrepented sin.[3]

A stranger in town who might have overheard the random telling of the gossip-riddled story would have thought I had committed some sort of heinous crime by handling the ordeal in a biblically prescribed manner. As a matter of fact, in a vain attempt to shift the focus off of himself, one of the men involved, who subsequently left the church, did in fact accuse me of that very thing. I kid you not.

The entire affair quickly took on a surreal quality. I felt like I needed to look down at a wide-eyed, shaggy little black dog sitting at my feet, gently pat it on the head, and whisper, "I have a feeling we're not in Kansas anymore, Toto."

It was while we were still wading through the immediate aftermath of that hellish scenario…
When it happened.

2

THE VISITATION

Are not all angels ministering spirits sent
to serve those who will inherit salvation?
—HEBREWS 1:14

Only a week or two after handling the upheaval, I was standing in front of the elevators on the first floor of the local hospital. The patient I planned to visit that morning was on the fourth floor. I had just pushed the "Up" button. I watched the lights flickering above the doors, indicating that my ride to the top would soon arrive. My mind was still reeling from the ordeal we had just been through. I found myself constantly questioning every detail of the matter. Had I handled everything exactly as I should have? Satan relentlessly tormented me through my overly critical thought process.

Finally, the door clunked open and I entered. Only one other person was on board—an elderly gentleman with a pleasant countenance. I nodded at him and smiled, expecting him to exit, because I assumed he had just come from one of the upper floors. But he didn't move. Instead, he simply returned the smile and asked, "What floor?"

He was dressed in a nice suit, and along with his perfectly styled, full head of wavy, gray hair and dignified presence, he had an unusually inviting aura about him. I had never seen this man before, but I felt as though there was an instant connection between us. It was an odd and unexplainable sensation—yet he exuded a truly comforting presence. The elevator door closed, and we lurched upward.

I started to introduce myself. However, instead of me leading the way in the typical "elevator chat," he spoke up first.

"You're Pastor Carl Gallups, aren't you?"

I was startled by the matter-of-factness of his opening salutation. "Yes, I am," I replied. "Do we know each other?"

I reached out to shake his hand, wondering how he knew me. I quickly flipped through the pages of my memory. *Nope. I had never seen him before.*

He shook my hand. "No, Pastor Gallups. You wouldn't know me. We've never met." He paused for a few seconds and then added, "But I know all about you." He smiled again, and looked straight ahead, staring at nothing.

I remember thinking: *What an odd thing to say to someone you've just met.* What did he mean that he knew *all about me*? How was that even possible? Don't forget, this happened in the days when we didn't have ubiquitous Internet services and in-depth "people search" capabilities, or social media. Before I could inquire how the man had come to know so much about me, he spoke again. It was as though he was staying one step ahead of my brainwaves.

"The truth is," he said, "I'm a *fellow minister* with you in this community."[4]

Ah! That was it…

Obviously, he was a pastor whom I simply had not yet come across. The community was still a small one. I thought I was at least familiar with almost all the pastors in our county. *But, maybe this pastor was brand new to the area.* I was opening my mouth to ask the gentleman what he "knew" about me when, again, as though he knew my intentions, he spoke up first.

"That horrible ordeal that you recently had to handle at your church…"

I smiled as I thought to myself: *Well, goodness! Everyone in the county knows about that! There's no secret there!*

"You need to know something, Pastor Gallups," he continued, "the Father has sent me to tell you this."

He now had my attention, but the next words that came out of his mouth truly stunned me.

The elevator arrived at the fourth floor. When the door opened, I smacked the "Hold" button. I was mesmerized by this man. What was it that he supposedly knew? And how could he presume to be speaking for "the Father" when, before this day, we had never even crossed paths?

At that moment the "minister" on the elevator revealed a particular piece of information about the ordeal. It was a very private detail—and, the man was *exactingly* specific. What was most shocking, however, was that the info he related was an element of the story that, at the time, only my wife and I were privy to.

Today, a small handful of my trusted church leaders also know about the specific piece of information I'm referring to. If you were to ask them, they would agree: There's no way that this "stranger on the elevator" could have known that specific detail when he was speaking to me. It would have been humanly impossible.

That should have been my first clue.

I was flabbergasted. How could this completely unfamiliar person know the intimate facts about something we had so carefully kept private? Yet this stranger, claiming to be a fellow minister, stood right there before me and, in just a few short sentences, unfurled the substance of the matter right into my lap. Again, as if he instantly knew my thoughts and the fact that I was physically unable to comment at that moment, he continued.

"The Father sent me to comfort you, Pastor Gallups, to tell you that you have handled the situation correctly. He wanted me to tell you to get on with your ministry. *Don't quit.*"

Like a baboon in a zoo cage waiting for another peanut to be tossed my way, I just stood there nodding my head. This conversation was increasingly surreal.

But he wasn't finished. "That horrible thing I told you that I knew about—it was actually an unclean spirit." He then named the spirit. The name he gave it further punctuated the fact that he knew exactly what he was talking about regarding this "unknown" detail.

Then he continued, "That spirit was sent as a ploy. It was meant to ensnare you, to destroy you. Its whole purpose was to have power over you and the church. But you walked right through the ruse. The Father is pleased."

When I look back on that day, I can think of so many questions I should have asked the man on the elevator. I certainly should have pressed for more details. After all, it was he who had invaded *my* life—and privacy—not the other way around.

I should have asked exactly where his church was and how long he had been in the community. I should have inquired as to how he came to possess such intimate and humanly unknowable information about the situation. But it was as though I had become mute. My mind was a swirl of inexpressible thoughts.

As if he was keenly aware of my dilemma, he simply smiled, stretched out his hand to shake mine, and exited the elevator. He turned towards the hall on our right and entered the big double doors of the hospital's rehab unit. I watched him until the doors flapped shut behind him.

I then turned to the left and stopped at the nurses' station to get the room number of my congregant. Armed with the information, I started down the hall, but I was still in a fog. *Who was that guy?*

The greatest shock was yet to come.

3

THE VANISHING

**My mind had trouble accepting what I
knew my eyes had seen and what my ears had heard.**

After visiting with our church member, I went straight back to the nurses' station right across from the elevator bank. The same two nurses who had seen us get off the elevator were still there.

"Excuse me," I said. "Who was the pastor on the elevator with me when we got off? I saw him go into the rehab unit. Has he come out yet? I really need to speak to him."

They looked at me with a strange expression, as though they thought I might be confused.

"There was no one on the elevator with you, Pastor Gallups," one of the women said. "You were the only one who came out."

I couldn't believe what I had just heard. "We were right here when you got off the elevator," she continued.

The other nurse asserted, "And no one has come through here from the rehab unit since then, either."

"I certainly don't remember anyone that fits the description you just gave us," the first nurse agreed.

I was mortified. For a moment, I began to doubt my own sanity. To this day, I don't recall how I explained myself to those poor nurses. All

I know is that I left them, went straight through the doors to the rehab unit, and inquired at that unit's nurses' station at the end of the long hall. I described my "friend" to them, hoping they had seen him. I was told the same thing: "No such person has come into this unit."

I left the hospital in a daze. My mind was having trouble accepting what I knew my eyes had seen and what my ears had heard. I had shaken the man's hand, for goodness' sake! He was real—flesh and blood! Could it be that I had peered behind a cosmic veil—if only for a moment?

I went home and told my wife what had happened. She responded in a matter-of-fact manner. "That's amazing! It sounds to me like you were visited by an angel."

Within days, I related the account to a few trusted pastors and deacons. They knew of no such minister in our community. I have since shared the story, on several appropriate occasions, with my congregation. Over the years, I have urged people to help me with this—even to prove me wrong, if possible. I have asked them to tell me what "minister" in our area that gentleman could have been. I have described him in detail and asked a number of people if they knew of any pastor, anywhere in our region, who even came close to meeting that description. Decades later, there has been no revelation in the matter. I've neither seen nor heard from him again. It is as though he simply vanished. Yet, he was with me on that elevator—and *he knew* what no one else knew.

As you might guess, I'm convinced that I was visited by one of heaven's *sons of God*.[5] These many years later, it would be difficult to persuade me otherwise.

I have come to grips with the clear biblical fact that angels disguised as humans truly move and minister among us at times.[6] Sometimes they are sent for the distinct purpose of undergirding our spiritual strength, especially in times of trouble.

That visitation occurred at a critical point in my ministry, and the message of it was even more significant: *The Father is pleased. You did the right thing. Now, press on. Don't even think about giving up.*

Looking back, I now realize the "word from our Father" was validated with the disclosure of that shocking, but crucial, bit of private evidence. Also, the words the man delivered were perfectly biblical. And, most importantly, the man/angel never even came close to exalting himself. His only concern was to do the will of the "Father" who, he claimed, had sent him—*to me*.

THE LESSON

Here's the main reason I've related the story. The truth is there has not always been a dimensional barrier between humanity and the divine realm.

That ominous veil was erected all the way back in the Garden of Eden.[7] Since that time, Satan has unleashed his hellish rage upon the human race, particularly the true born-again children of God.

We are *the seed of the Seed.*[8] As such, our presence on earth and our obedience to Jesus Christ represent the serpent's ultimate demise. We embody the new kingdom that is on its way. Collectively, we are the earthly deposits of the divine assurance that the glory of heaven will soon appear.

On that day, the dimensional barriers will be dropped and the sky will peel back like the unraveling of a scroll (Isaiah 34:4, Revelation 6:13–14, Mark 13:25–27). The stars will fall from the heavens,[9] and all of creation will be made new (Acts 3:21). It will be the glorious beginning of a new kingdom rule and the very last day of Satan's ignominious reign.

That's who we are!

And even though the enemy of God's people prowls around like a roaring lion, seeking whom he can devour (1 Peter 5:8), the truth is: *Greater is He who is in me than he who is in the world* (1 John 4:4). The Word of God is clear: We have been given the power and authority to overcome Satan—by the word of our testimony and through the blood of the Lamb (Revelation 12:11). And, from time to time, our heavenly Father even sends us angelic help along the way.

Those biblical truths cause my soul to cry out:

Our Father who is enthroned in heaven…*Holy* is your name!
Your kingdom come, your will be done on earth, as it is now—throughout the kingdom of heaven.
For yours, and yours alone, is the *genuine* kingdom…
And *all the power*.
And *all the glory* belong only to you.
Forever, and forever.
Amen.

Now, if you want to know what life is really all about, turn the page—
And, hang on.

PART TWO

The Perversion

These six things doth the LORD hate: yea,
seven are an abomination unto him:
A proud look, a lying tongue, and hands
that shed innocent blood, An heart that deviseth wicked
imaginations, feet that be swift in running to mischief,
A false witness that speaketh lies,
and he that soweth discord among brethren.
—Proverbs 6:16–19, KJV

4

OUT OF THE MIST

About 4,000 BC.
His words were smooth. Hypnotizing. Musical. Irresistible.

When they first laid eyes upon him, he had materialized out of an ethereal mist.

The young couple had heard him in the Garden before they physically saw him. In fact, they thought they had even *felt* his presence. It was as if he had been there among them—even before he was.[10]

As his form became increasingly visible, his swaggering saunter captivated them. It was as though he *floated* rather than walked. His slightly veiled visage shimmered as he moved, bathed in an emerald-colored, translucent light. How could a creature be so breathtaking—so stunningly lovely in countenance and deportment? His bodily movements were dancelike as he approached them. Other than the *Creator* Himself, nothing they had ever seen was as majestic as this one.[11]

They knew he had been appointed by the throne of Elohim to be the guardian of earth's newly created domain.[12] He was one of the holy cherubim. He was the *Royal Regent* of the Garden of Eden—that's what Creator had called him.[13]

Earth's first couple truly wanted to feel honored that this regal being from the divine council of Elohim[14] had come to them. But, they had also been cautioned about him. Apparently, something was beginning to go askew in paradise. From what they had gathered, it was suspected that this particular "mighty one"[15] was the author of the recent cloud of uneasiness that had previously been so foreign to the usual atmosphere of Eden.

Yet, here he was. Gigantic—and utterly beautiful. Standing right before them. What were they to make of this grand entrance?

Then, he spoke.

THE ENCOUNTER

"Well, well... *here* you are!" A childlike innocence engulfed his countenance. His voice was deep, rich, and sodden with condescension.

"I was just taking a stroll," he continued, "roaming to and fro through this magnificent domain of mine—" He paused midsentence, spreading his arms open wide as if everything they now beheld truly belonged to him. The morning mist swirled about his head as he spoke, causing the heavy droplets to sparkle like a luminous crown of diamonds.

He tilted his head to one side as though he just now noticed a great curiosity. His eyes scanned their forms from head to foot.

"*My*, the two of you certainly *are* very lovely! I don't think I ever realized just how exceedingly exquisite you are." His words were smooth. Hypnotizing. Musical. Irresistible. The lustful probing of his eyes continued to survey their figures.

The couple froze in their tracks. Eve blushed in the flattery of the moment. Adam leaned in and whispered in her ear.

"Eve!" he cautioned, "We were warned not to have anything to do with him. *You know this!* In fact, we were specifically instructed by Creator not to partake of the fruit this one would offer to us. We are not to even touch it."[16]

"I know that," she snapped. "But he hasn't *offered* anything yet. Let's hear him out. After all, he *is* Elohim's Royal Regent. In that regard alone, he's certainly deserving of our utmost respect. He's also worthy of our fullest attention—don't you think?"

Adam eased his head away from her ear and stepped back, still trying to size up the gravity of the meeting. *Why was Eve so mesmerized?*

There was no doubt about it: she was flatly enthralled by the Mighty One. She would later protest that she had been unfairly *beguiled* by him. But for now, she refocused her gaze, resting it upon this figure of abject beauty.

"Come now," the serpent hissed. "I'm so anxiou*ss* to introduce you to a multitude of amazing thing*sss*. Also—and please forgive me for not mentioning this before—I have gloriou*ss* knowledge at my disposal, information you have never imagined. Why, I *could* offer you…"

There it was! He was going to lay out a scheme, just as they had been warned that he might do.

With an uplifted hand, Eve interrupted him. "We are *not* to eat of the fruit you propose to us!" She seemed to have stepped up to a sober moment of consideration. She gathered her courage and continued.

"In fact, we are not to even *touch* whatever it is that you might offer. This is what Creator has commanded."

There. She said it. Now, in her nervousness, she struggled to catch her breath. Eve dropped her head as soon as she uttered the words. She was embarrassed that she had spoken so hastily. Had she done the right thing? *Why didn't Adam defend her position?* Instead, he just stood there like a lifeless lump of clay.

THE SEDUCTION

The keeper of the Garden gently knelt before them, as if Adam and Eve were his own dear children. They remained standing some distance from him, still hesitant to approach.

Satan enticed, "Come now. Come just a little clossser."

When he saw they were still reluctant to move closer to him, he continued. "Sssurely, Elohim did not sssay all of that? Why would He utter such a charge in the first place? Think about it for a moment… My dear little onesss, you don't even know what I am offering." Eve felt her face growing hot with embarrassment.

"Yes. *It certainly was* what He told us." Her voice trembled as she defended her memory of Elohim's prior conversation with them. She spoke much softer now. As she responded, she could not look directly at him.

Maybe…*was it possible?* Perhaps she had misunderstood Elohim as she and Adam had walked with Creator in the Garden a few evenings back? What if she was falsely accusing the Mighty One?

She shot an accusing glance at Adam, signaling her frustrated thoughts: *Why have you not yet said a word?*

"Well then, if Elohim really said *that*—" the Mighty One snapped, "then He *lied!* That's all there is to it!"

Eve gasped. Did she truly hear those words coming from this being's lips? Did he just call Elohim a liar?

None of this made sense. Her thoughts began to swirl with confusion. This was a fruit she had never before tasted.

"As a matter of fact," the serpent continued, "The problem is thisss. He knows that in the day you follow me, you'll become like usss—just like the angelic council of the Most High. You'll even be like Elohim Himssself! And…it appearsss He is purposely keeping thisss delightful morsel of enjoyment from you."

The mesmerizing cherub continued his appeal. "That certainly doesn't seem fair—does it? Don't you see how perfect this is, how beautiful? Behold how lovely…how sssweet to the tassste."

Eve beheld the object of temptation. It *was* beautiful, and alluring. He had at least spoken truth in that regard.

Before she could respond to his question, he spoke again. "What harm could come from only partaking in just one little tiny nibble? Ponder it for a moment! You'll soon come to understand that I *am* correct in this*s* matter! *You'll sssee…*"

Eve took a step closer. Adam followed.

The hook was embedded.

5

THE DESCENT

**The music of his presence softly
lit up the atmosphere around them.**

Eve, and Adam—the still-silent lump of clay—eased a few paces closer to the Mighty One. The trio stood just a few feet from each other.

"But…*but*," Eve whimpered as she approached, "Elohim also said… that if we did this…we would surely invite death upon ourselves."

"In fact," she protested, "He made it very clear that we would be separated from Him, and from His love, forever."

Eve wiped a tear that drained from her eye and trickled down her cheek. Here was something else she had never tasted: *sorrow.* It was bitter, and salty—and it caused an odd and dreary heaviness deep within her chest.

"I'll let you in on a little *sssecret*," the creature hissed. "You surely shall *not* die! I am here to straighten all of that out. *Trust me!* There's *sss*imply been a huge misunderstanding… Besides*ss*, it's utterly impossible for you to die! Have a little faith. I wouldn't *lie* to you …"

The distressed couple stepped back a few feet.

Confusion. Sorrow. Fear. From where were these emotions flowing? What was this sorcery that danced in the halls of their minds and souls?

As they cautiously backed away, the serpent could see that he might be losing them.

"No! Don't leave yet. I assure you…*no, no, no*…I *promise* you—" the serpent pleaded. He held up both of his hands as a sign of sincerity, "if you'll only eat this*s* fruit with me, all will be well. You'll *sssee…*"

How utterly gorgeous he was!

"It's such an effortless thing. And I assure you…there are no consequences whatsoever! What do you have to lose? If you don't like it, nothing is lost. I'll never ask you to do it again. I guarantee it…just one time. It won't hurt a thing." They stopped their retreat. The proposition sounded so reasonable.

"Such a *small* thing. Don't you think? Come now." Eve's expression changed. She was on the verge of succumbing. The Mighty One could see her beginning to melt to his will. It was also apparent that Adam would go wherever Eve led.

"And just think…you'll be *just like* the rest of us, once it's done!"

Here was that wonderful sensation again. It was magical, mystical… his words felt so right, so warm, so inviting.

THE FATAL STEP

How could something that felt so good be such a bad thing? Eve reasoned. *Surely, it couldn't! Surely this Mighty One was telling them the truth! Elohim had just made a simple mistake. This was all a big misunderstanding. Maybe it was she who had misunderstood from the beginning. In any case, the Mighty One promised he could fix everything…*

The serpent smiled. The ambient music of his presence softly occupied the atmosphere around them. Eve smiled back. Adam still had not registered a single spoken complaint, a reaction he would regret for the rest of his life.

So, with Eve leading the way, they once again moved closer to the *beguiling one.* As they did, they stretched out their hands like little children—and willingly took his. A surge of euphoric energy swept through them as they touched him. They were transfixed by his beauty. The Mighty One smiled. He had thoroughly charmed them.[17]

And so they ate.

Beautiful to the eye. Sweet to the taste.

Venomous to their souls.

They had walked right into his outstretched arms. It had taken much more effort than he had estimated to bring the thing to fruition. But, alas, they had eventually fallen for his scam. He prided himself in being such a tenacious hunter.

When the deed was done, Nachash[18] screeched out a fiendish cackle that echoed throughout the Garden, bouncing off every tree and boulder. The startled and horrified young couple bolted from his presence.

He watched them scamper off into the woods, frantically covering their nakedness as they ran. Now they knew...*they had been deceived.* But, it was too late—way too late. He sighed in ecstasy as he bathed himself in the exhilaration of the moment.

In one thrashing sweep, Satan had pulled off each of the six things Yahweh hates.[19] He had been successful in coaxing the first humans into crushing Elohim's heart. He congratulated himself.

He didn't relax, however. His plan was coming together nicely, but he still had a complex agenda to execute if he was to finally have his own kingdom. However, of one monumental thing he was certain: This day would, itself, completely rearrange the whole of Yahweh's creation.

Soon, Satan mused, *I will rule over the whole thing! It will all be mine!*[20]

The coup had begun. This is precisely what he had planned from the moment he first laid eyes upon the earthly work of Elohim's hand, when he first beheld the worshipful reaction of the rest of the divine realm. But now, Creator would have to turn His back on this newly crafted "paradise." After all, it had been thoroughly corrupted—*perverted,* and so perfectly and irreversibly profaned.[21]

Satan knew Yahweh's holiness would not abide what happened here this day. He would have to drop the veil on the whole thing. The result would be two distinctly different dimensions of reality[22]—a complete separation from the throne of God. Certainly, there would now be a cosmic clash of dimensional empires. But whatever else happened, he, Nachash, would be the ruler of *this* one.

Now... Everything about this brand-new creation... *Was. Finally. His.*

This was the moment he had longed for. This was his victory—or, so he thought.

Heaven's throne had yet to speak in the matter.

6

INTERVENTION

But first, there would be a purging.

The defilement process had begun.

The hideous corruption of Yahweh's paradise brought about through the darkness of Satan's repulsive lusts would continue through the ages with blinding indignation. The adversary was determined to drive a deepening wedge between humanity and Creator. He had come to kill, steal, and destroy. Thus far, he had been thoroughly successful in all three of his psychopathic aspirations.

But these were only the opening salvos of his diabolical strategy. The ultimate goal was to capture the throne of God itself. He would stop at nothing less. He *would be* worshipped among the humans, as well as among the divine ones. Every single one of them, one day, would bow to him.[23]

However, there was one hugely glaring obstacle. Yahweh had threatened him. In truth, He had more than just threatened. Yahweh had flatly vowed to destroy him for what he had done in the Garden. That declaration of judgment was delivered in the form of a complex riddle: *From the womb of a woman will come forth the Seed that will crush your head.*[24]

Those were the words Yahweh had used. But what, exactly, did He mean by them? It was clear that somehow a child would be born—in the *human way*. A human male-child that would destroy his freshly usurped kingdom? But how could that be—a mere child? Really? A *mortal* child at that? Impossible! Utterly ridiculous!

Where would this child come from; where would he be born? And *to whom* would he be born? *When* would this absurd idea of a cosmic dragon-slayer come into being? And, most important, *exactly how* would this miraculous and vain imagination defeat *his* divine power, much less utterly destroy him?

It was at the speaking of those threatening words that Satan *knew*. If his kingdom was to prosper—and ultimately be victorious—this mysterious child, heaven's bizarre plan of redemption, must be defeated. But there was still so much missing information.

A FALLEN WORLD

By the time several generations of humanity had begun to fruitfully populate the newly created planet, the flesh of both humans and animals had grown increasingly corrupt. Satan, and his allies from the rebellious angelic realm had seen to it. Gruesome aberrations among all living things had begun to manifest.[25] The indescribable beauty the planet had once enjoyed rapidly degenerated. Satan attempted to recreate as much of the planet as possible, but this time, the design was in his own twisted image.

Violence now engulfed the debased animal kingdom, as well as the altered human realm. Terror and dread had become the defining characteristics of daily existence. Gigantic, vicious men with deepening allegiance to the evil one brought their unspeakable horrors to every human encampment. An unholy alliance formed between the bulk of humanity and the cloaked demonic realm, those fallen ones who were masquerading as messengers of light among the populace of earth.[26]

But Yahweh also had a plan, a strategy that was unknown to the evil one. It had been in place since before the foundation of the universe itself. There was no doubt that Yahweh's tactic would succeed. He knew, from the moment He first created the now-fallen cherub, that every bit of this would eventually take place.[27]

First, there must be a purging. Everything would have to be destroyed—especially anything that had the corrupted breath of life in it, both man and beast.

The reset button would be pushed from heaven's throne itself. Elohim had declared it and the divine council had aligned themselves with the ominous decree. They would be the celestial witnesses of Elohim's authority and of His holy righteousness—both now and in the final judgment.[28]

However, this particular cosmic cleansing process had not been designed to immediately "correct" the situation. Rather, it would serve as a heavenly pattern of the ultimate judgment that was yet to come.[29]

There would still be scores of new human generations to live upon the earth. In the midst of those generations, kingdoms would rise and fall, and Jerusalem would ultimately be established as the very center of the nations, a testament to the coming restitution of the Garden of Eden itself. Not only would it be the epicenter of the earth, but in the very last days, it would once again become the focal point of the nations and their diabolical, geopolitical wrangling against heaven's throne.[30]

THE HARBINGER

To be sure, this primordial, global deluge would forever stand as an eternal harbinger to the future nations. It would be a sign of Elohim's overwhelming power and righteous indignation. But for now, at the decree of Yahweh, the cosmic "weeding out" process would commence. And now...the angels of heaven and the peoples of the earth, along with their kings, would be forced to choose sides. One kingdom, or the other. Each to his own desire.

This initial cleansing would be accomplished with water. Lots of water. Ultimately, though, it would be completed with blood. Holy blood. Offered by a very specific donor.

But not yet.

There was still the matter of a certain trap that must first be baited.

PART THREE

The Plan

*Oh, the depth of the riches of the wisdom and knowledge of God!
How unsearchable his judgments, and his paths beyond tracing
out! Who has known the mind of the Lord? Or who has been his
counselor? Who has ever given to God, that God should repay
them? For from him and through him and for him are all things.
To him be the glory forever! Amen.*

—ROMANS 11:33–36

7

THE IMPORTANT ONES

AD 30
Approximately 2,500 years after the Flood
During the time of the Roman Empire
Emperor: Tiberius Caesar Augustus
(known as *The Divine Son of God*)[31]
John the Baptist was at the Jordan River

Satan is now the one being hunted.

He doesn't know it yet. He only suspects it. But he'll soon figure it out.

When he finally realizes the divine safari—emanating from the throne of Elohim—is aimed squarely at the eventual toppling of his stolen kingdom, it will infuriate him. His suffocating conceit will not abide such a scheme. So, he will unleash his vicious counterattack, and it will be drenched in ravenous fury.

Satan has ruled as the *prince of the earth*[32] for thousands of years. He believes it is his rightful domain. In his perverted arrogance, he is certain his ownership came to him through a perfectly valid "legal" claim.

A number of the Roman Empire's governmental officials, including the emperor himself, were unwittingly acting as Satan's pawns. So were most among the ranks of the Jewish religious elite. Yes…this was *his* exclusive principality, and nobody in heaven or on earth would take it from him. Thus, Satan was willing to launch every power available to him in an attempt to thwart heaven's strategy to wrest the kingdom from his diabolical grip.

The saga unveils in the Judean countryside, down by the Jordan River. This is where the prince of darkness, as he observes the gathering throngs, first imagined that a grand scheme is finally taking a physical form. The crowds were daily rushing to the river's edge to listen to a bellowing preacher proclaim that God's kingdom was on its way. He assured the people that their "savior" would soon appear. This was not good news.

Satan furiously snatched at the strings of his earthly puppets. He summoned the power of the thrones that he and his demonic hordes manipulated. His mortal marionettes were all too eager to play their parts...to do his bidding. The cup of demonic power from which they drank was exquisitely intoxicating. So, they liberally imbibed—bathing in its glory.

This is how it began...

THE VISITORS

John shielded his eyes from the blazing Judean sun as he focused upon the advancing confederation of gloomy looking religious authorities.

"The Baptizer" had just lifted another convert out of the cool Jordan waters. Dozens stood in single file, in the waist-deep water. Thousands more lined the shores.

He knew the approaching black-robed men were powerful emissaries. They had been sent by the prestigious Sanhedrin Council, headquartered in Jerusalem. John had been warned of their imminent arrival. The word of his recent ministry endeavor had apparently spread faster than he had imagined.

But who could have missed this envoy? Adorned in their flowing orthodox garb and long phylacteries, their station in society was unmistakable. John wondered if they had even a clue as to who their real master was—the prince of this world.

In truth, John thought, they were a ridiculous-looking, swaggering gaggle of self-important men. They prodded, demanded, and pushed their way through the throngs with their usual air of entitlement and pomposity. If the scene had not been immersed in so much veiled evil, it would have been downright comical.

However, most of the people feared them. Knowing this, the approaching *important ones*, engrossed in the pageantry of their own grand entrance, basked in the crowd's obvious awe. Not only did these men hold places of prominence presiding over the religious and social life of the Jews, but they also represented the most powerful indigenous religious body—the Sanhedrin Council, one that held weighty connections to the local Roman governing authorities. Within the confines of proper procedure, the Sanhedrin, made up of seventy elite Pharisees and Sadducees, could even arrange for one of their own—a fellow Jew—to be crucified.

Seen from above, from the view of the *birds of the air,* this line of men, dressed all in black, slithering though the crowd, took the form of a viper. They appeared to be slipping and winding their way toward an unseen prey. The uneasy crowd deferred to them, almost genuflecting as the powerful men glided through their midst. Soon, the brood stood on the sandy shore of the Jordan, looking like a flock of vultures roosting in the top branches of a rotting, leafless, lifeless tree.

WHAT SHALL WE DO?

The Baptizer, resembling a rugged prophetic figure right out of ancient times, had been in the area of the Jordon River for several weeks. He would remain here for months. Every day, thousands had flowed out of the surrounding countryside to take part in the messianic fervor that had recently saturated the land. The crowds continued to move into the waters of baptism. This is why they had come.

Some in the multitude asked, "What should we do then? Since we are here to repent, where should we begin?"[33]

John answered them, "Anyone who has two shirts should share with the one who has none, and anyone who has food should do the same. Love each other. Care for each other's needs."

To the surprise of the masses, even a number of tax collectors came to be baptized by John. "Teacher," they asked, "what should *we* do?"

"Don't collect any more than you are required," John replied. "Treat the people fairly—as you would want your own family to be treated."

There were also a few Roman soldiers who came for baptism. They asked John, "And what should *we* do?"

He answered their query, "Quit extorting money from the people. You know in your hearts this practice is evil. And don't level false accusations against the people—be content with your pay. Serve your masters with dignity, and treat the populace with equity. These are the things that bring honor to the Lord and to the glory of His coming kingdom."

The crowds agreed among themselves. Never had they heard a preacher speak such bold and lovely words. However, sometimes he would also broadcast his blistering invectives with a divine authority that commanded rapt attention. So they listened to every word that fell from his lips. What would this preacher from the Judean wilderness say next?

This is why the religious authorities and their governmental counterparts were here. Because the people, thousands of them, were seriously considering everything this man preached.

Sanhedrin emissaries badly needed legal ammunition against this dangerous desert preacher. His zealous religious movement had the potential of going awry—quickly.

What they needed was evidence of sedition.

They would soon get the proof they wanted.

THE SONS OF SATAN

See how the people love him! This man must be stopped!

What they so desperately desired, John served up to them on a silver platter.

Satan's spiritually stupefied ambassadors, the federation of Sanhedrin moles, grew increasingly incensed as John preached what they considered to be unqualified heresy. They were certain their Jerusalem overlords, once the report was delivered, would agree with this assessment. *This man must be brought to account.*

Looking directly at the black-robed infiltrators, the Baptizer's booming voice split the air. *"You brood of vipers!"*

John's brow wrinkled in righteous anger as he spoke. He knew that by identifying these men as children of Satan,[34] he would be stirring an already bubbling vitriolic stew.

But one of John's missions was to "flush out" the great hunter of men's souls. Satan was the prime cosmic target of this operation, and the apostle had just fired the first shot into the demonic jungle—straight into another dimension.

But John's other goal—by far the most important—was to introduce the *One* for whom the people had been waiting...the long-expected

Messiah. For now, however, that indulgence would have to wait. There was a little matter of business that needed John's attention.

EXPOSED

John singled out the approaching rulers of the Jews by punctuating the air with the stabbing point of his index finger. With this caustic accusation, the approaching men stopped dead in their tracks.

John continued his tirade as he leveled his arm in their direction. "*You!* You hypocritical offspring of everything that is evil! Who warned *you* to flee from the coming wrath?"

They were appalled. Who was this loathsome beast—this lowly and disgusting itinerant evangelist—to point them out with his bony finger and bellow at them with such blasphemous indignity? Did he not understand who they were? Who they represented? Their far-reaching and fearsome power?

As if its presence had been orchestrated for this very moment, a circling hawk screeched overhead. A few in the crowd veiled their eyes from the sun and looked at the belligerent bird, gliding in the heavens just above them.

"You must produce fruit in keeping with repentance!" John shouted at them again. "And do not even *begin* to say to yourselves, 'We have Abraham as our father.' For I tell you that out of these stones God can raise up children for Abraham. The ax is already at the root of the trees, and every tree that does not produce good fruit will be cut down and thrown into the fire."

He stopped for a moment, taking a much-needed breath. He wiped the sweat from his brow. The dogs following the crowd were barking—some even howling—at the sharp report of John's commanding voice as he uttered words that seemed to crack open the atmosphere of the surrounding countryside.

The slight shivering of his body betrayed his raw spiritual emotions. It was as though the prophet could see something the crowd could not. It was as if he were peering into another realm.

Just then, a murmured curiosity rippled through the crowd. *Why had John so pointedly connected these religious leaders with the Garden of Eden?*[35]

What did the Baptizer see in these approaching men? His accusations were that they were somehow directly associated with the Garden serpent. John further identified these men as "bad trees" producing "bad fruit." With that comparison, the Eden imagery quickly became embarrassingly obvious, perhaps even hazardous to so boldly announce. These were, after all, the religious elite. A large number of the people still revered them. How could John have dared to address them in this obscene manner?

But there it was for all to hear. After the initial collective gasp of the crowd, the silence that followed was stifling. In the hush of the moment, all that was heard by the human ear were the screeching hawk, a few muffled murmurs in the crowd, the breeze moaning across their eardrums, and the tinkling, trickling flow of the Jordan River.

THE INQUISITION

As soon as the fearsome prophet finished delivering his invective, the consortium of important men drew even closer to the water's edge, seething with indignation as they came: *This desert preacher is clearly out of control. His crowds are enormous. His words are caustic...and look! See how the people love him! This man has to be stopped! He has to be silenced—now!*

One of the Levites in the group asked the next question: "So, you are claiming to be *Messiah*?"

In reality, the query was an accusation. Just one slip in John's next words could give them what they needed to bring charges against him. They held their breath and awaited his reply.

John answered emotionlessly. His penetrating gaze never wavered. "I am *not* the Messiah," he retorted. Their countenances collectively darkened in disappointment.

"What then? *Who* are you? Are you, perhaps, claiming to be the prophet Elijah?" one of them prodded.

Anything, one careless word, is all it would take. If John would just give them *something*, then they could begin the process of filing charges of blasphemy. But John wasn't playing their game.

"No."

The dry, monosyllabic reply was John's only answer. If they had not broken the silence, it appeared doubtful that John would have ever uttered another word to them.

In growing exasperation, they plied forward. "*What then*? Do you claim to be a prophet—*any prophet*?"

"No."

The circling hawk, riding the afternoon updraft, continued his relentless screeching. Almost annoyingly so. It was as though that lofty bird had purposely lent its voice to the harassment process going on just below him.

"Well then! Who *are* you? Give us an answer so that we may take it back to those who sent us! What do you say about yourself? In the name and authority of the Sanhedrin *we demand a reply*! Surely you have a title? Surely you have a mission?"

John countered with the words of the prophet Isaiah: "I am the voice of one calling in the wilderness, 'Make straight the way for the Lord.'"[36]

Now they were getting somewhere! The spokesperson asked, "Why then do you baptize if you are not the Messiah?" His words possessed a syrupy intonation.

"I baptize with water," John responded, "but *among* you stands one you do not know. He is the one who comes after me, the straps of whose sandals I am not worthy to untie."

Several among the "important ones" snapped their heads around, apparently expecting to gaze upon this "one among them" to whom John had just referred. Instead, they only saw a crowd of thousands of faceless, nameless people as far as the eye could see.

Yet, standing only a few feet away, unbeknownst to them, was the *One.* He had, just an hour ago, arrived from Galilee and stood at the water's edge. He gazed into their faces—even into their souls. They had no idea. They could not see past their own delusional self-importance.

But this Yeshua,[37] from Nazareth, did not stand out in the crowd. He had no features that would have drawn anyone there that day to believe He was the portentous one about whom John had spoken.[38] As Yeshua looked John's way and winked, a faint grin formed at the corners of the Galilean's mouth. The divine plan was beginning to come together.

John acknowledged the exchange with a gentle nod of his head, then turned and continued baptizing. He never again looked back at the Sanhedrin's submissive entourage. To him, it was as if they no longer existed. The throngs followed John's lead and pushed closer to the river's edge, ignoring the gaggle of black robes. They had now become irrelevant. And they seethed in the moment of their rude rejection.

The enraged "important ones" spun on their heels and glided back through the crowd. The serpent-like train headed back to Jerusalem to report what they had seen and heard.

This was going to be a long day.

But the coming days would grow even longer...*much longer.*

9

THE PLAIN ONE

**His vocal cords quivered out an answer,
"I heard… I saw…. *I believe* …."**

The next day John returned to the Jordan Valley.

The multitudes had also returned. Many of them had spent the night along the river's shore. Additional caravans had arrived from far-off communities after many days of travel.

Yeshua was there as well—among the people, yet still unnoticed.

When John entered the waters, the throng began to form a line, eager to partake of this growing national movement of repentance. It had been the historical teaching of the rabbis that the Jewish people, *en masse*, had to repent and express a sincere desire for their long-awaited Messiah to appear—only then would He finally come. They were hoping John's powerful urging of God's people to wholeheartedly participate in the nationalistic fervor would accomplish that goal.[39]

Here is where a great cosmic irony would soon take place. Their Messiah *would* truly appear to them—on this very day, in this very spot. John would even single Him out with an unmistakable pronouncement of His heaven-anointed messiahship. While some would be excited by at least the possibility of the moment, most would not even come close to receiving John's shocking disclosure in its fullest sense.

This man standing in their midst simply did not look like their notion of the true Messiah. What they desperately wanted was immediate deliverance from Rome's grip. They longed for the nation of Israel to burst back into life, to its former glory, and they needed it to happen now. It would be absolutely necessary, so they thought, for this miracle to come about wrapped in the visage of a militaristic, authoritative personality.

So, how could this *plain one* from Galilee be the leader to bring forth these long-awaited dreams? Many began to think they had come to these waters for nothing. Perhaps John really had lost his mind, exactly as the religious leaders were claiming.

LIFTING THE VEIL

Yeshua held out His hand and motioned to John, indicating He would be joining John in the baptismal waters. When He drew near, John leaned in to His ear, "What are *you* doing in these waters? I need to be baptized by you! The people must understand that *you* are the One—not me! You have no need to repent!"

Yeshua grinned. "John. I *must* do this," He said. "This act will fulfill all righteousness. From this moment forward, those who follow me must become one with me, as I am one with my Father. They must identify with me in this holy ritual. Today, I will lead the way, like a bride and groom exchanging rings at the altar of marriage. This must be done, John. Let it be so—*now*."

With a broad smile, Jesus nodded toward two young men standing close to the shore. "A couple of my true disciples are already here! They just don't know it yet… But they will follow me *to the end*. What we will do today is for them as well."[40]

With the Baptizer's gentle guidance, Yeshua went under. Jordan's waters glistened, then softly rippled around His submerged body. For

John, it was as if the moment had unfolded in slow motion and on a separate plane of reality.

The throngs suddenly faded into a mere blur in the background. The conglomerated sounds of life: men…women…children…dogs… the hawk…the water…all of it…were immediately blocked from John's ears.

Now, like the prophets of old, the Baptizer was transported to another place, yet he physically remained where he was—in the eyes of the crowd that surrounded him. A portal to heaven's seat had opened upon him, and enveloped him. John heard the voice of seven thunders pealing forth from heaven's throne: "This is my beloved Son. With Him I am very pleased!"[41]

John would later describe the scene:

I heard the voice! It was as clear to my ears as my own voice. It was as real as any man standing beside me. It was thunderous, and yet it was filled with an unearthly and indescribable loving softness. I could not see the actual face of the One upon the throne. His countenance was bathed in an unearthly glory. It was the most luxurious light I had ever beheld!

And, I recognized that voice as the very One who had spoken to me months ago telling me this day would soon arrive. He had assured me then that I would soon see and hear His very own confirmation upon the Messiah, the One that He Himself would bring to me at the Jordan.

It was at the booming of that voice at the river that I also saw the appearance of another bodily form. A holy countenance. He emanated from the throne of Yahweh and enveloped Yeshua, filling Him, covering Him.

The whole process was as though a gentle dove had landed upon His head. The event was beyond earthly description. That's when I knew…that's how I knew *that I knew*! This was Him!"[42]

Suddenly, John was snapped back to the present reality. From just beneath the water's surface, Yeshua's face peered into John's—in slow motion at first.

When His face finally broke through the water, everything returned to normal. The regular speed of earthly existence returned. The sound of the people, the barking dogs. The birds. The breeze. The rippling water. It was as if everything had always been at this normal pace of life.

Yeshua smiled. "*Now* do you believe, John? Did you *see* it, John? Did you *hear* it?"

John could barely breath, much less speak. His vocal cords quivered out an answer, "I heard…I saw…and yes … *I believe.*"

"That is why I told you, John, this *had* to be done. It had to be done for *them*," He nodded toward the throngs behind him. "And, just as importantly, it had to be done for *you*—for confirmation. *It had to be done for you.*"

Yeshua grasped John's shoulders and peered into his teary eyes. "You truly did hear from Yahweh! You *were* chosen for this very moment, John. From this day forward, you will minister with an unction you have never imagined. All of history will remember what you have done here this day, and they will tell of this moment and your faithfulness, forever."

John nodded and smiled. Now he understood. Immersed in a boldness he had never felt before, he cried out again—but this time with tears streaming down his face….

"*Behold!*" The voice cracked open the surrounding atmosphere and pierced the soul of the gathered crowd.

Not a person spoke. They simply waited, and watched. *What would John say next?*

On this otherwise serene morning, his thundering voice shattered the silence.

"*Behold! This* is the Lamb of God, who takes away the sin of the world! *This* is the One of whom I spoke! This is the One you have been waiting for! This is the One the Father has revealed to me! I baptized you with water. But *I assure you…* He will baptize you henceforth with fire—and the Holy Spirit!"[43]

Yeshua's eyes stayed fixed on John's as the Baptizer instructed the crowd. When John had finished, Yeshua reached out to him, and pulled him close. He whispered in his ear, "Well done, John. *Well done!* You are a good and faithful servant."

Yeshua turned to walk out of the water. He took a few steps, then stopped. He turned back to look upon the Baptizer, His all-knowing eyes piercing John's soul.

"Now, it begins, John! The enemy is at the gate, and he's there for both of us. He prowls around like a roaring lion, seeking whom he may devour. *Be strong.* Be alert."

John affirmed with another slight nod and a resolute sparkle in his eyes. "Now, it begins," he repeated.

With those last words, the "plain one" eased out of the water and once again melted into the crowd, largely unnoticed. For now.

He had someplace else He needed to be.

PART FOUR

The Plundering

*How can anyone enter a strong man's house
and carry off his possessions unless he first
ties up the strong man?
Then he can plunder his house.*
—MATTHEW 12:29

10

THE HUNTER

Judgment had arrived. In person.

He was seated upon a rock ledge.

He surveyed the gloomy Judean badlands stretched endlessly before Him. The atmosphere was laden with the presence of evil. Another ledge above Him formed an overhang—a roof, as it were, a shelter from the sweltering midday sun. This would be His base of operation for one month…and ten days.

Yeshua smiled. He remembered the look on John's face only a few days back when He first came up out of the Jordan's waters. It was a moment He would always cherish. That rugged man, wearing rough camel's-hair clothes over his bulging muscular frame, displayed the innocent look of a child's wonderstruck gaze. It was as if John, from atop a soaring mountain peak, had peered for the very first time upon the earth below.

Then Yeshua's thoughts turned more somber. *Dearest John. How I pray for you, that you will have an unwavering strength that will equip you for this mission that you must now endure…for my sake.*

Desolate. Treacherous. Deceptive. Isolated. The scant shrubbery was, at places, joined together like an interlocking and delicately green necklace. However, throughout most of the land, there was not a single green thing to be seen. The few diminutive "trees" that occasionally dotted the landscape wore the shape of the wind that had pummeled them over the ages. Other than those distinctive features, this place was brown and barren and seemingly lifeless. This was going to be a hellish ordeal. But that's why He was here in this fallen dimension. And it was why He had come to this specific place.[44]

This part of the plan *had* to be successfully completed before Yeshua could proceed with anything else. He had arrived here for the purpose of plundering Satan's house. He had come to commence the process of binding up the strong man.[45]

Yeshua was taking the first blow directly to Nachash, right at the front door of his demonic lair. A wilderness, teeming with wild animals. *How fitting.*[46] He chuckled at the thought of it. And He waited. He stirred the ground with a small stick as His eyes scanned the scene before Him.

The vultures always showed up first…

They scrutinized everything that stirred in the desert wilderness below. They floated on the currents of warm air rising from the blistering hot sand. They waited for things—*anything*—to die.

There would be forty days of this dreadful battle. No food. Scant water. No human companionship. No delivery of emergency supplies. Sizzling heat by day, frigid air by night—every single day. At least 960 grueling hours lay ahead.

THE DECREE

But this is how it had to be done. It could be accomplished in no other fashion.

The number *forty* had often been used, since the primordial times, as a divine signal of judgment, or testing. The enemy would know this all too well.

For forty days, the flood waters of Noah's day had deluged the earth.

Moses had fasted forty days on Sinai, only to descend and find the people of God dancing around the image of a golden calf.

For forty days the spies sent out by Moses had wandered into the Land of Promise only to return with a bad report. Yahweh's punishment upon them? One year of wilderness wandering for every day they had trod in faithlessness upon the soil of Canaan—*forty years*.

Years later, when the Israelites continuously did evil in the sight of the Lord, He gave them into the hands of the Philistines, their most hated enemies. They were subservient to the Philistines for—you guessed it—*forty years* (Judges 13:1).

Also, it was for a period of forty days that Goliath came forth and taunted the armies of God's people. On the fortieth day, the giant man lost his head due to his misplaced derisions.

Periods of forty were also used to mark God's hand of divine appointment. Deborah, the faithful judge of Israel, brought forty years of peace to her domain because of her fidelity in the service of the Lord (Judges 5:31). The same could be said for Gideon's days as the main judge of Israel (Judges 8:28).

It was King David who would bring the tabernacle and the Ark of the Covenant back to the heart of Israel, the city of Jerusalem, to reestablish sacrificial worship of Yahweh. Thus David would be given the divine appointment of reigning forty years (2 Samuel 5:4). The same with his son, Solomon, the one who built the Temple of the Lord; He, too, was given forty years of divinely appointed rule (1 Kings 11:42).

But that's not all. It would only be three years hence when Yeshua Himself would rise from the grave and spend exactly *forty days* walking the earth before His glorious ascension. Those forty days would be spent performing additional miracles and fellowshipping with His disciples. Each one of those days would be a signal to Satan: "Your judgment has been leveled. Your time is short. You will soon be reduced to ashes, and you will be no more. The Seed has arrived. He is here to destroy your kingdom."

In this way, Jesus' forty days in this barren wasteland, the domain of the strong man, sent a message that could not be missed: *The Stronger One is here.*[47]

THE SECOND ADAM

The next forty days would remind the ancient serpent of his profane defilement of the Garden.[48] The *second Adam* had now arrived. He was getting ready to set in motion the reclamation of Eden, the reality of which would eventually be delivered to heaven's throne as the grand prize in this cosmic war.[49]

Try as he might, the serpent would not be victorious in this garden-enticement scenario. The "tree of temptation" would have no sway over the second Adam. The "fruit" would not be eaten. The "lies and false prophecies" would not be believed. The beckoning to rule Satan's kingdoms would hold no sway.

This mission would not be "defiled."[50]

Nehushtan—"the brazen one"—would eventually appear. Of this fact there was no doubt.[51] In exactly what form he would manifest, Yeshua was uncertain. The serpent had several options from which to choose. But *show up* he would. This was the Garden serpent's fame; it was his characteristic mark of pretentiousness.

One day soon, that same flawed trait would prove to be his undoing… but right now he was out there, somewhere. Watching. Waiting. Calculating.

And this is why Yeshua was here as well. Seated upon a sparsely shaded ledge. Watching. Waiting. Calculating.

Through the human presence of the promised divine Seed, the repossession of the Garden of Eden was officially underway. Elohim's Garden promise was coming to pass.

Judgment had arrived. In person.

So, He sat…knowing that the ancient serpent would soon show himself.

11

THE BRAZEN ONE

**He materialized out of the shimmering
mist—as an angel of light.**

The past forty days in this wasteland had been unspeakably miserable.
Not a morsel to eat. Barely able, at times, to even wet His blistering lips. The scorching sun. The harsh, frigid nights. During the entire
ordeal, not another living soul had passed through the desolate area. The
overwhelming power of sheer loneliness had almost done Him in.

Yeshua's strength had long ago faded into a faint whisper. Heaven's
throne was purposely silent. This was, however, the plan from the beginning. This feat must be accomplished alone, inside the fleshly camou-
flage of a mortal being, wrapped in the enigma of a divine strategy.

A BATTLE OF THE MIND

In the midst of the torturous ordeal...*they came*. Every single night they
returned. The wild animals. Watching. Snarling. Threatening. Possessed
of otherworldly eyes. Creatures of the blackness.

Each day and each night had been a mortal battle of the mind and
spirit. Within the first few days, the thoughts that came to Him were

like the constant dripping of another voice from an unseen source. A dark, sugary-sweet, faintly vulgar voice—yet bathed in an almost musical intonation.

There it was again…the voice…

Look how you suffer. You really should give this up! Did Elohim truly sssay you were to come here? He knows you shouldn't have to do thisss thing… it's preposterousss! Surely, Elohim doesn't expect you to endure thisss brutality?

The temptations pounded ceaselessly upon His mind. But so far, the attack had only been through a voice whisking through the recesses of His subconscious. A powerful, persuasive, manipulative voice, to be sure. And one that attempted to coil itself around the depths of His inner being, but nothing more. So far.

However, that particular mode of attack was getting ready to change. The assault would soon be elevated to a much higher level. This was getting ready to become very personal.

A BATTLE OF THE FLESH

After the fortieth day—*He came.*[52]

Yeshua, resting upon His partly sheltered ledge, barely able to hold up His own head, first observed a slight shimmer in the eerily shifting atmosphere. The phenomenon had the appearance of a silken curtain flapping in a gentle breeze. It had drawn His attention because of a loud *snapping* sound that preceded the atmospheric disturbance. His senses shifted into a mode of high alert. He quickly surveyed His surroundings. Was this the arrival of the strong man?

Perhaps what He saw was just a mirage? An illusion borne out of the deprivation of nourishment? No. This was no illusion. Even the circling crows had scattered at the sound, squawking out their irritated protests as they fled.

There he was!

A discernable figure had appeared. He materialized out of the shimmering mist, from behind the "flapping curtain" of another dimension—like an *angel of light*. The *god of this age* had finally revealed himself.[53]

There was that eerie musical sound again. It had accompanied his arrival. Satan merely stood there…gazing…glaring…at Yeshua.

A fiendish arrogant smile formed upon the ancient serpent's face. This was the signal. What Yeshua had come for would now begin.

PERSPECTIVES

For the first time while in His earthly form, Yeshua was looking upon the seductive visage of Satan, the cosmic father of lies and murder. The Garden usurper had taken the bait.

So far, so good.

Yeshua's unabashed public appearance at the Jordan River had been the casting of the first lure. But His presence here, right in the center of Satan's Judean domain, had been more than the ancient dragon's curiosity could resist.

Had travelers passed by at that very moment, they would have beheld a singular man seated upon an imposing rocky ledge. They also would have observed this man to be in an apparent trance, a lonely soul merely lost in another world—a world unseen to the mortal onlooker's eye. Yet, a very real world indeed.[54]

The *prince of the power of the air*[55] knew fully well how to traverse these interdimensional planes of reality. He had long been known to roam *to and fro* over the face of the earth, yet also to appear in the heavenly dimension.[56]

Nachash knew how to bring one dimension in touch with another, either within the confines of a person's own mind or, sometimes, by manufacturing the thought into a literal, physical reality. He was the holder of the key to such secrets as these, secrets of the knowledge of good and evil. He was the tree that held that poisonous fruit within his gnarled branches. And he unfailingly used these ill-gotten powers to his own fiendish advantage, turning them into mere playthings of bewitchment. This was how he had operated, almost since the very beginning.

Today would be no exception.

12

THE GRAND ENTRANCE

Behold how even He has abandoned you!

He approached.

In fact, he almost floated, until he was standing just below the ledge where Yeshua sat. From there, the serpent gazed upon the fasting one, as a rattlesnake might scrutinize a quickly fading field mouse it was preparing to devour. A venomous lust for increased power consumed him. *This,* he thought, *might finally be my chance!*

In a flash, the ancient serpent[57] was seated right beside Yeshua on the ledge, attempting to make himself equal to this "Son of God."

His countenance was indescribably beautiful by mere mortal standards. But Yeshua knew that even this presentation was not the genuine thing. Something ineffably hideous was lurking behind the shimmering, soft glow of this master of profane masquerades.[58]

The *shining one* spoke.[59] "I presume that you're hungry?" Nachash sneered. "So horribly famished, I would guess. I can see it in your eyes! *Forty days?* For the life of me, I don't know how you pulled that off." He clapped his hands mockingly. "Bravo! Well done!"

Yeshua did not reply, nor had He yet acknowledged the actual presence of Nachash. It was a move meant to unnerve the adversary. And it was working.

As his smirk vanished, the serpent continued. "Why in the world did you do this to yourself? What can you possibly hope to accomplish by this vainglorious act of self-deprivation? All these theatrics—bringing you to the edge of utter starvation—it was so unnecessary."

A twinge of exasperation was embedded in the serpent's voice as he continued. "Surely you understand that your flesh will not tolerate this treatment much longer?"

Yeshua looked straight ahead, eyes still fixed on the horizon before Him. It would be dark in a few hours.

The sarcastic one mocked, "You know, if you don't eat something soon, you *shall* surely die. And what a horrible shame that would be."

Nachash picked up a stone, smiling as he held it. He condescendingly gazed upon the suffering wretch before him. He held the rock to his lips and began to lick it, almost in a vulgar manner, as if he were tasting a wonderful morsel of freshly baked bread. "*Umm*! So tasty!"

Yeshua still looked straight ahead, making no eye contact with the liar who sat beside Him. He closed His eyes and moved His lips slightly as He prayed.

"Oh, quit being *ridiculous*!" Nachash mocked. "There's no one there to listen to you! That ought to be apparent by now. Where is your help? Where is God now? Behold how even *He* has abandoned you! It's been forty days, and not one appearance from His throne. I know! I've been watching. By the way, where are His holy ones? Shouldn't they be here with you as well? *Hmm?*"

The mighty one's jabbing continued, as if he were physically plunging the barbs of insults into Jesus' own flesh. "Apparently, they have all forgotten you!" he said. "How is it that you can be the Son of God, when even heaven's throne refuses to acknowledge you? You may as well call upon *me* for help. After all, I'm sitting right here. And *they* are nowhere to be found! Say the word, and I'll have a feast spread before you. You are, after all, in *my* home."

Yeshua had still spoken not a word to His loquacious visitor.

Moving closer to Yeshua and leaning over into His ear, the serpent whispered, "How long will you cling to this*s* outlandishly inflated confidence—this delusion that you are somehow the Son of God? Do you truly believe those preposterous claims made about you at the Jordan? Use your head for a moment!" His breath smelled like the vile stench of rotting flesh.

Yeshua closed His eyes. Satan sat up straight and continued. "You were born in a cattle stable for goodness' sake! Yet *you* are the Son of *God*? Really? Please explain how *that* works! Just how delusional have you become?"

The condescending insults raged on. "And everyone knows you are nothing but the son of a poor, unsuccessful carpenter. On top of that, this same illustrious father of yours chose to raise you in a despicable little town—a nondescript little dot on the map—in *Galilee* of all places! And where is your father now? He's not even in your life anymore! *Pffft!*"[60]

Satan was on a roll. "Almost thirty years you spent there! And you know what everyone says: *Has anything good ever come out of Nazareth?*[61] Now, you want the world to believe that a 'voice from heaven' whispered only in *your* ears, and those of that empty-headed desert preacher, claiming that *you*, of all people, are the Son of God? A little presumptuous, don't you think? How embarrassed you must be."

BREAD OF LIFE

After a few silent moments, Nachash spoke again, words dripping with enlarged sarcasm. "Your days of hiding in this lonely place should end! Why linger for weeks in this desert, wandering among the wild beasts and lifeless boulders…ignored, unattended, unpitied, and at the point of starvation? Is this truly fitting for the supposed *Son of God*?"

Yeshua still did not respond.

But Nachash wasn't giving up. "Okay, have it your way. Obviously, you are completely deranged by now. No food. The heat. *I understand.* So, let's play your game then, shall we? Since you are the Christ, the Son of God—for that truly is what some are claiming about you—well then, surely you would have no problem."

He paused midsentence and held out the small, loaf-shaped rock he had picked up a moment ago. He flipped it around in his hand, taunting, thrusting it in Yeshua's direction. He continued to lick it, clutching it with both hands as if he were savoring some sort of actual taste and aroma.

"You should have no problem turning thi*ss* stone into a loaf of bread, for example. Imagine how a gloriously sweet-smelling chunk of warm, soft bread would ta*ss*te right now! Hmm? Here…just *ssay* the word. *Ssay* it!" He held out the stone to Yeshua. "Surely…you, of all people, can do thi*ss* one little thing?"

Here he was—the long-awaited prey.

Yeshua thought to Himself: *Finally! The deer has walked up to the pile of honey-mixed grain, right under the hunter's perch. Just like an overly confident beast slinking out of the woods, curious to sniff this strange intruder and not having a clue what this moment truly meant.*

This was exactly why Yeshua had come. The wait. The suffering. The elements. The insults. The taunting. The wild animals—and the cotton-mouthed thirst. Even the horrible, gut-wrenching hunger. It had all been worth the effort. With a slight smile, Yeshua prepared to speak His first words to Nachash.

"It is written: 'Man shall not live on bread alone, but on every word that comes from the mouth of Yahweh." He emphasized the word *Yahweh*.

A brooding darkness fell over the serpent's brazen countenance. *That word! That Name!* It pierced his ears with a racking pain… *Yahweh!*

It was Yahweh who had pronounced the prophetic primeval curse upon his head all the way back in Eden. Could it be this truly was the *Seed* whose mission it was to crush his head?[62]

In fact, the more he studied the matter, the possibility appeared to be growing, right before his eyes. *This was not good.*

But the serpent was determined to answer heaven's insult.

13

THE HIGH PLACES

The serpent recoiled in shock.

Who *was* this man?

This pitiful-looking human figure sitting upon the ledge… was this *indeed* the Son of God seated before him? Clothed in the frailty of mere *human flesh*?

Was this the best Elohim could throw at him? Nachash reassured himself: *Surely, Elohim is smarter than this. On the other hand, maybe He's not. Oh well, if He has made that mistake,* Satan thought, *then it will be to my fortuitous advantage!*

Nachash whipped his hand through the air as though he were slashing it with a knife. With that movement, he peeled back yet another cosmic curtain. The atmosphere *snapped* again, like the sudden crack of a bolt of lightning.

Instantly, far below, a panoramic view of the Temple courtyards in downtown Jerusalem burst into view. The sounds of everyday life echoed as worshippers bustled about in the matters of their daily routine, animals of sacrifice in tow.

Yeshua and Nachash clearly had not left the wilderness. Yet, they were most assuredly in Jerusalem, at the Temple Mount. Through the command of the serpent's wizardry, Yeshua was standing on the peak of the Temple edifice. They had crossed into yet another dimensional plane. They were in two different places at the same time. [63]

The *prince of the power of the air* brought Yeshua to this place not only to tempt Him, but also to parade his own possession of supernatural knowledge. He wanted this Suffering One to know beyond any doubt that he had mastered certain secrets that should not have been his to toy with in the first place. But, he was the cosmic master thief, and proud of it. He dripped with putrid vanity as he stood atop the Temple beside Yeshua.

The adversary spoke again. "*If* you are the Son of God— No, let me correct myself. *Sssince* it is so boldly claimed that you *are* the Son of God, prove yourself! Prove it to the people below. Throw yours*ss*elf down from here. For it is written: 'He will command His angels concerning you to guard you carefully; they will lift you up in their hands, so that you will not strike your foot against a stone.'"[64]

"You would quote Scripture to me?" More than asking a question, Yeshua posed a challenge.

Nachash looked at Him, feigning innocence, and shrugged.

"Well?" the serpent continued the taunt. "Will you do it? *Can* you do it? The promise is right there…it's in the Word."

Yeshua looked down at the throngs of worshippers below. He already knew the response He would give. But He wanted the old serpent to squirm for just a moment more…

After another few moments, Jesus matter-of-factly replied, "It is also said: 'Do not put the Lord your God to a foolish test.'"

The serpent's haughtiness turned to exasperation. *Nothing is working on this one!*

But, Yeshua also knew Satan had failed to quote the next and most important verse of that passage:

You will tread on the lion and the cobra; you will trample the great lion and the serpent. (Psalm 91:13)

No wonder that portion had been conveniently omitted. That verse perfectly described Yeshua's mission at this very moment. Today, fulfillment of the Garden prophecy had begun: The serpent's head would finally be trampled upon and eventually crushed. That great roaring lion, the devourer of humanity, would be destroyed.

But, not yet...

THE KINGDOMS OF THE WORLD

Snap!

The air crackled again.

In an instant, Nachash and Yeshua were transported from the Temple at Jerusalem to what appeared to be the highest imaginable mountaintop on the planet. A thick mist enveloped their ethereal perch. Smoke swirled above their heads as though the mountain had recently been on fire and was smoldering in the aftermath.

Out of that mist, a panoramic, glittering display appeared before their eyes. A cornucopia of shiny sparkles filled the air. Instantly, in a flashing moment, representations of all the kingdoms of the world, like trophies adorning a fireplace mantle, were made visible to Yeshua.[65]

"All this*sss* I will give to you," Nachash murmured, "if you would only bow down and wors*ss*ship me. This is mine to give. Only I can give it to *you!*" He looked deep into Yeshua's eyes, as though he were trying to read His thoughts, tilting his head slightly to one side in a peculiar expression of curiosity.

"It's only a little thing," the serpent tempted. "We *could* rule together! Yes! That's it! *Together!* As a matter of fact, what I was thinking was..."

"Away from me, Satan," came Yeshua's pointed command, spoken right in the middle of the drippy words that oozed from the serpent's deceitful mouth. Yeshua didn't even shout the admonishment. He merely gave the order. But, it was no plain order; His rebuke had been spoken with an unearthly assurance and a shocking absence of fear. His words and dismissive demeanor demoralized the serpent in the face of his abject arrogance.[66]

Nachash recoiled in shock. This was the first time the Suffering One had called him by that name, much less commanded *him*——the prince of the earth—with such unmitigated gall and air of authority.

Then, heaven's Son spoke again. "For it is written: 'Worship the Lord your God, and *serve Him only!*'" This time, His voice boomed… so that His words pierced the evening air, ricocheting from cliff to cliff.

"*Ahhhhhhghh!* Have it your way then!" Satan cursed, as a string of vile expletives began to flow from his blackened heart.

"You have no idea what you are doing! You may, in fact, be the *Son of God*—whatever *that* designation means. But understand this: You will never—I mean *never*—win this battle! This earth is mine! It is legally mine! I don't care *who* you are! And, in the end, *I will* ascend to the throne of the Most High!"[67]

Yeshua looked at the ancient serpent, His eyes piercing into the soul of the creature standing before Him. The serpent glared back and hissed: "Mark my words. This will not be the la*sss*t time you *sss*ee me—nor will it be the la*sss*t time you hear from me. I will come back to you. Over and over again I will return—in any form that I choo*sss*e…until you *sss*ubmit… *To. My. Will!*"

The air sizzled—then *cracked*. The serpent was gone. For now.

An uncanny silence followed. Yeshua was back on His ledge again, seated there as if He had never left.

No doubt, Yeshua would, in fact, see Nachash again. But that old serpent still had no idea what lay in store for his kingdom. The first divine snare had been set. The serpent had unwittingly slipped his head into the noose. And Satan knew no more now than he did by watching the activities at the Jordan, just forty days back.

A lone wolf howled in the distance. Others of its kind soon joined in the cacophony as though instructed by an unseen conductor. The sun slipped into the dust of the rugged horizon, bursting its multihued palette across the earth like a painter's masterpiece.

Then suddenly the fiery ball dropped out of sight, as if it had been snatched by a cord from underneath, by an unseen force. The darkness seeped across the landscape. The night creatures would soon begin rummaging through the wilderness, eyes occasionally sparkling in the ever-brightening moonlight.

Within moments, and in an instantaneous burst of blinding light, divine messengers from heaven's throne appeared beside Yeshua. They too had entered through a dimensional portal, one over which Satan had no authority. Those keys had been denied him…a very long time ago.

As Yeshua lay back upon the stone floor of the ledge, exhausted beyond words, the holy ones attended Him. Tomorrow would be a day of new beginnings and of a much longer road than the one He had already traveled.

The cosmic chess match had begun.

The prize was going to be the collective soul of humanity…and ultimately, the restoration of Eden itself.

But there were still three long years of grueling work to be done.

All of heaven and the generations yet unborn were counting on Him.

He would not disappoint.

PART FIVE

The Pummeling

For we do not have a high priest who is
unable to empathize with our weaknesses,
but we have one who has been tempted
in every way, just as we are—yet he did not sin.
—HEBREWS 4:15

14

PLUMBING THE DEPTHS

It is certain, whatever Satan might suspect, he did not fully know that the person he tempted was the true Messiah. Perhaps one grand object of his temptation was to find this out.

—Adam Clarke[68]

Exactly what did Satan *really* know about Yeshua?

This question has been bandied about by renowned scholars for hundreds of years. Yet, there are several important aspects to this dilemma that we are able to settle through a contextual examination of Scripture. Once the appropriate links are connected, the true depth of the biblical account of the cosmic war of the ages becomes much clearer.

Most commentators believe Satan already knew that Yeshua was, indeed, the Son of God at the time of, if not before, the wilderness temptation event. But here's the catch: Exactly what did the designation "Son of God" mean—and what were the specific details of His mission? Those things appear to be what Satan did *not* know…and for a very long time.

First on Satan's list was to determine exactly what kind of authority Jesus had over the elements of the earthly realm. Knowing that piece of information might help Satan determine what power this Son of God might wield over his domain. This would also explain why Satan's initial test of Jesus was to "turn these stones to bread…*if you are* the son of God!" (Luke 4:3, Matthew 4:3).

Have a look at how various scholars have addressed the matter of Satan's very first challenge.

Clarke's Commentary on the Bible

If thou be *the Son of God*—Or, *a son of God*, is here, and in Luke 4:3, written without the article; and therefore should not be translated The Son, *as if it were*, which is a phrase that is applicable to Christ as the Messiah: but *it is certain*, whatever Satan might suspect, *he did not fully know that the person he tempted* was the true Messiah. Perhaps one grand object of his temptation was to find this out.[69] (Emphasis added)

People's Bible Commentary

If thou be the Son of God. "If" suggests **a doubt**, and, perhaps, **a taunt.**[70] (Emphasis added)

Jamieson-Fausset-Brown: Commentary Critical and Explanatory on the Whole Bible

What was the high design of this? …That the tempter, too, might get a taste, at the very outset, of the new kind of material in man which he would find he had here to deal with.[71]

The Cambridge Bible for Schools and Colleges

If thou art… The same words were tauntingly addressed to our Lord on the Cross (Matthew 27:40). The Greek strictly means "*Assuming* that Thou art…"[72] (Emphasis added)

Gill's Exposition of the Entire Bible

> *If thou art*...or **seeing thou art [since you claim, or assuming you are]** in such a relation to God, **and so equal to him,** and possessed of all divine perfections... command this stone that it be made bread.[73] (Emphasis and brackets added)

Biblical Illustrator

> There seems little reason to doubt that Satan knew Jesus to be the promised One, whose advent the prophets had foretold. But although Satan was thus far in possession of the truth respecting Christ, **it does not follow that he "knew the whole truth" respecting him.** If *Satan had no just view* of the person of Christ, **of His true divinity,** he would necessarily have imperfect views of His perfect holiness.[74] (Emphasis added)

THE RECRUITS

Throughout Jesus' earthly ministry, we observe Jewish religious leaders demanding that Jesus should show them some sort of heavenly sign. Frequently, their caustic attacks were leveled by using Satan's very own wilderness taunts: "*If you are* the son of God..."

This scriptural detail is a huge clue, demonstrating that Satan knew a good deal about Jesus, but also that he certainly didn't know it "all." If Satan had known every detail about Jesus he desired to know, you can bet that Satan's human puppets would have been let in on the secret, too. Yet, we are shown the opposite throughout the biblical account.

EVEN THE ANGELS...

Of all of the biblical affirmations indicating that Satan *could not* have had total foreknowledge of the "Christ event," one of the clearest comes from the first chapter of 1 Peter.

> **Concerning this salvation, the prophets,** who spoke of the grace that was to come to you, **searched intently** and with the greatest care, **trying to find out the time and circumstances** to which the Spirit of Christ in them was pointing when he predicted **the sufferings of the Messiah and the glories that would follow.** It was revealed to them that they were not serving themselves but you, when they spoke of the things that have now been told you by those who have preached the gospel to you by the Holy Spirit sent from heaven. *Even angels long "to look into" these things.* (1 Peter 1:10–12, emphasis added)

The exacting details of redemption's plan were the exclusive *top secrets* of the throne of Elohim. The scholars agree this is, indeed, the very point Peter is expressing in his first letter to the early church.

Ellicott's Commentary expresses this important truth like this:

> Angels, who were present at every detail, and bore an active part in it all (see Matthew 1:20; Matthew 4:11; Matthew 28:2; Luke 1:26; Luke 2:9; Luke 22:43; John 1:51),—angels, of whom He "was seen" (1 Timothy 3:16),—covet now to exchange places with you that they may gaze into the mystery.[75]

Barnes' Notes on the Bible:

> The object of this reference to the angels is the same as that to the prophets. It had excited the deepest interest among the most holy men on earth, and even among the inhabitants of the [heavens]. They [the church] were [now] enjoying the full revelation of what even the angels had desired more fully to understand, and to comprehend which they had employed their great powers of investigation.[76] (Brackets added)

Pulpit Commentary

> The salvation which God's elect receive is so full of glory and mysterious beauty, that not only did the prophets of old search diligently, but even angels desire to look into it.… The verb [to look into] means "to stoop sideways;" it is used of persons standing outside a place who stoop in order to look in.[77]

We can, therefore, be confident that if the obedient divine beings had not been let in on every detail regarding the incarnation and redemption events, neither had Satan. Remember, as powerful as Satan is, he and his angels are not omnipresent. Nor are they omnipotent. And they certainly are not omniscient.

There is only *One* who fully embodies those attributes. And now, He was standing before humanity—in the flesh.

15

THE NEVER-ENDING WILDERNESS

**Neither Satan nor man was completely
privy to the mystery of it—yet.**

In reality, the continual demonic taunting and probing of the wilderness temptation never departed from Jesus, all the way up to that night in the Garden of Gethsemane, and then remaining upon Him until Calvary's cross. It was always there, slashing at His heels.

In light of what he didn't know at the time, Satan must have reasoned that if Jesus did possess certain limitations, then those constraints could be tactically used against Him. Thus, Satan's most insidious offer on that day in the wilderness was seductively dangled in front of Jesus: *If you will bow down and worship me, I'll give you the kingdoms of the earth.*

In his abject arrogance, it appears Satan must have rationalized: *If I can conquer this one, who just might be "God in human flesh," then I could very well conquer the throne of Elohim itself, and claim it as my own!*[78]

Succinctly put: The serpent needed to know exactly what he was dealing with.

Consider the position of the *Pulpit Commentary* in this matter.

Satan *might* well *have known* that [Jesus] was God incarnate, and yet *not have known* whether **as Man** he *might* **not yield.** [79] (Emphasis added)

Meyer's New Testament Commentary offers a similar view:

[If you are the Son of God]...[This] problematical expression **was to incite Jesus** to enter upon the unreasonable demand, and *to prove* himself the Son of God.... Whilst he himself, as the principle opposed to God, **has to combat the manifestation and activity of the divine.** [80] (Emphasis and brackets added)

Furthermore, while the Son of God was inhabiting the flesh of a mortal man, the satanic presentations that commenced in the wilderness were very real temptations indeed. Scripture bears out this truth:

For we do not have a high priest who is unable to empathize with our weaknesses, but we have one who has been tempted in every way, just as we are—yet he did not sin. (Hebrews 4:15)

Yet, in refusing to display His divine power in the wilderness, and thus perhaps avoid the sufferings of the cross down the road before Him (Hebrews 12:2), Jesus threw Satan off his game. Quoting Scripture was the only power Jesus used in defeating Satan's temptations. And, as He thus proved to humanity, that power alone was enough to repel the evil one.

It is fairly apparent then, that the question of how Jesus could be *all God* and *all human* at the same time was still a deep mystery that Nachash desired to unravel. However, the Word of God assures us that this miracle was God's *mystery of the ages,* known only to the throne and its closest allies.

No, we declare God's wisdom, a mystery that has been hidden and that God destined for our glory before time began. (1 Corinthians 2:7)

The mystery of God, namely, Christ, in whom are hidden all the treasures of wisdom and knowledge. (Colossians 2:2–3)

The entire affair of the wilderness temptation and every temptation thereafter was, in every sense of the word, a demonic testing and tempting of Yeshua—right up to the eternally significant choices that He would have to make in the Garden of Gethsemane.

The reason Yeshua's temptations were so real is because those enticements came to Him while He was in literal, human flesh. They also came while He was dwelling in the midst of a pervasively fallen world with all of its allurements, sufferings, and evil desires—which now brings us to a particularly significant theological conundrum.

16

CLOTHED IN FLESH

**He had every real opportunity to reject
the sufferings that were before Him.**

Here's another often-debated question: *Was Jesus inhabiting "fallen
flesh" during His earthly life and ministry—and, if so, does this mean
He entered the world with a "sin nature?"*

In several places in the Old Testament, we discover that God presented Himself to certain people in the *form* of a human man. However,
when He appeared in this form, He was never in mere human flesh.
Nevertheless, He *was* "God in the flesh."

One well-known example of an Old Testament theophany[81] is when
Abraham was talking face to face with Yahweh and the two angels that
accompanied Him, just before the destruction of Sodom and Gomorrah
(Genesis 18). Yet, to Abraham, they at first appeared to be mere men.

> And *Yahweh appeared* to [Abraham] by the oaks of Mamre....
> Abraham looked up and **saw** *three men* standing nearby....
> Then *Yahweh said* to Abraham, "What is this that Sarah
> laughed, saying, 'Is it indeed true that I will bear a child, now
> that I have grown old?' Is anything too difficult for Yahweh? At

the appointed time *I will return to you* in the spring and Sarah shall have a son." (Genesis 18:1, 2, 13–14; emphasis added)

ONLY BEGOTTEN

Most students of the Word of God are, of course, familiar with one of the titles Jesus gave Himself: the "only begotten Son of God." The term "only begotten" (Greek: *monogenés*) expresses the only time when God would present Himself to humanity as having first come through the womb of a woman. He had never done this before; *it was unique*. And, He would never do this again; it was His *one and only time* to appear to humanity in this manner.[82]

The *HELPS Word-studies* Greek dictionary defines *monogenés* as "One of a kind"—literally, "one (*monos*) of a class, *genos*" (the only of its kind).[83]

THE ENIGMA

However, the question of the "type of flesh" that Jesus inhabited presents an entirely different set of considerations. Some would argue that if He was indeed inhabiting sinful, fallen flesh—inherited through Mary—then He could not have been our "perfect" sacrifice. He could not have been the *Lamb of God* without blemish or spot (Exodus 12:5, 1 Peter 1:19).

On the other hand, if Jesus possessed no fallen sin nature whatsoever, then He would have had no "sin *within* Himself" over which He would have to battle. If this was so, then how could He have fully identified with us in our fallen human state, as Scripture so boldly declares that He did? How could He have been genuinely tempted?

So, was Jesus spotless and sinless, or did He have fallen human flesh that was subject to temptation? We simply can't have it both ways. At first glance, the enigma seems to be unsolvable. But, it's not.

The answer is right before us, laid out in the pages of the New Testament. Remember, we are able to get our answers from the perspective of having the entire Christ event *behind* us, thoroughly recorded in the pages of the New Testament. However, Satan did not have that advantage. He had to wade through the matter by trial and error, day by day. This is exactly why Jesus was continually pummeled by Satan's prodding and harassment. The enemy understood it was imperative to solve this mystery so that he might know exactly how to proceed in his own counterplan—thus, the reason for Satan's appearance in the wilderness and his haughty and repeated challenges of "*If you are* the Son of God" throughout Jesus' ministry.

Satan must have thought: *If this one who was called the "Son of God" could be coerced into sin…that would also have to mean that He too would fall. He too could be corrupted and separated from God's plan, just like with Adam and Eve.*

That was exactly what Satan intended to bring about: another Garden fall.

Except for one little stumbling block that was always nagging him, the matter of a certain ancient prophecy Nachash could never quite get out of his head. It was first given in the original Garden of Eden:

"The seed from her womb will crush your head."

UNTO US

"I am the Lord's servant," Mary answered.
—Luke 1:38

So, here are the questions of the ages. How could it be that heaven's *Son of God* was able to put on human flesh, born of a woman, yet still ensure that a fallen, human, sin nature was not inherited through that mortal process of conception?[84] And how could it be that the incarnation event would ensure that both the completely divine and the completely human would reside in one single person?

THE INCARNATION

The contextual answer to our question is given through the words of the angel Gabriel. On that glorious day when Gabriel appeared unto Mary to tell her of heaven's magnificent plan for her life, he also told her exactly how this miraculous plan would take place. Note the emphasized words of that pronouncement. They are the keys to unlocking the mystery:

> The angel answered, "The **Holy Spirit will come on you**, and *the power* of the Most High *will overshadow* you. So the *holy one* to be born will be called the Son of God." (Luke 1:35)

The power of the Holy Spirit was said to have "overshadowed" Mary. This divine presence from the throne of God would generate within Mary's womb the embryonic Christ child—out *of nothing*.

In the next chapter, you'll see more than a half dozen examples of the myriad renowned scholars who agree with this biblical revelation. But, before you might be tempted to balk at the notion, *think about this*: This is the very same language used in Genesis 1 at the Creation event.

Have a look at Genesis again. I've included some of my own explanatory commentary in brackets:

In the beginning **God created** [out of nothing, and by His Word] the heavens and the earth. Now the earth was formless and empty, darkness was over the surface of the deep, and **the Spirit of God** *was hovering over* [overshadowing] the waters. And **God said**, [He *spoke* into existence] "*Let there be* light," and **there was light**. (Genesis 1:1–3; emphasis added.)

Into Mary's womb God spoke: *Let there be a human embryo...*

OVERSHADOWING

Consider the Creation account of Adam. Elohim didn't need a human sperm and egg to bring Adam into being. He didn't even need a preexisting strand of DNA. Adam was formed by God's command and His direct creative power. All God required was His *Word* to be spoken. Furthermore, every time God created something in the Genesis account, His creative activity was always *overshadowed* by the Holy Spirit.

Now, consider this next contextual truth. The Word of God clearly identifies Jesus as the "second Adam" (Romans 5:14; 1 Corinthians 15:45–48). Just as the first Adam was called into existence solely by God's command, the second Adam would be formed in like manner.

The embryonic Jesus—Immanuel—was *spoken into existence* and then divinely situated inside Mary's womb. In this way, He was fully human.

At the same time, Jesus was also fully divine, owing His existence in Mary's womb solely to the *overshadowing of the Holy Spirit*, just as Adam was also created with a divine nature, never to die. He was born by the "will of God" and not by the will of man; it was an entirely supernatural event (John 1:13). Of course, in the first Adam's case, he forfeited his divine nature by succumbing to Nachash. This brings us right back to the wilderness temptation. Nachash was attempting to get the second Adam to succumb as well. His manipulation techniques had worked the first time, and Satan was betting his entire kingdom plan that his power of persuasion would work once more. He couldn't have been more mistaken. There was simply so much that Satan didn't know.

I AM YOUR FAITHFUL SERVANT

Once the amazing plan of the incarnation was pronounced by the angel, Mary gave her permission for the miracle to take place. She made it clear that she was more than willing to carry this divinely crafted embryo within her own womb. Obviously, in the long run, she had a choice. But, in the long run, God also knew that she would be obedient. He knew her heart.

> "I am the Lord's servant," Mary answered. "May your word to me be fulfilled." (Luke 1:38)

Mary would go down in history as heaven's anointed agent. She would assist the throne of Elohim in bringing to fruition the very beginning of the final destruction of the enemy of humanity and the ultimate restitution of all things (Matthew 17:11; Acts 3, 21).[85] The Creator of the universe would covertly step into His own creation through the human birth process. But, the *entrance* from the heavenly dimension to the earthly one would be through a child that was originally implanted in Mary's womb by the Word of God Himself. These truths have always been right before our eyes in Scripture.

We cannot get past the very first words of the Gospel of John without running right into the clear declarations:

> **He was in the world**, and **though the world was made through him,** the world **did not recognize him**. He came to that which was his own, but **his own did not receive** him. Yet to all who did receive him, to those who believed in his name, he gave the right to become children of God—children **born *not of natural* descent**, nor of human decision or a husband's will, ***but born of God.***
>
> **The Word** *became flesh* and made his dwelling among us. We have seen his glory, the glory of the one and only Son, ***who came from the Father***, full of grace and truth. (John 1:10–14, emphasis added)

After the mystery that God wrought had finally become apparent to all, the inhabitants of earth would celebrate it and sing of it for thousands of years hence.

> Christ, by highest Heav'n adored;
> Christ the everlasting Lord;
> Late in time, behold him come,
> Offspring of the virgin's womb.
> Veiled in flesh the Godhead see;
> Hail th'incarnate Deity,
> Pleased as man with men to dwell,
> Jesus, our Emmanuel.[86]

18

THE HOLY ONE

**By His word alone, God would create and
place a human embryo within Mary's womb.**

To further punctuate the truths we uncovered in the last chapter, note again that the angel Gabriel declared the Christ child to be "the holy one." At first glance, we might miss the gravity of that when reading the passage solely in the English language. The Word "holy" is translated from the Greek word *hagios*.

Helps Word-studies defines this word:

Hagios—properly, **different** (unlike), **other** ("otherness"), holy; for the believer, (hágios) means **"likeness of nature with the Lord"** because **"different from the world."**[87] (Emphasis added)

By His word alone, God would create and place a human embryo within Mary's womb. This child's body would be a one-of-a-kind creation that would never again be repeated. In creating the embryo in this manner, it would be separate from anything like it. This event was going to be a divine incarnation—in the purest understanding of the word.

POWER IN THE BLOOD

At this point, some might ask, "But what about Mary's blood, what about her DNA mixing with the baby's, and what about the sharing of these elements through the placenta during pregnancy? Wouldn't these contribute to Jesus inheriting a human sin nature through Mary?"

Here's the scientific truth: A mother's blood is completely separate from the baby's. This is why the baby's blood type is often different than the mother's. The mother's DNA is also distinct from the baby's. Soon after conception, the baby's unique DNA can be detected within the mother's bloodstream. They are two very separate individuals. Neither Mary's nor Joseph's DNA, or blood, was used in the creation of this embryo, so there was nothing *fallen* to be genetically passed from mother to child.[88]

It is true that the birth organ of the placenta allows oxygen and additional vital nutrients to travel from the mother's blood directly to the fetus' blood. The placenta is basically a biological "interface" between mother and child. However, the two circulatory systems are kept entirely separate. The amazing structure of the placenta allows this interchange to take place. The *placenta-exchange system* also allows for carbon dioxide and other biological waste to be dumped from the fetus' system. Those waste products are then transferred directly to the mother's system, and she is able to process and dispose of them on behalf of the baby.[89]

The bottom line is this: The blood, DNA, and even the body of the baby are uniquely different from the mother's, even in the normal human birth process. In the case of the divine incarnation of Jesus, the only thing that would be used would be the "baby carriage" of Mary's womb, as well as her parental care. But in so utilizing Mary's womb, the prophecy would be fulfilled that the Messiah would come through the seed of Abraham as well as through the line of David.

Mary and Joseph both came from that Abrahamic seed, and both came through the line of David.[90] Jesus Himself would come through the womb of Mary into the household of a man and woman who were joined together in a marriage covenant by heaven's decree. *Incognito. Mysteriously. Miraculously.*

The entire incarnation event would be carried out in perfect fulfillment of the prophecy first pronounced by Elohim Himself, way back in the Garden of Eden.

And I will put enmity between you and the woman, and between your seed and her seed. He will crush your head, and you will strike his heel. (Genesis 3:15, *Berean's Study Bible*)

THE SCHOLARS AGREE

Each of the essential elements we have connected in this chapter and the previous one is supported by numerous classical scholars. Especially note the words emphasized in bold print.

Barnes' Notes on the Bible

The power of the Highest…—**This evidently means that the body of Jesus would be created by the direct power of God.** It was **not by ordinary generation**…it was necessary that his human nature should be pure, and free from the corruption of the fall. **God therefore prepared him a body by direct creation** that should be pure and holy.[91] (Emphasis added)

Ellicott's Commentary for English Readers

Of the Holy Ghost…the words would at least suggest **a divine creative energy, quickening supernaturally** [to supernaturally bring to life] **the germ of life, as in Genesis 1:2.**[92] (Emphasis added, brackets added)

Pulpit Commentary

"The power of the Highest shall overshadow thee," reminds us of **the opening words of Genesis**, where the writer describes the dawn of life in creation in the words, "The Spirit of God moved [or, 'brooded'] over the face of the deep."

The Word was conceived in the womb of a woman, not after the manner of men, but by the singular, powerful, invisible, immediate operation of the Holy Ghost, whereby a virgin was, **beyond the law of nature,** enabled to conceive, and that which was conceived in her was originally and completely sanctified.[93] (Emphasis added)

Gill's Exposition of the Entire Bible

In the word, "overshadow"…there is an allusion to the Spirit of God moving upon the face of the waters, in Genesis 1:2.[94]

Expositor's Greek Testament

The embryo, Son of God; not merely because it is holy, but because **brought into being by the power of the Highest.**[95] (Emphasis added)

Matthew Poole's Commentary (Commenting on Matthew 1:20)

For that which is conceived in her is of the Holy Ghost. **That human body** which is in her womb, is **created in her**, and is of the Holy Ghost. The Holy Ghost, by his **almighty creating power**, hath supplied what is wanting as to ordinary productions of this nature.[96] (Emphasis added)

Matthew Poole's Commentary (Commenting on Luke 1:35)

But this phrase denotes an extraordinary special influence of the Spirit, changing the order and course of nature, and giving a power to...the **forming of the body of a child:** this is more mysteriously yet expressed, by the term overshadow thee...signifying **by a Divine creating power**, in a most miraculous manner.[97] (Emphasis added)

Benson's Commentary

For that which is conceived in her is **of *no human original,*** but produced by the miraculous and ***unexampled* operation of the Holy Ghost.** Thus, after Matthew has related how Christ was of royal descent, he now shows that he was also of much higher birth, **and *had a divine original.*** Now, although *no example be extant of such a wonderful nativity*, it nevertheless ought not to be rashly called in question by any especially.... Since...*Adam, the first man, was [also] produced without father or mother.*[98] (Emphasis added, brackets added)

Expository Notes of Dr. Thomas Constable

This delicate expression rules out crude ideas of a "mating" of the Holy Spirit with Mary. It is interesting that the same Greek word, *episkiazo*, translated "overshadow" here, occurs in all three accounts of the Transfiguration where the cloud overshadowed those present (Matthew 17:5, Mark 9:7, Luke 9:34). The Holy Spirit **would produce a holy offspring** through Mary. The deity and preexistence of the Son of God required a miraculous conception. His virgin birth resulted in His assuming a human nature without giving up His divine nature.[99] (Emphasis added)

Lange's Commentary on the Holy Scriptures: Critical, Doctrinal, and Homiletical

The laws of nature are not chains, wherewith the Supreme Lawgiver has bound himself…. **He can lengthen or shorten as His good pleasure** and wisdom dictate. And surely, in the present case, **an end worthy of divine interference** justified the deviation…. the new member **could only be introduced** into the human series **in an extraordinary manner**…. Who was **in the beginning with God**, and **who came of His own will** to sojourn in this our world, **could hardly enter it as one of ourselves would**…. **The same Spirit who formed the body of Christ,** forms also the corpus Christi mysticum, the Church.[100] (Emphasis added)

IMMANUEL

All of these truths, apparently, were completely misunderstood by the enemy…until it was far too late for him to do anything about it.

- In order that they may know **the mystery of God, namely, Christ**, *in whom are hidden* all the treasures of wisdom and knowledge. (Colossians 2:3, emphasis added)
- We declare God's wisdom, **a *mystery that has been hidden*** and that God destined for our glory before time began. ***None of the rulers* of this age understood it**, for if they had, ***they would not have crucified*** the Lord of glory. (1 Corinthians 2:7–8, emphasis added)

The full meaning and gravity of the Garden prophecy was wrapped in an enigma, shrouded by a mystery, and utterly hidden at the throne of God. It was the cosmic secret of the ages, known only to Elohim Himself.

> Concerning this salvation, the prophets, who spoke of the grace that was to come to you, **searched intently** and with the greatest care, **trying to find out the time and circumstances** to which the Spirit of Christ in them was pointing **when he predicted the sufferings of the Messiah** and the glories that would follow.... *Even angels long to look into these things.* (1 Peter 1:10–12, emphasis added)

Attempting to plumb the depths of this divine secret proved to be Satan's foremost goal.

But what the old serpent could not have known was that by Elohim simply speaking that original Garden prophecy, Satan's rebellious curiosity had been aroused. The fire of his arrogance had been stoked. He was already plotting an escape route and a path to his supposed diabolical victory.

But the whole thing had been a trap from the beginning.

And Satan would eventually walk right into it.

19

THE SECOND ADAM

**Never doubt, Jesus' fleshly temptations
were as genuine as they get...**

How do we answer the question, "Could it really be true that Jesus was genuinely tempted, as we are, if He didn't possess a fallen, human sin nature?"

Consider this important fact. Adam and Eve were also in an "unfallen" condition before they "fell." They had no "sin nature" either. There was nothing within their flesh with which they could have been tempted. Yet, they were genuinely tempted. And they genuinely fell. So the temptations thrust upon the first couple of creation would had to have come solely from the outward prodding of Satan's wiles, as well as whatever psychological temptations he could manufacture and then plant in their minds (Romans 12:2).

Yet, in spite of the temptations laid before Adam and Eve, they still had the unmitigated freedom to choose, or to reject, those temptations. And, while they were in that yet-unfallen nature, they still succumbed to the temptations Satan tossed their way, and thus, they thoroughly corrupted themselves. Just like Adam and Eve, Jesus did not have a fallen sin nature while He was in the flesh. However, the Son of God was most assuredly tempted in every way that we are tempted.

Matthew Henry's Commentary on the Bible

Jesus had no corrupt nature, therefore he was tempted only by the devil.[101]

This is why the Scripture refers to Jesus as the "second Adam" (Romans 5:14; 1 Corinthians 15:22, 45). This is also why scholars have long recognized that it was absolutely necessary for the second Adam to come into the fallen world in order to redeem it for His own.

Barnes' Notes on the Bible

When the first Adam was created he was subjected to the temptation of the devil, and he fell and involved the race in ruin: it was not improper that **the second Adam**—the Redeemer of the race—**should be subjected to temptation**, in order that it might be seen that there was no power that could alienate him from God.[102] (Emphasis added)

Meyer's New Testament Commentary

[Jesus] **is called, however, and is the last Adam in reference to the first Adam**, whose antitype He is as the head and the beginner of the new humanity.... For during his earthly life Christ **had a body of human flesh** (only **without sin,** Romans 8:3), which ate, drank, slept, consisted of flesh and blood, suffered, died, etc.[103] (Emphasis added)

HE COULD HAVE GIVEN IN

But here's the most important point. Jesus truly *could have* yielded to any temptation laid before Him, just as Adam, Eve, Satan, and the fallen angels, who began their lives in a completely sinless state, capitulated to the choice of evil. It was this fact that made Jesus eligible to be our substitutionary sacrifice.

That divine plan called for the Lord of glory to step into the fallen world while experiencing every pressure and temptation that we experience, but in an unfallen-flesh condition. However, He was required to *stay that way*—delivering Himself to the cross as the final and perfect sacrifice. Jesus would faithfully *choose* to accomplish what Adam and Eve did not.

> [Jesus] withdrew about a stone's throw beyond [His disciples], knelt down and prayed, "Father, if you are willing, take this cup from me; yet not my will, but yours be done." An angel from heaven appeared to him and strengthened him. And being in anguish, he prayed more earnestly, and his sweat was like drops of blood falling to the ground. (Luke 22:39–44, brackets added)

Unlike the first Adam, who had the freedom to make his choices within a pristine and perfect environment, the second Adam would have that same freedom of choice, but in a hostile, tempting, and viciously seductive environment that was universally corrupt and practically irresistible.

Never doubt, Jesus' fleshly temptations were as genuine as they get—and even more intense than anything we've ever endured. Practically every one of the most renowned classical scholars agrees with this assessment. Have a look at a sampling of those commentaries. Each comments on the biblical truths set forth in Hebrews 4:15:

For we do not have a high priest who is unable to empathize with our weaknesses, but we have one who has been tempted in every way, just as we are—yet he did not sin.

Forerunner Commentary

A [being from the divine realm] had never experienced life as a human being until the Word became flesh, when He was encompassed with the same kind of frame we are. He then also had a mind that was subject to Satan the Devil, if He would allow it.... [The writer of Hebrews] wants us to understand that Jesus' sinlessness was the result of conscious decision and intense struggle, not merely the consequence of His divine nature or the Father's protection or intervention.[104] (Brackets added)

Pulpit Commentary

Christ, in his human nature, partook of all the original affections of humanity ... his assumption of our humanity would have otherwise been incomplete. Such affections are not in themselves sinful; they only are so when, under temptation, any of them become inordinate, and serve as motives to transgression of duty. He, in virtue of his Divine personality, could not through them be seduced into sin; but it does not follow that he could not, in his human nature, feel their power to seduce, or rather the power of the tempter to seduce through them, and thus have personal experience of man's temptation.[105]

Gill's Exposition of the Entire Bible

There was no sin in his nature; though he was encompassed about with infirmities, yet not with sinful infirmities, only sinless ones; nor was there any sin in his temptations; though he was solicited to sin by Satan.[106]

Matthew Poole's Commentary

Was pierced and tried by all sorts of sufferings, **being outwardly tempted by the devil to sin; inwardly he could not**, being perfectly holy, John 14:30; but was outwardly with violence assaulted by him, Matthew 4:1–11: and tried by men beyond any man, **and tempted to the same sins whereby Adam fell, and others miscarry every day.** He felt the curse of sin, the wrath of God, agonies in his soul, violent pains in his body, sorrows to the death from the cradle to the cross: and **in every matter of grief and suffering** in soul, in body, from the world, from Satan, from God, **in all kinds of temptations spiritual and temporal;** experiencing the evils of this life, hunger, thirst, weariness, grief, Isaiah 53:3–10, even such as we are liable to, *all of them really and truly like ours, and more powerfully than ours.*[107] (Emphasis added)

Robertson's Word Pictures of the New Testament

He did not yield to sin. But more than this is true. **There was no latent sin in Jesus to be stirred by temptation** and no habits of sin to be overcome. But he did have "weaknesses" common to our human nature (hunger, thirst, weariness, etc.). **Satan used his strongest weapons against Jesus**, did it repeatedly, and failed. **Jesus remained "undefiled" in a world of sin** (John 8:46).[108] (Emphasis added)

Expository Notes of Dr. Thomas Constable

His temptations did not come from a sinful nature, as some of ours do, since He had no sinful nature, **but He suffered temptation as we do because He was fully human.** Since He endured every temptation successfully **He experienced temptations more thoroughly than we do when we yield to them before they pass.** Consequently He can sympathize (feel and suffer) with us when we experience temptation. The writer's point was that Jesus understands us, He sympathizes with us, and He overcame temptation himself.[109] (Emphasis added)

The answers to our original questions are obvious by now. But those revelations were not so apparent to Satan and his demonic horde as they observed this *One from heaven* delivering blow after crushing blow to their kingdom powers. Exactly who was this creature who willfully trespassed upon their sovereign domain?

Thus, the pummeling of Yeshua never ended—until it was far too late.

20

EVEN THE DEMONS

**Every challenge on their part, every question,
every probe, was still a "test" of Jesus'
actual power and authority.**

I f Satan didn't know who Jesus was, then how did the demons seem to
know?

This question is sometimes asked because not too long after the
wilderness experience, we find in Luke 4 the fact that certain demons
emphatically address Jesus as the "Son of God." Additionally, Luke par-
enthetically adds, "Because they *knew he was the Messiah.*"

> Moreover, demons came out of many people, shouting, "You
> are the Son of God!" But he rebuked them and would not allow
> them to speak, **because they knew he was the Messiah.** (Luke
> 4:41, emphasis added)

But here's the truth of the matter: For Jesus to be addressed by
Satan's minions as "the Son of God" or the "Holy One of God" would
have been nothing more than what Satan himself had already done

in the wilderness, or even what John had proclaimed at the Jordan River. The problem with this verse, according to some scholars, lies with Luke's additional observation that the demons "knew he was the Messiah."

However, even if that were true, we still face the question: "But did the demons know, early on, that Jesus would ultimately deliver Himself to the cross? Did they know the exact details of Jesus' mission and methods?"

It is apparent that Satan and his demonic horde suspected that Jesus was the true Messiah—the One who had come to destroy their kingdom. But as the context of Scripture indicates, they were not 100 percent certain of *exactly what* that designation encompassed, or how He would accomplish His mission.

Have a look at the other passages wherein demons speak to Jesus and assert that they possess some degree of knowledge concerning His divine nature:

- What do you want with us, Jesus of Nazareth? Have you come to destroy us? **I know who you are—the Holy One of God!** (Luke 4:34, emphasis added)
- What do you want with us, Jesus of Nazareth? Have you come to destroy us? **I know who you are—the Holy One of God!** (Mark 1:24, emphasis added)
- Jesus healed many who had various diseases. He also drove out many demons, but he would not let the demons speak **because they knew who he was.** (Mark 1:34, emphasis added)
- Whenever the impure spirits saw him, they fell down before him and cried out, "**You are the Son of God.**" (Mark 3:11, emphasis added)

The *Pulpit Commentary* offers a clear summation of what we are dealing with in regard to each of these demonic declarations:

It was given to them by [the Lord] who has supreme power over the spiritual as well as the material world, **to know as much as he saw fit that they should know**; and he was pleased to make known **as much as was needful.**...

But he made himself known to them, **not as he makes himself known to the holy angels**, who know him **as the Word of God**, and rejoice in his eternity, of which they partake. To the evil spirits he made himself known only so far as was requisite to strike with terror the beings from whose tyranny [Satan and his kingdom of the demonic realm] he was about to free those who were predestinated unto his kingdom and the glory of it.[110] (Emphasis and brackets added)

The *IVP New Testament Commentary* takes the matter even a step deeper:

The demon *asks* whether Jesus of Nazareth has come to destroy us.... In effect, **the remark, though it is posed as a question,** [actually] *poses a challenge.*

Given the note in the next verse about the man emerging from the exorcism unharmed...**the demon *does not think* he can be challenged** without the man's being harmed as well.... As James 2:19 suggests, **demons have *knowledge* about God but fail to respond** to that knowledge.[111] (Emphasis and brackets added)

In short, Satan and the demons knew a lot about Jesus by the time of these confrontations. At this juncture, they understood much more about Him than most of humanity knew. But they categorically *did not* know everything. And concerning what they did know, their diabolical arrogance and pride inhibited them from properly acting upon that information. They assumed, that somehow, they could ultimately defeat this One called the Messiah of God.

INTELLIGENCE GATHERING

Every future demonic challenge, every question, every probe was still a "test" of Jesus' power and authority. His supernatural authority was obvious. His ability to display the miraculous was undeniable. But the particulars of all that He would do and exactly how He would accomplish redemption's plan were not for the demonic realm to know. Not yet.

As Scripture reveals, the demonic realm did not know that Jesus was on the earth to purposely offer Himself as a living sacrifice on a Roman cross for the final redemption of humanity. And *there* was the vital key.

It will soon become strikingly apparent that Satan, the demons, and the demonically inspired religious elite of the human realm had convinced themselves that *they* were the ones who ultimately delivered Jesus to the cross. They thought that His death would be the end of all their problems.

What a horrific miscalculation that was.

But it was one that Jesus was certain they would make.

Indeed, heaven's redemptive strategy was counting on it.

THE CONFEDERACY OF EVIL

Jesus knew it. And, He called them out.

The thrones of power in Jesus' day—especially in Rome—had become thoroughly gripped by the demonic influence of Satan's kingdom.

Of course, those demonically manipulated authorities also involved the serpent's entanglement among the Jewish religious elite in Judea. The New Testament does not paint a very pretty picture in regard to this. A large swath of biblical narrative indicates the vast majority of the Jewish elite loathed the very existence of Jesus. As a result, at almost every turn, they sought to kill Him.

We do have evidence, however, that not all the Jewish leadership felt that way. Early on in His ministry, some of them even tried to warn Jesus of certain governmental/religious plots upon His life. One such plot had been perpetrated by Rome's hand-picked *King of the Jews*—Herod.

> At that time some Pharisees came to Jesus and said to him, "Leave this place and go somewhere else. Herod wants to kill you." (Luke 13:31)

Also, at the very end of Jesus' earthly ministry, right after His death on the cross, two Sanhedrin members, Nicodemus and Joseph of Arimathea, risked their lives and reputations in order to collect Jesus' body from the cross and entomb it with dignity.[112]

But, from the very beginning, the vast majority of the influential Jewish movers and shakers plotted the murder of this man called Jesus of Nazareth. Of course, the exposing of that demonic alliance was set in motion by Jesus Himself as He publicly identified those religious authorities for who they were—and more importantly, for whom they were really working.

THEIR REAL FATHER

Jesus' charges against the religious elite mirrored those of John the Baptist at the Jordan River. Have a look at several examples of Jesus' invectives:

- You are **doing the things your own father** does. You **belong to your father, the devil**, and you want to **carry out your father's desire.** He was a murderer **from the beginning,** not holding to the truth, for there is no truth in him. When he lies, he speaks **his native language,** for he is a liar and the father of lies. He who belongs to God hears what God says. The reason you do not hear is that **you do not belong to God.** (John 8:41, 44, 47, emphasis added)
- You **brood of vipers**, how can you who are evil say anything good? (Matthew 12:34, emphasis added)
- You **snakes!** You **brood of vipers!** How will you escape being condemned to hell? (Matthew 23:33–34, emphasis added)
- Woe to you, teachers of the law and Pharisees, you hypocrites! You travel over land and sea to win a single convert, and when he becomes one, **you make him twice as much a son of hell as you are.** (Matthew 23:15, emphasis added)

Now have a look at how a sampling of the classical scholars viewed Jesus' words of accusation against the Sadducees and Pharisees:

Expositor's Greek Testament

Being, of this parentage they deliberately purpose and **not merely unintentionally** are betrayed into the fulfilment of [Satan's] desires.[113] (Emphasis and brackets added)

Jamieson-Fausset-Brown Bible Commentary

Ye will do—are willing to do; not of any blind necessity of nature, but of pure **natural inclination**.[114] (Emphasis added)

Barnes' Notes on the Bible

Ye serpents—This name is given to them on account of their pretending to be pious, and very much devoted to God, but **being secretly evil, at the heart**, with all their pretensions, they were **filled with evil designs, as the serpent was [in the Garden of Eden]**. Genesis 3:1–5.[115] (Emphasis and brackets added. The Genesis 3 reference is in the original.)

THE ATTACK

The plot to deal with Jesus involved two main elements. The primary tactic was to insist that Jesus "prove Himself." Thus, the religious leaders continually mocked Him with the demands: "If you are the Son of God…" and "Show us a sign." Of course, these were the same temptations with which Satan hammered Jesus in the wilderness.

Here are a few examples:

- The Jews who were there gathered around him, saying, "How long will you keep us in suspense? **If you are the Messiah**, tell us plainly." (John 10:24, emphasis added)
- The Pharisees and Sadducees came to Jesus and tested him by asking him to **show them a sign from heaven**. (Matthew 16:1, emphasis added)
- The Pharisees came and began to question Jesus. To test him, they asked him **for a sign from heaven**. (Mark 8:11–12, emphasis added)
- Others tested him by **asking for a sign from heaven**. (Luke 11:16, emphasis added)
- At daybreak the council of the elders of the people, both the chief priests and the teachers of the law, met together, and Jesus was led before them. **"If you are the Messiah,"** they said, **"Tell us."** Jesus answered, "If I tell you, you will not believe me." (Luke 22:66–67, emphasis added)
- **The soldiers** also came up and **mocked him**. They offered him wine vinegar and said, **"If you are the king of the Jews, save yourself."** **One of the criminals** who hung there hurled insults at him: **"Aren't you the Christ? Save yourself and us!"** (Luke 23:36–37, 39, emphasis added)

Satan's accusatory probing tactics would endure, embodied within the serpent's human counterparts, right up to the night of Jesus' arrest.

And they would continue throughout the entirety of that dreadful day at Golgotha's hill.

22

GIVE US A PEEK!

They demanded to be an exclusive audience...

Show us a sign from heaven!
    Each time the Jews demanded that Jesus show them a sign "from heaven," there is a depth of meaning involved that the English translations simply don't express very well.

The word "from" in the Greek language of the New Testament is *ek*. For such a small word, the meaning is quite impressive. *Helps Word-studies* addresses the matter like this:

> Ek ("out of") is **one of the most under-translated** (and **therefore mis-translated**) Greek prepositions. (Ek) has a **two-layered meaning** ("out from and to") which makes it out-come oriented (out of the depths of the source and extending to its impact on the object).[116] (Emphasis added; parentheses in the original)

Strong's Exhaustive Concordance defines this word to mean: "Suggesting from the interior outwards."[117] *Thayer's Greek Lexicon* agrees: "It denotes exit or emission out of, as separation from, something with which there has been close connection. From the midst (of a group, number, company, community) of many."[118]

In other words, the Jews were demanding that Jesus should visibly command the doors of heaven itself to open and expose its interior. They demanded to be an exclusive audience to such a sign.

In effect, they were demanding of Jesus: "Show us what Moses, Isaiah, Abraham, Ezekiel, and Daniel saw. Show us the throne of God, like what John the Baptist claims he saw. If you can do that, then we will believe you are indeed the Son of God."

This understanding is certainly quite different from the more benign-sounding English rendering of "Show us a sign from heaven."

THE SECOND TACTIC

The various plots by the Jewish elite to kill Jesus started very early in His ministry. Jesus was aware of their plans. He even spoke parabolically about the demonic plot. He did this in order to make certain those with "eyes to see and ears to hear" would understand the stakes in this cosmic war:

> Listen to another parable.... But when **the tenants saw the son,** they said to each other, "This is the heir. **Come, let's kill him** and take his inheritance." **So they took him** and threw him out of the vineyard **and killed him.** (Matthew 21:33, 38–39, emphasis added)

Ellicott's Commentary on the Bible

> The words of the parable showed that [the Jewish religious elite] stood face to face with One who knew the secrets of their hearts, and **had not deceived himself as to the issue of the conflict in which He was now engaged.**[119] (Emphasis added)

Pulpit Commentary

Ancient prophecy, the signs of the times, the miracles and teaching of Christ, the testimony of the Baptist, pointed to one evident conclusion; **evidence had been accumulating on all sides. A latent feeling had grown up that he was the Messiah** (see John 11:49–52), and it was obstinate prejudice and perversity alone that prevented his open acknowledgment.... They plotted his destruction.[120] (Emphasis added)

Jamieson-Fausset-Brown Bible Commentary

Come, let us kill him, and let us seize on his inheritance—that so, from mere servants, we may become lords. This is the deep **aim of the depraved heart**; this is **emphatically "the root of all evil."**[121] (Emphasis added)

Satan's plan was to utterly destroy the "Son" from heaven. So, as it turned out, Satan would plan another *Eden-like* coup. Once again, his scheme would include murder.

But not just one death would be involved. They were going to try and cover all the angles. They were playing for keeps.

23

THE DEATH SENTENCE

They had actually planned a double murder.

From the opening days of His earthly ministry, Satan marked Yeshua as a "dead man walking."

Since this "Son of God" had dared to enter the realm that Satan thought was legally his, the primeval serpent was determined to bring about Jesus' death by manipulating certain thrones of earthly power.

Consider the biblical evidence:

- Then the Pharisees went out and began to plot with the Herodians **how they might kill Jesus.** (Mark 3:6, emphasis added)
- The chief priests and the teachers of the law heard this and began **looking for a way to kill him,** for they feared him, because the whole crowd was amazed at his teaching. (Mark 11:18, emphasis added)
- Every day he was teaching at the temple. But the **chief priests, the teachers of the law and the leaders** among the people **were trying to kill him.** (Luke 19:47–48, emphasis added)
- For this reason **the Jews tried all the harder to kill him;** not only was he breaking the Sabbath, but he was even calling God

his own Father, making himself equal with God. (John 5:18, emphasis added)

- Then the **chief priests and the elders** of the people assembled in the palace of **the high priest**, whose name was Caiaphas, and they **plotted to arrest Jesus in some sly way and kill him.** (Matthew 26:3–5, emphasis added)
- At this, [**the Jews**] **picked up stones to stone him**, but Jesus hid himself, slipping away from the temple grounds. (John 8:59, emphasis and brackets added)
- So from that day on they **plotted to take his life.** (John 11:53, emphasis added)
- Again **the Jews picked up stones to stone him**, but Jesus said to them, "I have shown you many great miracles from the Father. For which of these do you stone me?" "We are not stoning you for any of these," replied the Jews, "but for blasphemy, **because you, a mere man, claim to be God.**" (John 10:31–33, emphasis added)
- But the **chief priests and the elders persuaded the crowd to ask** for Barabbas and **to have Jesus executed.** (Matthew 27:20, emphasis added)
- "What shall I do, then, with Jesus who is called Christ?" Pilate asked. *They all* **answered, "Crucify him!"** (Matthew 27:22, emphasis added)

A DOUBLE MURDER

Are you ready for another biblical shocker? Satan even put it into the hearts of his Jewish-elite pawns to kill Lazarus as well! They had essentially planned a double murder. One plan was to kill Jesus; the other was to kill the living evidence of His power. Here's the biblical confirmation:

Meanwhile a large crowd of Jews found out that Jesus was there and came, not only because of him but also to see Lazarus, whom he had raised from the dead. So **the chief priests made plans to kill Lazarus as well,** for on account of him many of the **Jews were going over to Jesus and believing in him.** (John 12:9–11, emphasis added)

Here are a few examples of the scholarly attestation of the same:

Ellicott's Commentary on the Bible

The chief priests were for the most part Sadducees (Acts 5:17). They have been acting with the Pharisees from John 11:47 onwards. Their animus is shown in that, while no charge is brought against Lazarus, his life **is a witness to the divinity of him [Jesus] whom they have condemned to death.**[122] (Emphasis and brackets added)

Bengel's Gnomen

There was one doctrine, and **one miracle**, which especially **occasioned their killing Jesus**: the doctrine was that of Jesus being **the Son of God**; the miracle, the raising again of Lazarus.[123] (Emphasis added)

Pulpit Commentary

They **deliberated to kill Lazarus as well as Jesus.** It was not enough that one man should die; another and another must follow **if their plan is to succeed.**[124] (Emphasis added)

Jamieson-Fausset-Brown Bible Commentary

> [Jesus raising Lazarus from the dead] led to a plot against the life of Lazarus also, as the only means of **arresting the triumphs of Jesus** (see John 12:19)—**to such a pitch had these chief priests come of diabolical determination** to shut out the light from themselves, and **quench it from the earth.**[125] (Emphasis added)

Additionally, we have the witness of heaven's throne itself, given to John the Revelator. Revelation 12 tells us that from the beginning of Jesus' life, Satan clearly intended to kill this "Son of God":

> **The dragon stood in front of the woman who was about to give birth, so that it might devour her child the moment he was born.** She gave birth to a son, a male child, who "will rule all the nations with an iron scepter." (Revelation 12:1–4, emphasis added)

Cambridge Bible for Schools and Colleges

> [Revelation 12] Symbolizes the enmity of the serpent against the seed of the woman, beginning with the intended treachery of Herod, and massacre of the Innocents; but including also the malice that pursued him through life, the temptation, and at last the Cross.[126] (Brackets added)

If you didn't see it before, do you see the pattern now? It's pretty apparent once the proper contextual links are made.

Ask yourself another question: "Doesn't it stand to reason that if Satan worked so hard to kill Jesus, wouldn't this fact indicate that Satan thought by killing the Holy One from heaven he would somehow come out on top?" Of course it does. No matter how one tries to slice and dice the analysis of the matter, that is the undeniable, foundational truth. And what a revelation that is!

However, there was still at least one more eternally significant piece of information that Satan did not possess. That information has always been right before the eyes of every student of God's Word—and the evidence of it is found not only in the New Testament, it's in the Old Testament as well.

THE MISSING PIECE

The whole thing had already been planned at the throne of Elohim—without Satan's knowledge.

What Satan didn't know would eventually prove to be his undoing. Everything we have explored thus far makes even more sense when we consider that Satan obviously thought Calvary's cross and the torture, crucifixion, and death of Jesus were *his* ideas. This is no small consideration.

We now know it was Satan who "filled Judas" with the idea of betraying Jesus unto death on a cross (Luke 22:3). But why would Satan have done such a thing if he knew the crucifixion would turn out to be his own demise? The answer is that he wouldn't have done it—of course. The only reasonable conclusion is that he purely didn't know the gravity of the mistake he had made.

On the other hand, Jesus not only knew who would ultimately betray Him, but He also knew who would prompt that betrayer to accomplish the deed. The power behind Judas "the betrayer" was none other than the old serpent from the Garden of Eden.

Yeshua would use this knowledge to the advantage of heaven's plan—and, ultimately, for our deliverance and salvation.

For Jesus had **known from the beginning** which of them did not believe and **who would betray him.** (John 6:64–65, emphasis added)

Jesus reminded His disciples that He was the One who chose *them*, not the other way around. This was His way of affirming that everything was ultimately in His hands.

You did not choose me, but I chose you and appointed you. (John 15:16, brackets added. Also see John 6:70, John 13:18, and Acts 1:2)

ARRANGING THE PUZZLE PIECES

The whole thing had been planned at the throne of Elohim, and without Satan's knowledge. Considering the biblical evidence that clearly supports this fact, it is increasingly apparent that there truly was much about Jesus that Satan did not know, but he was desperately trying to figure it out, right up to the end.

Bengel's Gnomen also asserts the case just made, beginning with the words of Jesus in John 6:64:

The very time of this discourse is marked, although Jesus, **even before that time, had always known** what was about to be.[127] (Emphasis added)

The following biblical declarations further prove that Jesus' mission to Calvary's cross was foreordained at the throne of God before Adam drew his first breath.

All inhabitants of the earth will worship the beast—all whose names have not been written in the Lamb's book of life, **the Lamb who was slain from the creation of the world**. (Revelation 13:18, emphasis added)

...but with the precious blood of Christ, a lamb without blemish or defect. **He was chosen before the creation of the world**, but was revealed in these last times for your sake. (1 Peter 1:19–20, emphasis added)

And let us not forget that it was Peter, at the birth of the church, who also declared this same truth in his first sermon:

This [Jesus] was **handed over to you** [through Judas] **by God's deliberate plan and foreknowledge**; and you, **with the help of wicked men**, put him to death by nailing him to the cross. (Acts 2:23, emphasis and brackets added)

Now, let's snap another piece of this puzzle into place. When we do this, the picture grows increasingly clearer.

FORETOLD BY THE PROPHETS

Most students of the Word are familiar with the Old Testament prophecies that foreshadow the crucifixion of the Messiah (i.e., Psalm 22, Isaiah 53, and Zechariah 12). However, there are also ancient biblical prophecies that reveal the place of Judas Iscariot within heaven's redemptive schematic.

Peter declared this truth in his Pentecost sermon:

Brothers and sisters, **the Scripture had to be fulfilled** in which the Holy Spirit spoke long ago **through David concerning Judas,** who served as guide for those who arrested Jesus. [Psalm 41:9] (Acts 1:16, brackets and emphasis added)

Jesus also told His disciples that Judas' role had been foretold by David:

I am not referring to all of you; I know those I have chosen. But this is **to fulfill this passage of Scripture:** "He who shared my bread has turned against me." [Psalm 41:9] (John 13:18, brackets and emphasis added)

The prophet Zechariah lays out very specific details of Judas' betrayal, including his tossing of the money back to his tempters at the Temple and his direct connection with Potter's Field.[128]

I told them, "If you think it best, give me my pay; but if not, keep it." So **they paid me thirty pieces of silver.** And the Lord said to me, "Throw it to the potter"—the handsome price at which they valued me! So I took **the thirty pieces of silver and threw them to the potter at the house of the Lord.** (Zechariah 11:12–13, emphasis added)

Now look at Matthew 27:5–10 from the *Aramaic Bible in Plain English* translation:[129]

And he cast the silver into The Temple and departed, and he went and hanged himself. But the Chief Priests took the silver, and they said, "It is not legal to put it into the treasury, because it is the price of blood." And they took counsel, and they bought with it the field of a potter as a graveyard for the burial of strangers.

Therefore that field has been called, "The Field of Blood," until this day. **Then was fulfilled what was spoken by the Prophet** who said, "I took thirty silver coins, the price of the Precious One on which they of the children of Israel had agreed. And I gave them for the potter's field as THE LORD JEHOVAH commanded me." (ABPE, emphasis added)[130]

What we have uncovered thus far is truly amazing. These biblical truths explain why Satan manipulated his earthly emissaries to do his bidding of bringing Jesus to a sentence of death. Satan was obviously convinced that the Son of God, as long as He was in human flesh, could truly be *killed,* thus eliminating heaven's influence over his own demonic kingdom.

So the serpent pushed forward, thinking he had devised the perfect plan of retaliation. Judas would be his key to unraveling Elohim's design, and would serve as a puppet of his influence and manipulation. But Nachash could not have been more mistaken. The whole thing was a divine setup.

HIDDEN IN PLAIN SIGHT

A legal case had to be made.

Here's the clincher that verifies our thesis concerning Judas: Jesus affirmed that the traitorous Judas Iscariot was "possessed" by Satan.

But, why would Satan think Judas would be a key player in his overall plan? It was because the serpent was attempting to physically destroy the Son of God. He thought Judas could be used to that end. Satan just didn't realize how quickly his plan would go awry, then finally come back upon his own head.

The Bible Exposition Commentary—New Testament

> Satan thought that he had succeeded when he used Judas to betray the Lord and handed him over to be crucified. But the Cross was actually Satan's defeat![131]

It was this proud assumption that would ultimately unwind everything else Satan had carefully constructed through the ages, ever since the unfolding of his diabolical plot that began in the Garden of Eden.[132] If curiosity killed the cat, then it would prove to be pure unadulterated arrogance that would eventually kill the serpent.

But, because of Judas' deep character flaws, he eventually became Satan's willing puppet. Satan honed in on Judas' prime weaknesses: his love of money, his overzealous and haughty religious spirit, as well as his lustful desire to eventually sit upon a throne of earthly power.

However, in His omniscience, Jesus, as well, had chosen Judas for this very purpose. The monumental difference was that Jesus didn't override Judas' will. He didn't *make* Judas betray Him. He didn't manipulate Judas in any way. Judas was not Jesus' puppet. He knew from the beginning that Judas would do it.[133]

Scripture speaks of the omniscient nature of Jesus—a fact that proves His absolute divinity:

> But Jesus would not entrust himself to them, for he knew all men. He did not need man's testimony about man, for he knew what was in a man. (John 2:24–25)

Barnes' Notes on the Bible

> [He knew what was in man] This he did because he had made all (John 1:3), and because he was God, John 1:1. There can be no higher evidence than this that he was omniscient, and was therefore divine. To search the heart is the prerogative of God alone (Jer. 17:10); and as Jesus knew what was in "these disciples," and as it is expressly said that he knew what was in MAN—that is, in "all people"—so it follows that he must be equal with God.[134]

The Bible Exposition Commentary—New Testament

> [Jesus] did not accept human testimony. Why? Because, being God, He knew what was in each person's heart and mind.[135]

Jesus already knew the exact path Judas would ultimately choose:

> Then Jesus replied, "Have I not chosen you, the Twelve? Yet one of you **is a devil!**" (John 6:70, emphasis added)

This startling revelation was Jesus' way of assuring His disciples: "I've got this! I know things that you don't know. Trust me in this matter."

THE CHOICE

This speech, made in the company of all His disciples, including Judas, was Jesus' discreet way of letting Judas know *I'm onto you. You need to repent now, before you make this eternal mistake.*

Judas didn't heed the advice. He didn't repent. Though this is a tough matter to reconcile within the confines of our purely human reasoning, even reputable scholars have seen this same truth:

Pulpit Commentary

> By these warnings the Lord **was giving [Judas] chance after chance of escaping** from what, even to the Lord's prophetic human foresight, looked like his destiny. **We may compare Christ's severe rebuke to Peter,** when, after the grand confession (Matthew 16:16), he counted himself worthy to disapprove the methods of his Lord's mercy, "**Get thee behind me, Satan:** thou art an offence to me; thou savourest not the things that be of God, but the things that be of men."
>
> Judas did far worse—he wanted to use the Divine power of his Master for his own personal ends.... This "choice" is repeatedly referred to (John 13:18; John 15:16; cf. Luke 6:13;

Acts 1:2, 24).... **Yet this choice, to Christ's human nature and self-consciousness, was early seen to be one which was not softening but hardening the heart of Judas.**[136] (Emphasis added)

POSSESSED

We have to believe that the omniscient Jesus knew Judas would not repent. However, it was still Judas' decision to make, just like Adam and Eve had a decision to make in the Garden of Eden. In the same way, Judas was confronted with a similar choice. The same serpent from the Garden was alive and well...now tempting Judas. He chose the path of rebellion. A legally exposed door through which Satan could "possess" Judas was thrust open.

However, because of Jesus' very real offer and Judas' genuine opportunity to make the right choice, Judas could never say before the throne of God that he "didn't know," or that he was never given the option to turn back. In this way, in the end, heaven's final judgment of Judas would be brought to bear in absolute righteousness.

Meyer's New Testament Commentary on John 6:70 illuminates the meaning of Jesus' heartbreaking words concerning Judas' alliance with Satan:

[Jesus said that Judas was] Not an informer, not an adversary or betrayer, **but, [a] devil,** whereby antagonism to Christ is **set forth in its strongest manner...in keeping with its demoniacal nature.**[137] (Emphasis and brackets added)

Gill's Exposition of the Entire Bible likewise addresses the depth of Jesus' declaration:

And **one of you is a devil** or like to one, is a deceiver, a liar, and a murderer, as the devil is from the beginning; all which Judas was, and appeared to be, in the betraying of his master. Judas, who, notwithstanding his profession of faith in Christ, **was in the hands and kingdom of Satan, and under his influence and power.**[138] (Emphasis added)

Vincent's Word Studies states the matter of Jesus' woeful words in the most succinct of ways:

It is of **the very essence of the devilish nature** to oppose Christ.[139] (Emphasis added)

There are still additional passages in the New Testament that pointedly speak to Judas' demonically influenced condition.

Now the Feast of Unleavened Bread, called the Passover, was approaching, and the chief priests and **the teachers of the law were looking for some way to get rid of Jesus,** for they were afraid of the people. **Then Satan entered Judas,** called Iscariot, one of the Twelve. And Judas **went to the chief priests** and the officers of the temple guard and discussed with them **how he might betray Jesus.** (Luke 22:1–4, emphasis added)

Meyer's New Testament Commentary testifies to the literal nature of Luke's choice of words:

The part played by the devil, who is conceived of as an actual intrusion, as the [Greek] word [used here] is constantly used to express **the intrusion of demons into bodies** (Luke 8:30; Luke 8:32 f., Luke 11:27, emphasis added).[140]

At the Last Supper, Jesus speaks of the soon-coming personal appearance of Satan. A number of scholars see this as Satan's physical arrival in the person of Judas.

I will not say much more to you, for **the prince of this world is coming.** He has no hold over me. (John 14:30, emphasis added)

Ellicott's Commentary for English Readers

The prince of evil is here regarded as **working in and by Judas,** who is carrying out his plans and doing his work.[141] (Emphasis added)

Expositor's Greek Testament

"The ruler of this world" is Satan, see John 12:31. He "comes" **in the treachery of Judas** (John 13:27) and all that followed.[142] (Emphasis added)

Cambridge Bible for Schools and Colleges

The powers of darkness are **at work in Judas** and his employers.[143] (Emphasis added)

Pulpit Commentary

The activity of evil was then at work. **Satan entered into Judas;** the spirit of evil was rampant in all the machination of the leaders of the people.[144] (Emphasis added)

Matthew Poole's Commentary

He cometh by the evil angels, or rather by vile and wicked men, as his instruments, Judas and the soldiers.[145]

Although John's Gospel uses the word "prompted" to describe Satan's sway over Judas, John also uses the words "entered into him," just a few verses later:

The evening meal was being served, and the devil had already **prompted** Judas Iscariot, son of Simon, to betray Jesus. (John 13:2–3, emphasis added)

As soon as Judas took the bread, **Satan entered into him**. "What you are about to do, do quickly," Jesus told him. (John 13:27, emphasis added)

John, an eyewitness to the event, says that at that particular moment, Judas was literally possessed by Satan.

Meyer's New Testament Commentary

So that he was therefore from **henceforward a man possessed by the devil**, Mark 5:12–13; Mark 9:25; Luke 8:30; Matthew 12:45.[146] (Emphasis added)

Cambridge Bible for Schools and Colleges

At first Satan made suggestions to him (John 13:2) and Judas listened to them; **now Satan takes full possession of him.**[147] (Emphasis added)

Pulpit Commentary

> [John, the Gospel writer] **clearly saw what he thus described—** he saw the malign and unrelenting expression on Judas's face; he suspected that some devilish plot was hatched, some hideous purpose finally formed. It is **the evangelist's way of saying what he personally saw and afterwards concluded.**[148] (Brackets and emphasis added)

Heaven's throne had ordained the plan even before the foundation of the world. Jesus already knew where the plan would lead. He even knew the horror of the road set before Him. He fully understood what it would require. He was completely aware of the fact that the players would include every power and authority Satan commanded. Jesus also knew He would have to draw Satan into a trap. A legal case had to be made. The plan would call for divine patience and holy cunning—and most especially, it would call for resolute faithfulness.

John witnessed the demonic possession of Judas. What a painful thing that must have been for softhearted John to have experienced. Yet, there it was, right in front of him. He would never forget it.

Satan had finally manipulated Judas into delivering Jesus to the stake of flogging—then to the cross of crucifixion, one of the cruelest deaths ever devised by humanity.[149]

Satan could not have known, at this point, the devastation to his own kingdom that he had ultimately set in motion.

If he had, he would never have acted so foolishly.

26

DIDN'T HE KNOW THE PROPHECIES?

**He could never have understood this was
Jesus' plan from the beginning.**

Why didn't Satan just read the Bible? After all, the foretelling of the coming Messiah, His place of birth, the miracles He would work, the fact that He would be betrayed, His suffering on the cross, His resurrection, and His ultimate victory—it was all right there in front of Satan's face. *Right?* Could Nachash have really been so foolish as to not be able to figure out the biblical clues?

Remember though, the very earliest New Testament documents weren't written and distributed among the Christians until several decades *after* the resurrection of Yeshua and the birth of the church. Obviously, Satan had no prior access to the invaluable information that Scripture contained regarding the full details of heaven's redemptive plan. By the time it was finally circulated, that material evidence was mere hindsight to Satan.

So, we are left with *this* question: Why didn't Satan know the *Old Testament* prophecies concerning the coming of Messiah and the details of God's plan of redemption contained therein?

SUPERNATURALLY CLEVER

It is quite evident that Satan knew Scripture. He even quoted Scripture to Jesus during the wilderness temptation episode. But, as we've already discovered, he didn't completely comprehend all the passages that specifically pertained to Messiah and the details of how Yeshua would ultimately carry out His mission.

"But," you might ask, "How could this be? Isn't Satan transcendentally intelligent?"

Yes. But even Satan, with all of his superior acumen, lacked one key ingredient to the final mix. He didn't have the Holy Spirit illumination that is necessary to decode the deep mysteries of God's word. Satan's heart was blackened with pride and greed. His hatred for Yahweh had blinded him to the ability to crack the codes that were long ago implanted in God's word. They were there only for those who had "eyes to see." Satan certainly did not have those spiritually acute eyes.

Think of the "highly educated" ones in our own day who are not only unbelievers, but who also openly mock God's glory. In all of their intellectual brilliance, the deep things of the Word of God are still unfathomable to them. They see God's wisdom as mere foolishness. It was the same principle with Satan—maybe even more so, considering the immeasurable vanity and arrogant condescension that are the essence of his character.

> Brothers and sisters, think of what you were when you were called. Not many of you were wise by human standards; not many were influential; not many were of noble birth. But God chose the foolish things of the world to shame the wise; God chose the weak things of the world to shame the strong. (1 Corinthians 1:26–27)

Regardless of Satan's poring over Scripture—if in fact he ever did such a thing—he never realized that Messiah had already planned to deliver Himself to the cross and would willingly suffer and die for the sins of fallen humanity—until, that is, it was much too late for Satan to do anything about it.

NOT ALONE

The misinterpretation about the Messiah of Scripture was often shared by the significant players of the New Testament days as well. Consider the following groups who consistently misunderstood the revelations of God:

The Pharisees and Sadducees

Obviously, this group categorically rejected the idea of a suffering and crucified Messiah. In fact, humanly speaking, they were instrumental in putting Jesus on the cross in the first place. They mocked anything Jesus said that even hinted at His real mission and its details.

The Jewish People

> [Jesus said] Now is the time for judgment on this world; now the prince of this world will be driven out. And I, **when I am lifted up** from the earth, will draw all people to myself." He said this to show the kind of death he was going to die. **The crowd spoke up,** "We have heard from the Law that the Messiah will remain forever, so **how can you say, 'The Son of Man must be lifted up'? Who is this 'Son of Man'?"** (John 12:31–34, emphasis added)

The Jews then responded to him, "**What sign can you show** us to **prove your authority** to do all this?" Jesus answered them, "**Destroy this temple, and I will raise it again in three days.**" They replied, "It has taken forty-six years to build this temple, and **you are going to raise it in three days?**" But the temple he had spoken of was his body. (John 2:18–21, emphasis added)

Jesus' Declaration from the Cross

Father, forgive them, **for they do not know** what they are doing. (Luke 23:34, emphasis added)

One renowned commentator stated the truth of Jesus' statement like this:

If they had [known who Jesus really was], they would not have crucified him, as we cannot suppose that they would knowingly put to death their own Messiah, the hope of the nation, and him who had been so long promised to the fathers.[150] (Brackets added)

Jesus' Disciples

- But the temple he had spoken of was his body. **After he was raised from the dead,** his disciples recalled what he had said. **Then they believed the scripture** and the words that Jesus had spoken. (John 2:21–22, emphasis added)
- While everyone was marveling at all that Jesus did, **he said to his disciples,** "Listen carefully to what I am about to tell you: **The Son of Man is going to be betrayed** into the hands of men." **But they did not understand** what this meant. (Luke 9:43–45, emphasis added)
- **Jesus took the Twelve aside** and told them, "We are going up to Jerusalem, and everything that is written by the prophets about the Son

of Man will be fulfilled. He will be handed over to the Gentiles. They will mock him, insult him, spit on him, flog him and kill him. On the third day he will rise again." **The disciples did not understand any of this. Its meaning was hidden from them, and they did not know what he was talking about.** (Luke 18:31–34, emphasis added)

- Simon Peter asked him, "**Lord, where are you going?**" Jesus replied, "Where I am going, you cannot follow now, but you will follow later." (John 13:36, emphasis added)

- From that time on Jesus began to **explain to his disciples that he must go to Jerusalem and suffer many things** at the hands of the elders, the chief priests and the teachers of the law, and that he **must be killed and on the third day be raised to life. Peter took him aside** and began to **rebuke him. "Never, Lord!"** he said. "**This shall never happen to you!**" (Matthew 16:21–22, emphasis added)

- "And if I go and prepare a place for you, I will come back and take you to be with me that you also may be where I am. **You know the way to the place where I am going.**" Thomas said to him, "**Lord, we don't know where you are going**, so how can we know the way?" (John 14:3–5, emphasis added)

- **Philip said, "Lord, show us the Father** and that will be enough for us." Jesus answered: "**Don't you know me, Philip, even after I have been among you such a long time?** Anyone who has seen me has seen the Father. **How can you say, 'Show us the Father'?**" (John 14:8–9, emphasis added)

- **Now Thomas**…one of the Twelve, was not with the disciples when Jesus came. So the other disciples told him, "We have seen the Lord!" But he said to them, "**Unless I see the nail marks in his hands** and put my finger where the nails were, and put my hand into his side, **I will not believe.**" (John 20:24–25, emphasis added)

But that's not all.

Surprisingly, there were still other key "unbelievers."

THE INNER CIRCLE

The whole matter was a mystery to him.

E ven more astounding than the unbelief among Jesus' own disciples is the crisis of faith we find in none other than John the Baptist. *You know,* the one who saw heaven opened and heard the voice of God. The same one who witnessed the bodily presence of the Holy Spirit emanate from the throne of Elohim, then overshadow the person of Yeshua.

> When John [the baptizer], who was in prison, heard about the deeds of the Messiah, he sent his disciples to ask him, *"Are you the one* who is to come, **or should we expect someone else?"** (Matthew 11:2–3, emphasis and brackets added)

Think of it! Peter, Thomas, Philip, Judas, and even John the Baptist were all part of Jesus' inner circle. But they never understood the fullness of His mission until *after* the resurrection.[151] In fact, at the crucifixion, all the disciples left Jesus in fear for their lives—that is, all except John (John 19:26–27).

The men seized Jesus and arrested him.... Then [all the disciples] deserted him and fled. (Mark 14:46–50, emphasis and brackets added)

SEALED

The point is fairly obvious: If Jesus' own disciples did not immediately grasp the gravity and details of what the Son of God had come to accomplish, then neither did Satan, even with the prophecies and Scripture right before him. To Satan, those passages were meaningless words steeped in silly Jewish tradition. Here's the scriptural evidence of exactly why Satan missed the crucial points of what Yeshua was doing:

- This is what we speak, not in words taught us by human wisdom but in **words taught by the Spirit**, explaining spiritual realities with Spirit-taught words. **The person without the Spirit does not accept the things that come from the Spirit of God but considers them foolishness**, and **cannot understand them** because they are **discerned only through the Spirit.** (1 Corinthians 2:13–14, emphasis added)
- This grace was given me: to preach to the Gentiles the boundless riches of Christ, and to make plain to everyone the administration of **this mystery, which for ages past was kept hidden in God**, who created all things. His intent was that now, **through the church**, the manifold wisdom of God **should be made known to the rulers and authorities in the heavenly realms**, according to **his eternal purpose** that he accomplished in Christ Jesus our Lord. (Ephesians 3:8–11, emphasis added)
- [The angel] replied, Go your way, Daniel, because the words are rolled up and **sealed until the time of the end.** Many will be purified, made spotless and refined, but the **wicked will continue to**

be wicked. None of the wicked will understand, but **those who are wise will understand.** (Daniel 12:9–10, emphasis and brackets added)

Because of the serpent's obscene arrogance and condescending rebelliousness, he couldn't fathom that Jesus would transport Himself to Calvary's cross on purpose. The whole matter was a mystery to him. Today, that fact is still being revealed to the world through the church's preaching of the Gospel of Jesus Christ—to the shame and embarrassment of the ancient serpent.

The truth is now evident. Instead of trying to thwart the divine plan of the mission of the cross, Satan unwittingly lent himself to the process of delivering Jesus to it. And in so doing, he fell right into the hands of heaven's eternal plan.

Imagine that.

28

THE RULERS WHO LOST

He was filled with rage when he discovered it.

Because Satan did not fully understand the messianic prophecies, he apparently thought he could pull off his ultimate counter strategy while God was "imprudent" enough to be "trapped" in human flesh. But, in the end, it was *not* Elohim who would prove to be the tricked one.

Jamieson-Fausset-Brown Bible Commentary (Revelation 20:3)

> **Satan imagined that he had overcome Christ on Golgotha,** and **that his power was secure forever,** but the Lord in death over-came him by His ascension as our righteous advocate cast out Satan, the accuser from heaven.[152] (Emphasis added)

With very little contextual argument otherwise, the Scriptures pointedly bear out this truth.

We do, however, speak a message of wisdom among the mature, but not the wisdom of this age or of **the rulers of this age,** who are coming to nothing. No, we declare God's wisdom, **a mystery that has been hidden** and that God destined for our glory before time began. None of the **rulers of this age** understood it, for if they had, they **would not have crucified the Lord of glory**. (1 Corinthians 2:6–8, emphasis added)

Thayer's Greek Lexicon says of the "rulers of this age" in the 1 Corinthians 2 passage:

[The rulers of this age] The **rulers of nations**, universally, of magistrates; especially judges, members of the Jewish Sanhedrin, **and perhaps also, [that] one who has great influence among the Pharisees** [and those other earthly powers]...**the devil, the prince of evil spirits.**[153] (Brackets added for context to the entire commentary; emphasis added).

The New Testament supplies us with a number of passages wherein Satan and his demonic realm are referred to as the true "rulers" who work behind the scenes in conjunction with the earthly powers.[154]

- To make plain to everyone the administration of this mystery, which for ages past was kept hidden in God, who created all things. His intent was that now, through the church, the manifold wisdom of God should be made known to the **rulers and authorities in the heavenly realms.** (Ephesians 3:9–10, emphasis added)
- For our struggle is not against flesh and blood, but against the rulers, against the authorities, against the powers of this dark world and against the spiritual forces of evil in the heavenly realms. (Ephesians 6:12)
- For in him all things were created: things in heaven and on earth, visible and invisible, whether thrones or powers or rulers

or authorities; all things have been created through him and for him. (Colossians 1:16)

- They are demonic spirits that perform signs, and they go out to the kings of the whole world, to gather them for the battle on the great day of God Almighty. (Revelation 16:14)
- Now is the time for judgment on this world; now the prince of this world will be driven out. (John 12:31)
- I will not say much more to you, for the prince of this world is coming. He has no hold over me. (John 14:30)
- …and about judgment, because the prince of this world now stands condemned. (John 16:11)
- But the Pharisees said, "It is by the prince of demons that he drives out demons." (Matthew 9:34)

THE FINAL WORD

Of course, the crucifixion, and most especially the resurrection, demonstrated to the fallen spiritual realm that Satan had lost the battle and that the cross was Elohim's plan from the beginning—not Satan's. This was Elohim's final word. Satan had not killed *God in the flesh*. He would not be ascending to the throne of heaven as he intended. He would not even be the ultimate ruler of this earthly domain.

Jesus declared the final impeachment from the cross, the very cross Satan had mistakenly thought he alone controlled. That divine indictment was declared with these words, words that still echo through the corridors of history and fall hauntingly upon the ears of Nachash…

It. Is. Finished.

29

WHY GO TO ALL THAT TROUBLE?

His only strength is his incessant, slanderous accusations against the throne of heaven.

What Jesus completed at Calvary also answers another age-old question.

The query goes something like this: Why didn't God just kill Satan instantly—immediately after he corrupted everything in the Garden? Why go to all that trouble and suffering and allow thousands of years of evil and devastation to prosper?

The fullest answer is much deeper than what we have room for here, but following is the long and short of the matter. If Yahweh had only wanted to destroy Satan, it could have been done in a nanosecond. But God's purpose was far beyond the seemingly obvious convenience of Satan's instantaneous destruction.

Heaven's plan involves three main purposes. The first one includes you, me, and the billions who came before us—and, perhaps, the billions who will come after us. He wanted you to understand life with Him as it was intended to be experienced, beginning in the Garden of Eden. He didn't have to handle the matter in this way, but it was because of His great love for you that He did. Had He destroyed Satan thousands of years ago, you wouldn't be here. You never would have received the opportunity to rule and reign with Him and to be a joint heir with Jesus for eternity! (Revelation 20:4–6, Romans 8:17)

Secondly, His plan included your free choice. Just like the choice Adam and Eve had before them. Just like Satan and the fallen divine beings had to make. And just like Jesus dealt with—in the flesh. And now, because of heaven's "slow" and methodical plan, you now have that opportunity.

> But do not forget this one thing, dear friends: With the Lord a day is like a thousand years, and a thousand years are like a day. The Lord is not slow in keeping his promise, as some understand slowness. Instead he is patient with you, not wanting anyone to perish, but everyone to come to repentance. (2 Peter 3:8–9)

But there's another reason God did not end Satan's existence a long time ago: Yahweh would not have His righteous character eternally besmirched by the father of lies and murder. In the Garden of Eden, Satan called God a liar. He declared God to be blatantly unfair and even deceptive toward His brand-new creation.

But the truth is, Satan possesses no literal "power" that can defeat Yahweh. His only *strength* is his incessant, slanderous accusations against the throne of heaven. Satan was the original "deep state," the original "fake news." That was his weapon of choice then, and it still is…to this very day.

Imagine if Satan, knowingly facing God's judgment, had declared to the fallen heavenly and earthly realms something like, "God is a raving lunatic! He only cares about himself! He's an uncontrollable tyrant!"

Now imagine if God, desiring to end everything on the spot, had stared Satan down and said, "Go ahead. Make my day!" Then envision that God had instantly disintegrated *old smutface* into an instantaneous burst of glittering stardust.

What if God then turned to the rest of His creation at that staggering moment of unmitigated power and challenged, "Anyone else want to say anything? You want some of this too? No? I didn't think so!"

Even though Satan would have been annihilated, his blasphemous denunciations against Yahweh would have rippled throughout eternity: "See, I was right! Look what He did! This proves my accusation!"[155]

But Calvary's cross, Yeshua's unspeakable suffering, heaven's plan to redeem your divine nature,[156] and Yahweh's endless patience, grace, and mercy ultimately proved Satan's charges to be abject slander.

Along these same lines, theologians Roger T. Forster and Dr. Paul Marston wrote an excellent synopsis of the matter in their book, *God's Strategy in Human History*:

> We may indeed accept that he had the sheer power to stop or even destroy Satan. The problem is that in this case, even as Satan sank under God's wrath and destruction, he would have gone with a sneer on his lips as though to say, "I told you so."
>
> Such a "solution" would have left forever unanswered Satan's accusation that God's kingdom was based (like his own) on force and expediency. It was not lack of power that prevented God from crushing Satan—it was a matter of principle. It is, perhaps, comparable to the moral restraint that makes it impossible for God to lie. Satan's accusations must be answered, and they cannot be truly answered by a force that simply crushes the accuser.[157]

Or, as theologian James Rochford, author of *Evidence Unseen* so succinctly states, "Instead of destroying Satan in an instant, God sets forth His plan to refute him forever."[158]

THE HEAVENLY SPECTACLE

In Jesus Christ, Yahweh's work of redemption was accomplished. Heaven's strategy had been obeyed. Prophecies had been fulfilled. His life had been successfully lived in the frailty of the flesh, yet without sin. His teaching was completed. The Word had been made flesh. The perfect sacrifice had been offered. Every jot and tittle of the Law had been fulfilled in Him. Jesus' last human-flesh tie had been severed on the cross (John 19:26–27); the end had come. Satan had lost. Heaven had won. Truly, *it was finished*. Elohim had spoken.

Following is the biblical attestation of this truth:

> When you were dead in your sins and in the uncircumcision of your flesh, God made you alive with Christ. He forgave us all our sins, **having canceled the charge of our legal indebtedness**, which stood against us and condemned us; **he has taken it away, nailing it to the cross**. And having **disarmed the powers and authorities, he made a public spectacle of them, triumphing** over them **by the cross**. (Colossians 2:13–15, emphasis added)

Barnes' Notes on the Bible

> The "principalities and powers" here referred to, are the formidable enemies that had held man in subjection, and prevented his serving God. There can be no doubt that the apostle refers to the ranks of fallen, evil spirits which had usurped a dominion over the world.[159]

Jamieson-Fausset-Brown Bible Commentary

> The **"principalities and the powers" refers back** to Colossians 2:10, Jesus, "the Head of all principality and power," and Colossians 1:16. In the sacrifice of Jesus on the cross, God **subjected**

all the principalities to Jesus, declaring them to be powerless as to His work and His people.[160] (Emphasis added)

Matthew Poole's Commentary provides a copious amount of scriptural context to this passage in Colossians:

Christ disarmed and despoiled **the devil and his angels**, with **all the powers of darkness.** We have seen that by principalities and powers **are meant angels**, Colossians 1:16, with Romans 8:37, Ephesians 1:21; and **here he means evil ones**, in regard of **that power they exercise in this world** under its present state of subjection to sin and vanity, Luke 4:6, John 12:31, 2 Corinthians 4:4, Ephesians 2:2, 6:12, 2 Timothy 2:26; whom Christ came to destroy, and effectually did on his cross defeat, Luke 11:22, John 16:11, 1 Corinthians 15:55, Hebrews 2:14, 1 John 3:8; **delivering his subjects from the power of darkness**, Colossians 1:13, **according to the first promise**, Genesis 3:15.[161] (Emphasis added)

DEAD WRONG

Why were the cross and resurrection a "triumph" and a "spectacle" over Satan? The answer is now apparent. Because Satan thought the cross was *his idea*. Because Satan thought he was somehow thwarting Elohim's attack upon his kingdom by "killing" the Son of God.

But Satan was wrong about the entire passion event. *Dead wrong.* In "killing Jesus," Satan had set the process of his own demise into an unstoppable progression. What Nachash had done to Elohim and humanity in the Garden of Eden was now turned back upon his own head. He would finally get a taste of his own poisonous medicine.

The divine judgment had begun.

And he was filled with rage when he discovered it.

PART SIX

The Perspective

*Whom the heaven must receive until the times of
restitution of all things, which God hath spoken by the
mouth of all his holy prophets since the world began.*
—ACTS 3:21, KJV

30

THE AWAKENING

My Father's house has many rooms; if that were not so, would I have told you that I am going there to prepare a place for you?
—JOHN 14:2

Let's now open another door of revelation.

We have lightly touched upon the matter of the multilayered dimensions within which Satan and the divine realm move and operate. This truth is made apparent in the wilderness temptation event and attested to by numerous classical scholars, inasmuch as they could understand and articulate the idea within the confines of the scientific information of their day.

I know this can be a difficult concept to grasp, especially as we are bound within the day-to-day framework of our own limited dimension of earthly existence. Yet, the certainty of several different dimensions of physical reality is an oft-recurring biblical theme, from the opening pages of Genesis to the closing words of the book of Revelation.

A PARABLE

Please allow me to take a moment to illustrate the truth of how several very different dimensional realities can exist side by side, yet one dimension can be oblivious to the existence of the others. As with any allegory, the example will not be a perfect representation. This is because we are attempting to use mere human conceptualizations to illuminate the deep and utterly mysterious truths involved with the unseen realm. Nevertheless, as you read the following parable, see how many metaphorical biblical truths you can spot.

THE FISH TANK

Call me Eddie Red.

I'm a goldfish.

Or at least I used to be a goldfish. Eddie Red is the name I was given when I lived within the confines of that fish-tank existence.

However, at the present moment, I exist as something so much more. My current situation almost defies explanation. I am standing on the outside of the tank where I used to live. Yes, I have a new body, one like yours. And I'm standing on two legs and two feet. Later, I'll tell you more about how that happened.

Suffice it to say, in my present state I am now able to see everything more clearly; I can even communicate with you in a language you're able to understand. I guarantee what I'm about to relate to you will forever change your perspective of life and reality. It certainly has done so for me!

THE MANSION

My former fish tank is mounted into an entire wall of a single room. That room is located inside a magnificent mansion. The tank is a monstrous thing—at least, from my old point of view, I used to think so. My previous family is still there. They are going on with their meager fish lives not even imagining that I'm currently observing them from an entirely different perspective. The same is true with all my former fish compadres, friend and foe alike. If they only knew what I now understand. I used to think that my old existence was the sum total of all that was real. At the time, how could I have considered the matter in any other fashion?

I was always vaguely aware there was *something* outside my watery life. I understood that I could never enter whatever was above the surface of my world and survive. I also knew very little about the *other side*. Everything outside the tank existed in shadows and blurry images. I suppose that's why we, inside the tank, thought our existence was the ultimate reality of all things, because our physical world was the only one we could clearly see, understand, and experience.

From time to time, something from the *other side* would appear inside my world. Now I know that what I saw was only a portion of a hand, maybe a finger or two. I could not have imagined the reality that was attached to those fingers. But, I understand it now, because I am just like one of them—I am a human. It's as if I was reborn, or perhaps awakened from a long, dream-like slumber. I have no other words with which to describe the matter.

CAUGHT UP

Here's where my story takes an amazing turn. One day, while going about my daily fish life, I was *caught up*; I was taken out. *The Hand* appeared and gently took hold of me. It lifted me up through the surface and brought me into a new world. My eyes were filled with a burst of magnificently blinding light.

In the very moment when I thought all was hopelessly lost, I was transformed—*in the twinkling of an eye*. How the transformation took place, I don't know. All I know is that I instantly stood beside the one who had lifted me out, the one who had given me new life. And now, I was very similar to him. I was in the image of what I eventually came to understand to be a *human being;* I was no longer a lowly fish living in a boundary-laden tank.

I had no anxiety in that moment of transformation, only a feeling of indescribable love. I was enveloped in warmth and light. Yet, I was still aware of who I was and from where I had come. I was still *me*, but, at the same time, I was something completely altered. I had been glorified. I had been changed.

My eyes darted around the room, trying to take in every sight at once, afraid I might miss something vitally important. All of the previously shadowy images leapt into full focus. In my new body, with my new mind, communicating in my new language (which I comprehended and used instantaneously), everything began to make sense. Every item in the room was fitted for human existence.

I now understood that the fish tank was only one component of that room. But that wasn't even the beginning of the full truth.

There were still amazing revelations yet to come …

31

THE FAMILY

For this reason I kneel before the Father, from whom every family in heaven and on earth derives its name.
—Ephesians 3:14–15

The thought exploded upon my consciousness as I considered my former fish-tank life: *This has to be paradise!*

But just when I thought I was finally beginning to fathom my newly given existence, my world would be further shaken to the core.

The *One* who had brought me to this place and had changed me into His likeness took me on a fantastic journey through a multitude of physical realities. These realities had apparently surrounded my lowly fish existence all along, yet they were completely unknown to any of us inside the tank.

MEETING THE KINFOLK

First, I was introduced to *The Family*. These are the humans who live in the mansion. They assured me that since I had now become like one of them, I had been officially adopted. I was called an heir, a beloved child, a member of their family!

The magnificence of these discoveries was beyond my comprehension. I would never have been counted worthy of such a wondrous transformation merely upon my own merit, yet here I was. How does one describe this type of unmerited love?

I gazed around the place where I was standing, and I inquired, "Is this my new home?" The others laughed through eyes of love, like those laughing at a child discovering a puppy for the first time. "It's only a small part of it!" they assured me. "Let us show you what lies beyond this room."

I could not believe my ears. There was *more*? This was only a *room*?

THE DOORS

A door creaked open. When I saw it, I could barely speak. Before me lay a multitude of larger rooms! Apparently, these were merely additional spectacular components of even more dimensions of reality within the confines of this glorious place. Section by section, I was shown the mansion, upstairs and downstairs. Even this grand edifice was multidimensional! All of the accommodations were magnificently appointed. I was stunned as I beheld the inexpressible wonders before my eyes. However, these revelations turned out to be only a small part of yet another tiny reality when compared to what would be disclosed to me next ...

The Family led me to another one of the mansion's many doors. This one, however, was larger than the others and ornately decorated. They opened it slowly so as not to overwhelm me. When the door was opened, the glories I had previously beheld almost faded into oblivion.

That is when I first laid my new human eyes upon the "outdoors." The sun splashed my face with a magnificent warmth; it was a brilliant fiery ball of radiant beauty that lit this alluring new world. It was hanging above me, upon "nothing!"

When my eyes finally focused properly, I saw trees, flowers, gardens, beautiful lawns, birds, butterflies, animals, children, automobiles, and the sky. I was mesmerized at the sight of airplanes, clouds, and the majestic mountains on the sun-bathed horizon.

At night, standing on the mansion's lawn, I marveled at the star-splashed heavens and the dazzlingly radiant full moon. The very next morning, I witnessed my first rain shower and the rainbow that followed! The sights, the sounds, the smells, the feelings…they were overwhelming, too wonderful to describe! My fish mind could never have come close to imagining such a paradise. Yet…here I stood. And now I understood—this was *all* right here—all around me the entire time we were living in the fish tank. But how could I have known?

Next, I was informed that our family unit was just a very small part of a much larger community. It was a world, they told me, that contained seven billion other human beings, as well as twenty-five million forms of other living species. How could I have conceived such a thing? All of these wonders would have been considered impossibilities, science fiction, even out-and-out lies—if they had been even remotely mentioned by any of us living within my previous existence. Yet, I was experiencing every bit of it—in living color—and breathing the air! But my journey of discovery was still not complete, not by a longshot.

THE MIND CANNOT CONCEIVE

In the days that followed, I was treated to rides on a jet airliner, miles above the vast expanses of our foundational existence. I also took submarine expeditions to the depths of the boundless oceans. I engaged in extensive automobile trips, twisting through picturesque landscapes and whisking along broad highways at exhilarating speeds.

I meandered through lush, endless forests. I went swimming in icy-cold and crystal-clear mountain streams. I spent countless nights gazing through a telescope, exploring an even larger universe of realities of incalculable extensiveness. My mind reeled with the stunning revelations that unfolded before me with each passing day.

Just when I thought I had seen it all, I was introduced to a microscope. *Phew!* More worlds! More realities! More unseen forces! More dimensions of physical realities! Wonders upon wonders! Where does it all end? Where did it all *begin?*

I am now so ashamed of how desperately I had embraced the lowly fish tank existence, as though it was all there was to life. Yet my embarrassment is overshadowed by the love my new family pours out on me with each passing day.

PARADIGM SHIFT

As I pondered all that was happening, two other striking realities dawned upon me. The first was that I possessed absolutely no desire to go back to the fish tank. That existence was my reality only in times past. *This* was my reality now, and this life was light years ahead of anything I could experience in the fishbowl. While I still held a fondness for my memories of that past life, they just didn't mean the same thing they did in the fish life. That was a completely different kind of life. But, *this* state of being is truly *living!*

The second notion that occurred to me was that my former fish community would presently declare me to be dead, or *gone*. But, neither of those descriptions would be anything nearly accurate. I am more alive in this moment than I've ever been! I am completely different, but, at the same time, I am still…*me.* How could they ever comprehend such a wonderful truth? Further, not only am I not *gone*, but for the first time in my life I know exactly where I am and where *they* are in relation to everything else. That knowledge is yet another piece of the puzzle that my former fish compadres could never understand within their present frame of reference.

SPIRITUAL EYES

Do you see it now?

Multiple dimensions of physical realities that exist all around us completely outside of our physical grasp are possible, and this is exactly what Jesus came to *demonstrate* to us (John 14:19). This truth is what the Bible declares from the beginning word to the very last paragraph.

Are we not repeatedly promised that there are indeed supernatural "portals" to a new life and a glorified bodily existence, but they are only available through Jesus Christ? The answer to these questions is a resounding *yes*.

Now we understand why the Bible declares that no one will *enter into* the dimension called heaven, or paradise, without first coming through Jesus Christ (1 John 5:11, Acts 4:12, John 14:6). He is the only One who is *the way*. He alone is *the door*. No one but Jesus is *the gate*. No one else holds the keys! In other words, Jesus is *the only portal* to that dimension. And only He has the power to physically transform us into a glorified state fit for the new life of that new dimension.

Jesus appeared in the fish tank with us, in the form and the flesh of a lowly *goldfish*, to demonstrate to us the unbounded magnitude of the Father's love, to show us the way, the truth, and the real life. He came into our world to assure us that something much bigger exists outside our earthly existence. He wants us to come into that dimension of paradise with Him. He reaches down into our fish tank and offers to transform us *into His likeness* (Romans 8:29, 2 Corinthians 3:18).

Because of our Creator's loving activity in our life and world, occasionally, some of us get to experience a glimpse of the divine—even in an angelic visitation straight from the unseen realm.

When that happens, our lives are rarely ever the same.

32

DIMENSIONS, PORTALS, AND TIME TRAVEL

*Whatever has happened, will happen again; whatever has been
done, will be done again. There is nothing new on earth. Does
anything exist about which someone might say, "Look at this! Is this
new?" It happened ages ago; it existed before we did.*
—ECCLESIASTES 1:9–10, ISV

Hopefully, the astounding truth of multiple dimensions has been
made a little clearer through the parabolic experiences of Eddie
Red.

It is through the understanding of these matters that the biblical
texts and the myriad supernatural mysteries therein begin to pop off
the pages. Only then do we truly begin to see, with wide-open spiritual
eyes, the bigger picture of life and the broader panorama of the complete
biblical message.

We can't get past the third chapter of Genesis without learning that
after the Fall, the former earthly dimension of the Garden of Eden was
sealed and a veil was dropped, separating humanity from it (Genesis
3:23–24).

By the time we arrive at the New Testament, we hear Jesus tell of a
rich man and Lazarus, an account wherein Jesus again declares there are
several dimensional realities after we leave this physical world. They are

dimensions where living souls truly exist. He even tells us of the chasm or the un-openable portal that exists between those dimensions (Luke 16). We'll explore those truths a little later on.

Then, as we close the final pages of Scripture, Revelation 21–22 tells of the brand-new dimension of the recreated earth and the opening of the veil to the Garden of Eden where the Tree of Life has *always* been (Revelation 2:7), awaiting the restitution of all things (Revelation 22). In fact, almost the entire book of Revelation was given to John only after he was allowed to enter through a portal (Revelation 4) that transported him to another dimension, the throne room of Yahweh.

THE SCIENCE

Before we go any further, let's have a look at several important scientific foundations. As you read through these, think back on the temptation of Jesus in the wilderness. See if some of that scenario makes a little more sense as we compare what the Bible says with what some of the very latest science claims.

A *Discover Magazine* article titled "Three Totally Mind-bending Implications of a Multidimensional Universe" reveals the following:

Nearly a century ago, Edwin Hubble's discovery of red-shifting of light from galaxies in all directions from our own suggested that space itself was getting bigger.... Hubble's discovery implied that **the cosmos exists in more than the three dimensions we're familiar with** in everyday life.... **We don't see** or feel **more dimensions**; nevertheless, **theoretical physics predicts that they should exist.** [162] (Emphasis added)

Now, lets' go a little deeper.

Dr. Michio Kaku is a world-renowned theoretical physicist. He is the cofounder of string field theory[163] and continues Einstein's search to unite the four fundamental forces of nature into one unified theory.[164] He holds the Henry Semat Chair and Professorship in theoretical physics and a joint appointment at City College of New York and the Graduate Center of City University of New York.

Dr. Kaku writes:

> It sounds preposterous that **electrons and atoms can be in many states at the same time, but this is the foundation of modern civilizations.** [The theory] has been **tested to 1 part in 100 billion in accuracy, making it the most successful physical theory of all time.... The idea that you can be in many places at the same time can be proven indirectly,** by looking at the properties of many atoms, **but testing it** on single atoms and single photons **was beyond reach. Until now.**[165] (Emphasis and brackets added)

The following excerpt is from an article posted at the scientific news site *Nautilus—Matter | Physics*. It is titled, "How Big Can Schrödinger's Kittens Get?" However, it's the subtitle that truly gives away the article's premise: "Scientists are slowly scaling up quantum effects *from atomic to human size*."

> Most scientists agree that technical difficulties will prevent us from ever putting a basketball, or even a human, in two places at once. But **an emerging understanding of the quantum-classical transition also suggests that there is nothing in principle that prohibits it**—no cosmic censorship separates our "normal" world from the "weird" world that lurks beneath it. **In other words, the quantum world may not be so weird after all.**[166] (Emphasis added)

Here's another example. This excerpt is from an article titled "A Universe of 10 Dimensions" at the quantum physics news site *PHYS.org*.

> When someone mentions "different dimensions," we tend to think of things like **parallel universes—alternate realities that exist parallel to our own....** However, the **reality of dimensions** and how **they play a role in the ordering of our Universe** is really quite different from this popular characterization.... We are immediately aware of the three dimensions that surround us on a daily basis—those that define the length, width, and depth of all objects in our universes. **Beyond these three visible dimensions, scientists believe that there may be many more.** In fact, the theoretical framework of **Superstring Theory posits that the universe exists in ten different dimensions.**[167] (Emphasis added)

Following is yet another important assertion from the science of quantum physics. These are the opening two paragraphs from another *PHYS.org* article, titled, "Record Quantum Entanglement of Multiple Dimensions":

> **An international team** [of quantum physicists] **has managed to create an entanglement**[168] **of 103 dimensions** with only two photons. **The record had been established at 11 dimensions.**
>
> The states in which elementary particles, such as photons, can be found have **properties which are beyond common sense.** Superpositions are produced, such as **the possibility of being in two places at once,** which defies intuition. In addition, **when two particles are entangled a connection is generated: measuring the state of one affects the state of the other particle instantly, no matter how far away from each other they are.**[169] (Emphasis and brackets added)

Dr. Michio Kaku explains the scientifically proven phenomenon of quantum entanglement in this easy-to-grasp manner:

> If I have two electrons close together, they can vibrate in unison.... Now, separate **those two electrons** so that they're hundreds or even **thousands of light years apart**, and **they will keep this instant communication bridge open. "If I jiggle one electron, the other electron 'senses' this vibration instantly,** faster than the speed of light."[170] (Emphasis added)

Did you catch that? The quanta particles of an atom—i.e., *electrons*—can "communicate" with each other and instantly respond to that communication at the speed of light. Furthermore, this communication process between subatomic particles occurs whether they are in the very same dimension, within the same atomic structure, or even if they are separated by any distance imaginable, effectively putting that particle in a totally different "dimension" of reality altogether. Mind blowing? Perhaps, but it's a scientifically proven fact.

Think about it. Instantaneous communication, at the speed of light, from one dimension to another dimension. That sounds awfully close to the supernatural concept of prayer, doesn't it? It even comes fairly close to putting a "scientific twist" on the concept of God the Father being located in the dimension of heaven while at the same instant existing in human flesh on earth.

Just a few things to consider.

But, we're not finished yet.

33

OPEN DOORS

**Out of this door might come something,
or we might send something through it.**[171]

Now, let me really blow your mind—that is, if you're not already aware of the stunning claims concerning the renowned CERN[172] Hadron Collider located in Switzerland.

Have a look at the excerpts of the science articles that follow. The first one is written by Adam Milton-Barker, a network engineer and intel software innovator in the fields of artificial intelligence, internet of things, and virtual reality.

Mr. Milton-Barker asserts:

The Large Hadron Collider or LHC is the world's most powerful particle accelerator, [located] 300 ft. below the ground at the CERN Control Centre in Geneva, Switzerland.[173] The machine is the result of thousands of scientists and engineers planning and building over the last few decades. **To explain simply what the machine does, it sends sub-atomic particles at the speed of light** hurtling around the loop in opposite directions and then **smashes them into each other.**

CERN wants to use the LHC to find out the **fundamentals of our universe** and **how it was created**. [They are also] **expecting to find other dimensions** and [then] **open portals** to these dimensions.[174] (Emphasis and brackets added)

Another publication, claiming to be "a leading global online tech publication with more than nine million monthly unique browsers worldwide," had this to say about the work at CERN:

A top [scientific researcher] at the Large Hadron Collider (LHC) says that the titanic machine **may possibly create or discover** previously unimagined scientific phenomena, or "unknown unknowns"—for instance "**an extra dimension.**"

"**Out of this door might come something, or we might send something through it,**" said Sergio Bertolucci, who is Director for Research and Scientific Computing at CERN.[175] (Emphasis and brackets added)

So…we don't know *what* might come out of one of these dimensional portals that we're now on the verge of opening? Hmm. Kind of spooky, wouldn't you say? That's probably why Albert Einstein labeled the study of particle physics "spooky action at a distance."[176]

Not to be outdone, the rising global superpower of China now wants in on the action concerning the parting of the potential *multiple dimensions* and discovering those portals of entry. Gee, what could go wrong with that?

For about a decade, the biggest machine on the planet has been the Large Hadron Collider (LHC).… The main body of the collider is a giant ring over five miles in diameter and the entire facility employs thousands of people. But according to a new announcement from China's Institute of High Energy Physics, it might not be the world's largest machine for long.

The Chinese institute announced plans to build its own particle accelerator over the next decade, and it's designed to surpass the LHC in every way. According to the report authored by the institute, the upcoming collider will be over five times more powerful and over 20 miles in diameter.

This second-generation collider might even be able to create new particles we've never seen before.... The mysteries of the universe likely won't stay hidden for long.[177]

THE STUFF OF LIFE

From the little we *do know* about quantum research, now everyday technologies have burst forth, including lasers, computers, Internet technologies, cellular technology, atomic clocks, and smartphones, not to mention transistors, semiconductors, Blu-ray technology, CD-player technology, HD DVDs, GPS, MRI technology, super artificial intelligence (AI), laser and satellite weapons guidance systems, 3D optical holograms, Bluetooth technology, biometrics technology, quantum computing, quantum encryption technologies, and more.[178] And there's so much more to be discovered right around the corner. As a matter of fact, those reading this book in the years to come might giggle at the "outdated" technologies I've just listed as the "latest-greatest." Our world is changing at warp speed.

However, there is still a much larger point regarding the matter we are examining. It begins with the question: *How does what we have discovered thus far help us understand the beginning of all things and its connection to the overall biblical message?*

Great question!

34

THE LAW OF BEGINNINGS

So that what is seen was not made out of what was visible.
—HEBREWS 11:3

According to the Bible, God created the different dimensional planes of existence in the first place.

God is a multidimensional being. He doesn't dwell in a singular dimension alone. He traverses all dimensions *at one time*. He *created* the universe; He doesn't *live* in the universe. He created the "invisible" quantum particles and their mind-bending properties. He is not *subject* to them; He *controls* them, at His will.

THE GOD OF THE COMPUTER

As an illustration, consider the computers we use every day. The "god" that created the computer does not live inside the computer; he dwells outside of it. He's not running around inside the computer changing the images that appear on the screen. Rather, he is entirely different than and separate from the computer he created. He can traverse any other dimension the world has to offer. He is not bound by the inner dimensions of the computer that he created. On the other hand, the components of the computer may "communicate" with a certain portion of the "outside world," but those components will forever dwell only within the confines of the computer.[179]

Furthermore, the one who crafted the computer is the same one who infused it with "knowledge and memory." He also programmed it to "think." In that sense, the computer was created "in his image." (Hang in here with me!)

Additionally, the computer's creator formed the machine by first "thinking" about its potential existence, then by *acting* upon that thought. If it wasn't for the "god" who created the computer—by first *thinking* about it—the computer would never have come into existence in the first place. The computer's inventor, at some point, said, "*Let there be* a computer." Do any of these truths have a familiar ring?

- By the word of the LORD the heavens were made, their starry host by the breath of his mouth. (Psalm 33:6)
- For this is what the LORD says—he who created the heavens, he is God; he who fashioned and made the earth, he founded. (Isaiah 45:18)
- But they deliberately forget that long ago by God's word the heavens came into being and the earth was formed. (2 Peter 3:5)
- And God said, "Let there be light," and there was light. (Genesis 1:3)

Now, if you really want your brain to be teased, consider the following information from a Space.com physics article. Notice how close the quoted scientist comes to explaining the truth of "God" as being outside of and utterly independent of our universe as we know it.

The universe we live in may not be the only one out there.
In fact, our universe could be just one of an infinite number of

universes making up a "multiverse." Though the concept may stretch credulity, **there's good physics behind it.** And there's not just one way to get to a multiverse—**numerous physics theories independently point to such a conclusion.** In fact, some experts think the existence of hidden universes is **more likely than not....**

Max Tegmark of MIT...proposed this brain-twisting idea. **"I really believe that there is this universe out there that can exist independently of me that would continue to exist even if there were no humans."**[180] (Emphasis added)

A universe that can exist independently of us? Why...of course! The same is also true of Elohim. He is outside of our universe. He is not "in" our universe, nor is He "of" our universe. On top of that, God and the universe exist, whether we are here or not. This is truth the Bible has proclaimed for many thousands of years.

- But in these last days he has spoken to us by his Son, whom he appointed heir of all things, and through whom **he made the universe.** (Hebrews 1:2, emphasis added)
- By faith **we understand that the universe was formed at God's command.** (Hebrews 11:3, emphasis added)
- In the beginning, God **created the universe.** (Genesis 1:1, ISV, emphasis added)
- For since the creation of the world **God's invisible qualities—** his **eternal power** and divine nature—**have been clearly seen,** being understood **from what has been made,** so that people are **without excuse.** (Romans 1:20, emphasis added)
- Behold, heaven and the highest heavens [the universe] **cannot contain Thee.** (1 Kings 8:27, KJV, emphasis and brackets added)
- The Almighty is **beyond our reach.** (Job 37:23, KJV, emphasis added)

- **He is before all things** [the universe], and in him all things [the universe] hold together. (Colossians 1:17, brackets and emphasis added)

The late Stephen Hawking (January 8, 1942–March 14, 2018) was probably the most renowned physicist the world has known to date. As far as I have been able to determine, Dr. Hawking was not a professing believer in the biblical message of Jesus Christ. Yet, even through the lens of an evolutionary model of humanity's existence, he still theorized that the universe as well as the concept of time had a beginning. Following is an excerpt of a lecture he gave.

> The conclusion of this lecture is that **the universe has not existed forever.** Rather, **the universe, and time itself, had a beginning** in the Big Bang, about 15 billion years ago. The beginning of real time, would have been a singularity, at which the laws of physics would have broken down. Nevertheless, **the way the universe began would have been determined by the laws of physics.**[181] (Emphasis added)

However, as an example of how complex the topic really is, consider the very latest from Dr. Stephen Hawking. The following was published *after* Dr. Hawking's death, in March of 2018. It is quite different than the position he held for most of his scientific life. In fact, it is almost a complete reversal of the foundation of his previous statement:

> When Stephen Hawking died on 14 March [2018], the famed theoretical physicist had a few papers still in the works....
> In the new paper, Hawking and Thomas Hertog, a theoretical physicist at the Catholic University of Leuven (KU) in Belgium, attempt to stick a pin in a bizarre concept called eternal inflation.... **But what they're driving at is something even**

more basic: They're claiming that our universe never had a singular moment of creation.[182]

So which is it? A singular moment of creation of the universe or an eternally existing universe? They can't both be correct. Oh well, I guess the modern evolution textbooks will need a major rewriting. Yet again.

Here's the bottom line. We don't even know *what we don't know!* This universe and the God who created it are still beyond our comprehension. We are swimming in a fish tank trying to describe what is outside the doors of the mansion. And we don't even know about the mansion we're living in—much less the multitude of "doors" that access that mansion. There are worlds of dimensions we have never seen, nor are we capable of ever comprehending them as long as we are in these physical bodies. In fact, we are just now beginning to learn that they are "there" in the first place.

FUNDAMENTAL CONCEPTS OF COSMOLOGY[183]

As we continue to move forward, have a look at an excerpt from a *New York Times* science article, titled "Beyond Energy, Matter, Time and Space," which asserts the following:

It is almost taken for granted that **everything from physics to biology**, including the mind, ultimately comes down to **four fundamental concepts: matter and energy interacting in an arena of space and time.**[184] (Emphasis added)

Now have a look at one of the most familiar verses in the Bible. Remember, this passage was written a couple thousand years before humanity began to discuss the fundamental concepts of physics and the foundational elements of cosmology.[185]

The passage in question is the very first verse, Genesis 1:1. I have put in parenthesis what science now tells us should be "taken for granted":

In the beginning (time) God created (energy) the heavens (space) and the earth (matter). (Genesis 1:1)

However, I would add one more factor to the foundation of the discipline of cosmology, because without this vital factor, everything else is unexplainable from a logical and truly scientific viewpoint. Have a look:

In the beginning (time), God (*intelligence*) created (energy) the heavens (space) and the earth (matter).

Let me put it another way. The computer could not have built and then programmed itself. Neither did a random explosion of matter create the computer. Those scenarios are utter impossibilities. Rather, an intelligent designer who exists outside of the computer—completely independent of it—planned and directed its existence and implanted within it the *intelligence* the device needs in order to operate.

Think of it! The supreme and personal Intelligent Designer, whom the Bible reveals as Yahweh/Elohim, brought humanity into existence. Then He gave us the intelligence necessary for us to create the computer! Yet, even with that same intelligence, a significant portion of the world's population still believes the universe and all of its unfathomable and elaborate intricacy burst into existence by a jolt of happenstance. How incongruous with reality. How sad.

The Word of God directly addresses this paradox:

For since the creation of the world God's invisible qualities—his eternal power and divine nature—have been clearly seen, being understood from what has been made, so that people are without excuse.

For although they knew God, they neither glorified him as God nor gave thanks to him, but their thinking became futile and their foolish hearts were darkened. Although they claimed to be wise, they became fools. (Romans 1:20–22)

I couldn't have said it better myself.

By the way, as we move on, *do you have any idea what time it is?*

35

TIME

A thousand years in your sight are like a day that has
just gone by, or like a watch in the night.
—PSALM 90:4

Scientific research in the field of particle physics has repeatedly demonstrated that our concept of time is actually only half of a dimension in breadth. This is because time can only move forward. Moving backwards in time, thus far, appears to be scientifically impossible.[186]

This fact proves the multidimensional nature of God. If God only existed in one dimension of time, then He Himself would had to have been created at some point within that time-dimension. Yet the Word of God is clear: God was not created; He has always existed.

Simply put, Yahweh/Elohim has existed from eternity past and will continue to exist into eternity future. He is the same yesterday, today, and tomorrow. He is the first, the last, and the One who is to come (Psalm 90:2, Revelation 1:8).

The Bible also tells us that God was acting long before our understanding of time began (1 Corinthians 2:7, 2 Timothy 1:9, Titus 1:2, Jude 1:25). These biblical assertions confirm that God exists either outside of time altogether, or that He exists in *at least* two dimensions of time at once. There's no other reasonable scientific way to explain the matter.

In addition, the Bible states that God can compress or expand our timeline based upon his sovereign will. For God to turn a day into a thousand years or a thousand years into a day, as the Bible declares, would require that God exists utterly separate from our mere singular dimension of time (2 Peter 3:8, Psalm 90:4). This is a biblical fact that nearly all classical commentators acknowledge as well.

Cambridge Bible for Schools and Colleges

To God there is no before and after; no past and future; all is present. To Him "was, and is, and will be, are but is." It is only the weakness of the finite creature that "shapes the shadow, Time."[187]

Pulpit Commentary

For a thousand years in thy sight are but as yesterday. Time has no relation to God; it does not exist for him.[188]

Ellicott's Commentary for English Readers

Distinctions of long and short time are nothing in the sight of God.[189]

Expositor's Greek Testament

The sense of the duration of time in the Divine Mind is not the same as in the human. One day is the same to God as a thousand years, and a thousand years as one day.[190]

Jamieson-Fausset-Brown Bible Commentary

With the Lord [time] is irrespective of the idea of long or short. His eternity exceeds all measures of time: to His divine knowledge all future things are present.[191]

Renowned astrophysicist Dr. Hugh Ross gives further scientific and biblical insight into our subject:

By definition, time is that dimension in which cause and effect phenomena take place. **If time's beginning is concurrent with the beginning of the universe**, as the space-time theorem says, then the cause of the universe must be **some entity operating** in **a time dimension completely independent of and pre-existent to the time dimension of the cosmos.** This conclusion is powerfully important to our understanding of who God is and who or what God is not. It tells us that the creator is *transcendent, operating beyond the dimensional limits* of the universe. **It tells us that God is not the universe itself,** *nor is God contained within the universe.*[192] (Emphasis added)

The Word of God settles the matter. Elohim knows how to bend, manipulate, turn, and/or use any of the laws and dimensions that He created. He can do so for any purpose He desires.

Which leads us to the next stunning revelations.

36

HOW DO THEY KNOW?

**We *know* these elements exist—
but we have not actually *seen* them.**

The Word of God declares it was Elohim who created the laws that govern the quanta particles—which He also created. Those particles are the smallest of the elements and forces that make up the atoms that form the molecules that transform our existence into a physical world of matter and energy…a world we now physically experience.

> By faith we understand that the universe was formed at God's command, so that what is seen was not made out of what was visible. (Hebrews 11:3)

Benson's Commentary

> That is, they were not made of any pre-existing matter, but of matter which God created and formed into the things which we see; and having formed them, he placed them in the beautiful order which they now hold, and impressed on them the motions proper to each, which they have retained ever since.[193]

Furthermore, the physical realm in which we live just so happens to operate by a set of scientifically settled laws—*the natural laws of the universe*.[194] Yet those natural laws are completely different from the laws that govern the movement and operation of the quanta particles. And, those precise movements of the quanta particles are what make the natural laws possible in the first place.

It's difficult to conceptualize, *I know,* but this is exactly how our world operates, and it is the foundational stuff of modern research within the various fields of quantum sciences.

Now. Think about these questions…

How do those quanta particles "know" what to do in the first place? How do they know that they *must* always "do" the same thing *or else* we would cease to exist?[195] What power holds all this together? Are these elements "thinking" or are they merely obeying the preprogrammed instructions of the original *Thinker*?

Was the "beginning" truly a random celestial explosion that took place billions or trillions of years ago without any intelligent input whatsoever, as the evolutionists would have us to believe? Was it all a simple lucky throw of a set of accidently generated cosmic dice?

Here's what the Word of God declares in these matters:

- **In the beginning *God created*** the heavens and the earth. (Genesis 1:1, emphasis added)
- For *in* [Jesus Christ] *all things were created*: things in heaven and on earth, *visible and invisible*, whether thrones or powers or rulers or authorities; **all things have been created through him and for him. He is before all things**, and *in him all things hold together*. (Colossians 1:16–17, emphasis added)
- By faith we understand that **the universe was formed at *God's command*,** so that *what is seen was not made out of what was visible.* (Hebrews 11:3, emphasis added)

- In the beginning was the Word, and the Word was with God, and the Word was God. He was with God in the beginning. **Through him all things were made**; without him nothing was made that has been made. (John 1:1–2, emphasis added)

The Bible declares that Jesus Christ—*God with us*—is the "power" that holds everything together. He is the intelligence behind the initial eruption of matter and the resulting physical universe. It all began with him merely speaking the words "Let there be…" His very "Word" was the ultimate "unseen" element that produced the creation of all that is now "seen."

The Word of God also tells us that everything we "see" and experience surged ahead from those divinely "spoken-forth" subatomic elements and powers we cannot "see." Of course, this sounds very close to what we currently know about quantum physics. We *know* these elements exist, but we haven't actually *seen* them. The National Science Teachers Association explains the matter like this:

You've seen drawings of atoms. How did people decide what those drawings should look like? Part of the answer has to do with experiments similar to throwing rocks at the walls of a dark room.

This experiment, plus many others like it, plus observations of chemical reactions, nuclear reactions, and the light that substances emit, all combine to give us a particular picture of what atoms look like. Just as with that dark room in which you can't turn on the lights, though, we cannot isolate a single atom and look directly at it to see if our drawings are correct.

The important thing is that everything we observe is consistent with our current view of atoms. The same statement goes for all sorts of other scientific models, such as quarks, electric and magnetic fields, and black holes.[196]

SATAN'S ABILITY

Through examining the biblical texts relating to the wilderness temptation of Jesus, we learn that Satan knows these truths as well. We also
learn that he has been *allowed* to traverse several dimensions and manipulate certain elemental properties of the creation, at least for a while.
Again, this is exactly what the Apostle Paul asserted in his letter to the
Ephesians:

> Put on the full armor of God, so that you can take your stand
> **against the devil's schemes.** For **our struggle is** *not against flesh
> and blood* [not of this earthly dimension of reality], but against
> the rulers, against the authorities, **against the powers** [physics
> properties of which we have no knowledge] **of this dark world**
> and against the **spiritual** *forces* of evil *in the heavenly realms*
> [other dimensions of reality that we cannot see or enter]. (Ephe-
> sians 6:11—12, emphasis and brackets added)

Even from the Old Testament we get a hint of Satan's capability of
traveling through various different dimensions of time and space.

> And the LORD said to Satan, "From where have you come?"
> Then Satan answered the LORD, and said, **from going to and
> fro in the earth**, and from walking up and down in it. (Job 1:7,
> ESV, emphasis added)

Benson's Commentary

This representation teaches us, that Satan, the great apostate
spirit, is **entirely under the dominion of the sovereign Lord** of
all things, and not suffered to act without control; and that he is

chiefly confined to the limits of this earth; agreeably to which he is called, in the New Testament, the Prince of this world, John 12:31.[197] (Emphasis added)

This commentary acknowledges that Satan is also able to move freely through multiple dimensions of reality. Satan had just come from the earthly realm, and now, in Job 1:7, we find him standing before the throne of Yahweh in the heavenly realm. But he is only allowed to do these things *with the permission* of Yahweh/Elohim.

Barnes' Notes on the Bible reveals another stunning aspect of the use of the words "to and fro." His description, again, gets awfully close to speaking of God-like transportation through multiple dimensions—devoid of any constraints of time.

In Zechariah 4:10, [the phrase "to and fro"] is [also] applied to "the eyes of Yahweh," which are said to "run to and fro through the earth," that is, [God] surveys all things as one does whose eye passes rapidly from object to object.[198] (Emphasis added)

Gill's Exposition of the Bible appears to express the same notion of Satan's currently "allowed" ability to experience relatively unbridled dimensional traversing:

Satan answered the Lord and said, **from going to and fro** in the earth, and from walking up and down in it; this he said as swaggering and boasting, as **if he was indeed the God of the whole world**, the Prince and King of it, and had and exercised a sovereign dominion over it, and as such had been making a tour through it, and taking a survey of it, see Matthew 4:8, and as if *he was at full liberty to go where he pleased,* and *was under no control.*[199] (Emphasis added)

We shouldn't be surprised when we discover the myriad declarations of multiple dimensions of reality, hidden portals, and time travel in the Word of God. The truth is, in one way or another, each of these concepts is found throughout the pages of Scripture. And, to one degree or another, each of these same concepts has been scientifically proven to exist— or at least to have a very high probability of existence.

Of course, the Word of God doesn't use the same terminology as our scientific community. Those particular terms of science have been invented by relatively modern humanity in an attempt to label the newly discovered energy forces and observed phenomena of physics that impact our world. Even though we are still making further discoveries, we're nowhere near the point of catching up with what the Bible has already described. But isn't it interesting that the *concepts* of these modern discoveries were already spoken of as absolute fact by the Word of God more than three thousand years ago?

Even the classical scholars—who lived many years before our modern world of string theory, multiverse theory, and the scientific facts of certain quantum principles were discovered—understood there were powerful physical properties at work in our universe and in our world. They agreed that these properties were often demonstrated throughout the Word of God and described as supernatural events.

Which brings us to our next chapter.

37

ROLLED UP LIKE A SCROLL

**The book of Revelation tells us why this
dimensional shift will take place.**

We've read the words many times before. They're right there in Scripture. But seldom do we give these biblical declarations their full significance. The Word of God speaks of things we are just now beginning to discover as genuine scientific possibilities, even in the area of multiple dimensions and dimensional "shifts."

Prior to our knowledge of these very real possibilities, biblical interpreters struggled a bit as they attempted to comment upon the contextual interpretation of such passages. Were these descriptions, assertions, and promises meant to be taken literally, or were they merely symbolic? They sounded like expressions of pure science fiction during the lives of commentators who lived any time over just a hundred years ago. However, with the knowledge they possessed in their time, many spoke about certain interdimensional changes that would, in fact, accompany the time of the end.

CLOSING THE BOOK

Have you ever noticed that the Bible speaks of the days of the return of
the Lord as involving the sky—or the *heavens*—being "rolled up like a
scroll?" These verses also tell of the corresponding phenomenon of the
"stars falling" from the sky. Have a look for yourself:

- All the **stars in the sky** will be dissolved and **the heavens rolled
  up like a scroll**; all **the starry host will fall** like withered leaves
  from the vine, like shriveled figs from the fig tree. (Isaiah 34:4,
  emphasis added)
- **All the host of heaven shall rot away**, and the **skies roll up like a
  scroll.** All **their host shall fall.** (Isaiah 51:6, ESV, emphasis added)
- And **the stars in the sky fell** to earth, as figs drop from a fig
  tree when shaken by a strong wind. **The heavens receded like
  a scroll being rolled up**, and every mountain and island was
  removed from its place. (Revelation 6:13–14, emphasis added)
- [Jesus said] However, after the tribulation of those days, "The
  sun will be darkened, and the moon will not give its light; **the
  stars will fall from the sky**, and the **powers of the heavens will
  be shaken.**" At that time they will see the Son of Man coming
  in the clouds with great power and glory. (Mark 13:25, Berean's
  Study Bible, emphasis added. See also Matthew 24:29.)

Myer's New Testament Commentary gives a sweeping perspective of
the phenomenon described in the preceding passages:

While **the whole world is being convulsed** (Matthew 24:29,
after Joel 3:3 f.; Isaiah 34:4; Isaiah 24:21), the heaven-sent Messiah appears in His glory (according to Daniel 7:13) to judge,"
etc.… **To be understood literally…** meaning: the *whole of the
stars* together… the powers of the heavens (the *powers which*

uphold the heavens, which stretch them out, and produce the phenomena which take place in them, etc.) will be *so shaken as to lose their usual stability*.... also with the whole connection which refers to **the domain of physical things.**

It is not political revolutions (Isaiah 13:10; Isaiah 34:4; Ezekiel 32:7 f.; Joel 3:3 f.) that are in view, but **the new birth of the world, and the establishment of the Messiah's kingdom.**[200] (Emphasis added)

What is the reaction of earth's inhabitants when they see the heaven's parted like a scroll, the stars falling from the sky, and the face of God appearing in the heavens and visible throughout the planet? Scripture answers that question as well:

I watched as he opened the sixth seal.... Then the kings of the earth, the princes, the generals, the rich, the mighty, and *everyone* else, both slave and free, **hid in caves and among the rocks of the mountains.** They called to the mountains and the rocks, "Fall on us *and hide us from the face of him* who **sits on the throne** and from the wrath of the Lamb! **For the great day of their wrath has come**, and who can withstand it?" (Revelation 6:12, 15–17, emphasis added)

It certainly appears that through an interdimensional peeling back of time and space, the unbelieving inhabitants of earth will at last get a glimpse "behind the curtain," like the rolling up of a scroll. They will behold the "face of God." As a matter of fact, in the Hebrew language, the word "scroll" is translated from *megillah,* which shares the same root as the phrase "to reveal."[201]

This peek into another dimension would be similar to the experience of John the Baptist at the baptism event of Yeshua or the experience of Stephen, the early church's first martyr, as he was being stoned to death (Acts 7:55–56). The difference is that this *last-days' glimpse* into God's literal face will be a dreadful day—a time of eternal reckoning, a day when God Himself physically demonstrates his power over the many dimensions of reality that He alone created. It seems the unbelievers will finally get that "sign *from* heaven" they've always demanded. But by this time, they'll wish they had never asked for it.

THE CLASSICAL SCHOLARS

The majority of the conventional conservative scholars, writing more than one hundred years ago, knew very little of the modern scientific principles of quantum physics. So, in what specific terms of our language did they portray the biblical concept of the heavens rolling up like a scroll?

Have a look at a sampling of their responses, which I think are amazing considering the tiny portion of scientific information they had, relative to our own:

Benson's Commentary

It appears as if the whole body of **the heavens were about to be *utterly dissolved*,** he intends to signify, that, during these destructive judgments, the confusion and consternation of mankind would be as great as if **all *the frame of the creation* were *broken into pieces*.**[202] (Emphasis added)

Barnes' Notes on the Bible

The heaven above us is "an expanse" (Genesis 1:8; Psalm 104:2) which is spread out; and which *might be rolled together*, **and thus pass away....** A destruction that would be well represented by *the rolling up* of the firmament, and the *destruction of the visible heavens* and their host.[203] (Emphasis added)

Jamieson-Fausset-Brown Bible Commentary

Violent convulsions of nature are in Scripture made the images of *great changes* **in the human world** (Isa 24:19-21), and *shall literally accompany* them **at the** *winding up* of the present dispensation…. The stars shall fall **when the heavens in which they are fixed pass away.**[204] (Emphasis added)

Matthew Poole's Commentary

So great shall be the confusion and consternation of mankind, as if *all the frame of the creation were broken into pieces.*[205] (Emphasis added)

Pulpit Commentary

The heavens shall be rolled together as a scroll; *literally, as a book.* Such *a rolling together* **of the widely extended heavens** is here intended.[206] (Emphasis added)

Forerunner Commentary

This event is the most puzzling (Revelation 6:14). The apostle compares it to **a scroll rolling up**, or we might think of it in terms of *opening a spring-loaded window* blind. Joseph A. Seiss, in his *The Apocalypse: Exposition of the Book of Revelation*, comments: "**Great, massive, rotary motion in the whole visible expanse,** is signified, as if it were *folding itself up* to pass away forever."[207] (Emphasis added)

The truths we have unfolded in this chapter are also revealed, albeit in slightly different words, through the declarations of Peter. He speaks of the very "elements" themselves *disappearing*, accompanied by a massive dimensional shift of our current physical reality.

Let's take a closer look at Peter's understanding of the matter at hand.

38

DISAPPEAR WITH A ROAR

But in keeping with his promise we are looking forward
to a new heaven and a new earth…
—2 PETER 3:13

lthough the words "like a scroll" are not mentioned in the verse, a corresponding passage speaks of the same event: *the day of the Lord.* Once again, most of the classical commentators see the apparent connection. The verse in question is found in 2 Peter 3:10:

> But the day of the Lord will come like a thief. **The heavens will disappear** with a roar; **the elements will be destroyed by fire,** and the earth and everything done in it will be laid bare. (Emphasis added)

Jamieson-Fausset-Brown Bible Commentary

"The day of the Lord" comprehends the whole series of events, beginning with the pre-millennial advent, and ending with the destruction of the wicked, and final conflagration, and general judgment…. **It is likely by "elements," mentioned after "the** heavens," are meant "**the works therein**," *namely, the sun, moon, and stars.*[208] (Emphasis added)

Vincent's Word Studies

Here the word is of course **used in a physical sense**, meaning the parts of which this system of things is composed.[209] (Emphasis added)

Pulpit Commentary

The meaning seems to be that the elements or rudiments, **of which the universe is composed** and compacted, **will be loosed; that is, the framework of the world will be disorganized.**... *The heavenly bodies* are constantly mentioned in the descriptions of the awful convulsions of the great day (Matthew 24:29; Mark 13:24; Luke 21:25; Acts 2:20; Revelation 6:12, etc.)[210] (Emphasis added)

Several classical scholars also see a conspicuously direct connection of the verse in 2 Peter with the passages that speak of the last days as being like the "rolling up of a scroll," particularly as mentioned in Isaiah 34 and Revelation 6.

Ellicott's Commentary for English Readers

The expression occurs nowhere else in the New Testament, but some such idea **as that in Isaiah 34:4, Revelation 6:14,** is probably indicated—not the roar of flames or the crash of ruins, but the parting and **rolling up of the heavens.**[211] (Emphasis added)

Meyer's New Testament Commentary:

> [2 Peter 3:10] must be understood of the constituent **elements of the heavens, corresponding to the expression:** [the forces of the heavens], **Isaiah 34:4**; Matthew 24:29; **Revelation 6:12–14.**[212] (Emphasis added)

Expositor's Greek Testament:

> [The passage] Would therefore **mean sun, moon and stars…**Cf. **Isaiah 34:4**, Joel 2:30–31, Matthew 24:29, **Revelation 6:12–14.**[213] (Emphasis added)

WHY IT WILL HAPPEN

The book of Revelation tells us *why* this dimensional shift will occur when everything is "rolled up" like a scroll and the "elements" disappear with a roar:

> Then I saw "a new heaven and a new earth," for the first heaven and **the first earth had passed away,** and there was no longer any sea.… **For the old order of things has passed away.** (Revelation 21:1, 4; emphasis added)

Practically every single one of the classical commentators—*dozens of them*—agree that these verses from Revelation are meant to be taken in a literal manner. Each of the scholars states, in his own way, that *something* will happen in the end of days wherein a brand new and literal dimension of reality will be brought to us, and we to it. The door to Eddie Red's house will be opened. The fish-tank world will be gone forever! A complete *restitution of all things* will finally appear, and we will inhabit that new physical dimension of pristine reality (Acts 3:21, Revelation 21–22).

MacLaren's Expositions

So, **throughout Scripture, the re-constitution of the material world,** by which it passes from the bondage of corruption into "the liberty of the glory of the children of God" **is taught,** and the final seat of the city of God is set forth **as being, *not some far-off, misty heaven in space,* but "that new world which is the old."**[214] (Emphasis added)

Ellicott's Commentary for English Readers

The word (kainos) is employed to describe [the new heaven and earth]. Now, it is this [Greek] word which is used **throughout this chapter,** and, indeed, throughout the book of Revelation. **[Kainos relates to the "quality" of the newness and not the "time" of the newness].**

The **newness which is pictured** is **the newness of freshness:** the old, decaying, enfeebling, and corrupting elements **are swept away** [rolled up like a scroll?] **.... *there must be some correspondency between the old and the new*,** when the new things are called new heavens, new earth, New Jerusalem.[215] (Emphasis and brackets added)

The Apostle Peter also relates this truth:

But in keeping with his promise we are looking forward to a new heaven and a new earth, where righteousness dwells. (2 Peter 3:13)

Even the Old Testament speaks of the reality of everything being "made new." More than likely, this is the scriptural promise to which Peter was referring:

See, I will create new heavens and a new earth. The former things will not be remembered, nor will they come to mind. (Isaiah 65:17)

In relation to Isaiah's prophecy, the classical commentators also saw the contextual reference to some sort of a dimensional shift taking place.

Cambridge Bible for Schools and Colleges

The thought of **a new creation** is **nowhere expressed so absolutely as here.**... Here there can be no doubt that the words are **to be interpreted literally.** At the same time **the new creation preserves as it were the form of the old,** for the next verse shews that **a New Jerusalem is the center of the renovated earth.**[216] (Emphasis added)

Barnes' Notes on the Bible

Calamity and punishment in the Bible are often represented by the heavens growing dark, and **being rolled up like as a scroll,** or **passing away.**... The figure of **great transformations in material things** is one that is often employed in the Scriptures.[217] (Emphasis added)

Jamieson-Fausset-Brown Bible Commentary

As Caleb inherited the same land which his feet trod on (De 1:36; Jos 14:9), so Messiah and **His saints shall inherit the**

renovated earth which once they trod while defiled by the enemy (Isa 34:4; 51:16; 66:22; Eze 21:27; Ps 2:8; 37:11; 2Pe 3:13; Heb 12:26-28 Re 21:1).[218] (Emphasis added)

Now that we know what we are looking for, Scripture begins to make a lot more sense—even in the scientific understanding of it all, not that we need science to verify anything God has told us. Rather, we are just now discovering that science is always catching up to the Bible, and certainly not the other way around.

The truth of multiple dimensions, especially the ability of the *evil portions* of the divine realm to breach those dimensions, shines a brand-new light upon several of the wilderness temptations Satan dangled in front of Jesus, and upon the reasons why Jesus submitted Himself to them.

That's where we discover that the Holy Spirit *led* Jesus into the wilderness temptations (Matthew 4:1). But, it's also where we discover the evil one staged a temporary "abduction"—we are told Jesus was "taken" (Matthew 4:8, Luke 4:5).

Apparently, even Jesus Himself, while in human flesh, voluntarily submitted to the supernatural power's interdimensional transference that was possessed by the prince of the power of the air.

39

TAKEN

In other words, there was a genuine multidimensional "transportation" involved.

The informed reader of the Bible should now understand the scientific possibilities of quanta particle theory, which truly appears to be in play within the pages of Scripture. It's almost an impossible hurdle to ignore. But the most important thing is that as the Word of God represents these descriptions throughout its pages, we were categorically instructed to accept these realities by "faith," long before the *fact* of their existence was discovered by modern scientific research.

In fact, in the book of Hebrews, not only are we told that we absolutely must have "faith" in these matters; we are also told why:

> Now faith is confidence in what we hope for and assurance *about what we do not see*. This is what the ancients were commended for. By faith we understand that **the universe was formed at God's command**, so that *what is seen* was not made out of *what was visible*....

And **without faith it is impossible to please God**, because anyone who comes to him **must believe that he exists** and that he rewards those who earnestly seek him. (Hebrews 11:1–3, 5–7; emphasis added)

During the many decades I have been preaching the Word of God, I've given my various groups of listeners what I consider a working definition of the word "faith":

Taking God at his word, even if there is no evidence before us that we can grasp, and even if we don't have a clue how He is going to bring his word to pass. Like a trusting child jumping into the arms of his loving father, from the edge of a pool. We may not know how to swim, and we might even be terrified of the water. But we do not fear our loving father. He is only trying to teach us to swim. We are *not* "leaping into the darkness." We know he will catch us as we jump. That is faith.

PHILIP WAS TAKEN

Students of the Word are quite familiar with the Holy Spirit of God instantly "taking" Philip to another location.

After they had come out of the water, the Lord's Spirit took Philip away. The official never saw him again, but he was very happy as he went on his way. (Acts 8:39, CEV)

Here is one of those "faith" passages where we are shown a supernatural power of the divine realm, the power wherein a person can be "transported" from one place to another.

Even the classic commentators acknowledge this power.

Myer's N.T. Commentary

The Spirit snatched him away (comp. John 6:15), in which act not only the impulse and the impelling power, but also the mode, is conceived of as miraculous—as *a sudden unseen trans-portation* as far as Ashdod, Acts 8:40.[219] (Emphasis added)

Expositor's Greek Testament

The reference is evidently to the same divine power as in Acts 8:29…the disappearance, as the context shows, was regarded as supernatural.[220]

Jamieson-Fausset-Brown Bible Commentary

To deny the miraculous nature of Philip's disappearance, is vain. It stands out on the face of the words, as just a repetition of what we read of the ancient prophets, in 1 Kings 18:12; 2 Kings 2:16. And the same word is employed to express a similar idea in 2 Corinthians 12:2, 4; 1 Thessalonians 4:17.[221]

JESUS WAS TAKEN

When we read the wilderness temptation events as described in Matthew 4 and Luke 4, how do we interpret these verses that would have us accept by "faith" that Jesus Himself was "taken" to the temple in Jerusalem? Or, how should we understand the ones that tell us He was "taken" to a mountain from where He was supposed to be able to see all the kingdoms of the world *at once?*

In order to accept the texts of the wilderness temptation at face value, we have to assume Satan was at least "allowed" some sort of limited jurisdiction over these unearthly abilities of instantaneous and multidimensional transportation. Either that, or we have to say that these "temptations" were only "in Jesus' imagination" and that somehow Satan was allowed to "get inside Jesus' head."

The *Pulpit Commentary* addresses the implausibility of such an interpretation:

> Some think that, as at the end of the temptation Christ is in the wilderness, this removal to Jerusalem is solely mental, without any motion of his body. *Improbable*; for to make such a temptation real, our *Lord's mind must have suffered complete illusion.*[222] (Emphasis added)

In other words, there truly was a genuine multidimensional and physical "transportation" involved, but by a means that was over and above what is naturally available to mere humanity. Even before the classical commentators had any real knowledge of the science of particle physics and interdimensional relationships proven by quantum science, they knew Satan apparently had access to a certain class of fearsome powers that exceeded anything possessed by humans. But why should we be surprised at this particular notion? Scripture is abundantly plain in warning us of this truth.

Notice how close *Gill's* commentary comes to describing what we now recognize as the foundation of quantum mechanics and particle physics.

Gill's Exposition of the Entire Bible

> Satan, by *divine permission*, and with the consent of Christ, which shows his great humiliation and condescension, *had power over his body*, to *move it from place to place; in some such*

like manner as the Spirit of the Lord caught away Philip, Acts 8:39.[223] (Emphasis added)

Before scoffing at *Gill's* learned speculation, consider this: Modern scientists are already "transporting" the smallest elements of atomic particles from one dimension into others. Even though our current science is yet unable to duplicate that feat with large objects, our most recent understanding of quantum physics gives us the scientific foundation for the potentiality of harnessing those same "powers." And today's physicists are working feverishly toward those ends.

Observe this excerpt from a *PHYS.org* article:

Little did [Texas Tech University professor of chemistry and biochemistry] Bill Poirier realize as he delved into the quantum mechanics of complex molecules that he would fall down the rabbit hole to **discover evidence of other parallel worlds** that might well be **poking through into our own,** showing up at the quantum level.... **Particles at this atomic and subatomic level can appear to be in two places at once.**

Poirier postulates that small *particles from many worlds seep through to interact with our own,* and their interaction accounts for the strange phenomena of quantum mechanics. Such phenomena include particles that *seem to be in more than one place at a time,* or to communicate with each other over great distances without explanations.

There is no fuzziness in his theory. Particles do occupy well-defined positions in any given world. However, **these positions vary from world to world,** explaining why they appear to be in **several places at once.** Likewise, quantum communication of far-away particles—something Albert Einstein called "spooky action at a distance"—is **actually due to** *interaction of nearby worlds.*[224] (Emphasis added)

If our previously quoted scholar, Mr. Gill, had only known how scientifically accurate his biblical analysis had been! Along these same lines, let's look at the considerations of a few more scholars:

Meyer's NT Commentary

[Satan] *places* Him, which *implies the involuntary nature of the act on the part of Jesus*, and *the power on the part of the devil*. A more precise determination of **what is *certainly a miraculous occurrence*** is not given in the text, which, *however, does not permit us to think of it as something* [merely] *internal taking place* [as in] the condition of a trance.[225] (Emphasis and brackets added)

Meyer's agrees with *Gill*. However, the former source makes a special point of having us understand that what happened to Jesus was a literal and physical moving of His body by an unknown power to another location altogether. *Meyer's* insists this experience was not merely in Jesus' "mind," nor was it the result of a "trance." Jesus was physically transported to Jerusalem, to the top of the Temple on the Temple Mount.

Bengel's Gnomen

A *marvelous power was granted to the tempter*, until our Lord says to him, in Matthew 4:10, "Depart."[226] (Emphasis added)

Vincent's Word Studies

The preposition παρά (with, by the side of), implies **taketh along with himself, or conducted.** It is **the same word** which all three evangelists use of **our Lord's taking his chosen apostles** to the Mount of Transfiguration (Matthew 17:1; Mark 9:9; Luke 9:28).[227] (Emphasis added)

Ellicott's Commentary for English Readers

> **Taketh him up into** the holy city—The analogy of Ezekiel 37:1; Ezekiel 40:2, where the prophet is **carried from place to place** in the vision of God, leads us to think of **this "taking"** as **outside the conditions of local motion.**[228] (Emphasis added)

Ellicott uses the words of his day, "outside the conditions of local motion," to describe the obvious supernatural condition of the literal transporting of Jesus to the Temple at Jerusalem. We now understand this "carrying from place to place" most likely had something to do with the laws of quantum mechanics and Satan's ability to travel through multiple dimensions.

This information should help the modern Christian to understand the sheer power of the one we're up against. It also should be a warning to us to steadfastly heed the advice of Ephesians 6.

> Finally, be strong in the Lord and in his mighty power. Put on the full armor of God, so that you can take your stand against the devil's schemes. For our struggle is not against flesh and blood, but against the rulers, against the authorities, against the powers of this dark world and against the spiritual forces of evil in the heavenly realms. Therefore put on the full armor of God, so that when the day of evil comes, you may be able to stand your ground, and after you have done everything, to stand. (Ephesians 6:10–13)

However, as already noted, the Temple in Jerusalem was not the only place to where Jesus was *taken...*

40

ALL THESE KINGDOMS

**The event of taking Jesus to a supernaturally
high place was literal.**

How high did that mountain have to be?

The Bible says Jesus was *taken* to a high mountain upon which He was able to see all the kingdoms of the world *in an instant*. Yet, there's no such mountain on earth.

So, what is the Word of God trying to convey in this description? You've probably guessed it by now. It was, most likely, yet another inter-dimensional experience. Why should we consider this account to be any different than what happened at the Temple in Jerusalem?

As a matter of fact, the Apostle John, when given the Revelation of Jesus Christ, was also "taken to a high mountain." John was shown the New Jerusalem coming down out of heaven in the very last days at the restitution of all things:

> **And he carried me away in the spirit to a great and high mountain,** and showed me that great city, the holy Jerusalem, descending out of heaven from God. (Revelation 21:10, emphasis added)

Even the classical commentators understood the connection between this "high mountain" in Revelation with something similar that Satan employed for the temptation of Jesus. This "high mountain" experience is certainly something of an interdimensional nature, and not a literal mountain upon this present earth.

Consider the following from *Ellicott's Commentary for English Readers*:

The tempter showed to our Lord the kingdoms of the world and the glory of them; the comforting angel shows to our Lord's prophet [John the Revelator] the city that hath the foundations, and the glory of it—the city that is of God, its builder and maker.[229] (Emphasis added)

Gill's Exposition of the Entire Bible sees the same correlation:

"The Spirit brought me"; not the evil spirit Satan, who took up our Lord corporeally, and carried him to an exceeding high mountain, and showed him all the kingdoms of this world, and their glory, Matthew 4:8 but either a good angel, or the Spirit of God: to a great and high mountain.[230] (Emphasis added)

Obviously, the angelic realm—both the holy and evil dimensions—have access to certain multidimensional portals. Now, let's look at a sampling of the classical scholars as they comment upon what happened to Jesus when He was taken to that "high mountain."

Jamieson-Fausset-Brown Bible Commentary

That **a scene was presented** to our Lord's **natural eye seems plainly expressed.**... It remains, then, to gather from the expression, *"in a moment of time"*—which manifestly is **intended to** intimate *some supernatural operation*—that **it was permitted to the tempter to extend preternaturally for a moment our Lord's range of vision**, and throw a "glory" **or glitter** over the scene of vision: *a thing not inconsistent with the analogy of other scriptural statements regarding the permitted operations of the wicked one.*[231] (Emphasis added)

The *Jamieson-Fausset-Brown* entry for this passage is quite adamant in asserting that the event of taking Jesus to a supernaturally high place was literal. The account of the "moment in time" was also literal and was accomplished through the manipulation of the dimension of time itself—by Satan's *permitted* "supernatural operation."

Gill's Exposition of the Entire Bible

Again, **the devil taketh him up** into an exceeding high mountain.... That is, **he took him off** from the pinnacle of the temple, **and *carried him through the air*...** which **Satan was permitted** to make...where he proposed **an object externally to his sight**, and internally to his imagination, which represented, in appearance, the whole world, and all its glory.... If this could be thought to be a true and **exact account of** *a moment*, or point of time, it was a **very short space of time indeed**, in which **the devil showed** to Christ **the kingdoms of this world**[232] (Emphasis added)

Once more, without having any knowledge of today's discoveries in the field of quantum particle science, *Gill* used the best words he had at his disposal to describe the literal nature of what happened with Jesus. It was accomplished by the "power" of Satan.

Are you a "believer" yet?

41

TWO PLACES AT ONCE

**As far as the science of the matter goes,
a single atomic particle can be in two places at one time.**

In the opening chapters of this book, I mentioned the possibility that, to a passerby, it might have appeared that Jesus was right there in the wilderness—alone, yet, at the same time, He was also in another dimension, at Satan's directive. But, how could this be? Was my suggestion merely the stuff of improbable science fiction?

The *Pulpit Commentary*, commenting upon Luke 4, brings forth yet another rather shocking assertion, especially considering when it was written.

Had he been **observed by any spectator** whilst the temptation **was going on,** *he would have appeared all through it motionless upon the soil of the desert.* **But** though the conflict **did not pass out of the** *spiritual sphere,* it was *none the less real.*[233] (Emphasis added)

Ellicott's Commentary also recognized, long before science began to back the idea, the supernatural potential for simultaneous events to occur in at least two different realms of reality. The following is in reference to Satan's appearance before the throne of Yahweh, in the book of Job:

> Sons of God—the phrase probably means the angels; or at all events an incident **in the unseen spiritual world** is referred to **simultaneous with a corresponding one on earth.** (Comp. 1 Corinthians 11:10.)[234] (Emphasis added)

Ellicott also presents this enlightening observation. He is addressing the Apostle Paul having been "caught up" to paradise, and then describing his "out of body experience," in 2 Corinthians 12:2:

> No words can describe more accurately the phenomena of consciousness in the state of trance or ecstasy. It is dead to the outer world. **The body remains**, sometimes standing, sometimes recumbent, but, in either case, motionless. **The man may well doubt, on his return to the normal condition of his life, whether his spirit has actually passed into unknown regions in a separate and disembodied condition,** or whether the body itself has been also a sharer in its experiences of the unseen.[235] (Emphasis added)

Again, *Ellicott* speaks of Paul's experience as being not only a dimensional shift (an unknown and unseen region), but also as being potentially in two places at once.

Likewise, the *Benson's Commentary* ventures into the same arena of supposition concerning Paul's supernatural "transport" experience:

> It is equally possible with God…as seems to have been the case with Ezekiel in the visions mentioned Ezekiel 11:24, and Ezekiel 37:1; and with John in those recorded Revelation 17:3; Revelation 21:10; or, as the Spirit caught away Philip, (Acts 8:39,) **to transport both soul and body for what time he pleases to**

heaven; or *to transport the soul* only thither for a season, and *in the meantime to preserve the body fit for its re-entrance.*[236] (Emphasis added)

THE SCIENCE

As far as the science of the matter goes, today's field of quantum mechanics has certainly shown—at least at the subatomic level—that a single atomic particle can be in two places at one time. Observe an excerpt from a *New Scientist* article titled, "Science: How a Photon Can Be in Two Places at Once."

> Physicists in New Zealand have devised an experiment which could **demonstrate once and for all** that quantum theory correctly predicts the weird nature of the subatomic world.... **The experiment will show that a single photon—a particle of light—can be** *in two places at once.*[237] (Emphasis added)

Another article at *PHYS.org*, titled "Atoms Can Be in Two Places at the Same Time" confirms the same truth:

> **Objects of the quantum world**...can simultaneously take different paths and **end up at** *different places at once.* Physicists [call this phenomena] *quantum superposition* of different paths.[238] (Emphasis and brackets added)

THE SECOND ADAM

In addition to the amazing connections we've just made, numerous scholars also agree the wilderness temptation experience was the first heavenly step in reclaiming what was lost in the Garden of Eden.

In the wilderness, in Jesus Christ, the *second Adam* was truly present. And Satan knew it. This is why the serpent showed up in a similar, if not the same, visage as he did in the Garden of Eden. The two dimensions of the fallen Eden and the Eden "behind the veil" were simultaneously coming into direct contact with each other. The *head-crushing seed* of Genesis 3:15 was here, in Satan's domain.

Whedon's Commentary on the Bible

We can view this transaction neither as a mere train of thought, as a vision, as a parable, nor a myth; **but as a great *verity*, occupying a most significant place in the system of sacred *realities*. The first Adam** truly was tempted, and fell; *the second Adam* was as truly tempted, and won the victory.[239] (Emphasis added)

Expository Notes of Dr. Thomas Constable

The impact of Satan's temptation is that Jesus, like Adam... had a justifiable grievance against God and therefore ought to voice his complaint by "murmuring" and ought to provide for himself the basic necessity of life.... Satan, in other words, sought to make Jesus groundlessly anxious about his physical needs. *In short, the devil's aim was to persuade Jesus to repeat the apostasy of Adam.*[240] (Emphasis added)

The matter appears to be biblically settled. Through certain *supernatural* powers, Satan was able to traverse and manipulate various quantum spheres of physical reality. Yet, each of these powers was *allowed* by Yahweh, regardless of Satan's vain imaginations otherwise. Most importantly, unbeknownst to Satan, Jesus was in the wilderness as the second Adam. He was there to be tempted by Satan and to utterly defeat the ancient serpent at his own manipulative game.

Having explored this vein of scientific and biblically connected study, you might still find yourself asking something along these lines: "But are there other examples in the Word of God that illustrate the possibility of such phenomena as *portals* into *other dimensions* and actual *time travel*?"

Turn the page and get ready for some additional surprises.

42

BACK TO THE FUTURE

**The Apostle John was "warped"
into the throne room of God.**

If you think about it, there is a very real sense in which almost all of the prophets were "time travelers," especially those who appear to have been transported to a specific period of time that was far into their future, and who were then given striking details of specific events they could not have known otherwise.

The prophets would often refer to these experiences as "visions." Some, however, even questioned whether they were "in their body" or "out of their body" (2 Corinthians 12: 2–3) during their *supernatural transportation*. In other words, they knew they were physically located in a real place, yet they were in a very different dimension of reality, one not otherwise available to mere humans. Because we live on the other side of many of those prophetically foretold events or, in some cases, because we live right in the midst of them, we stand as a generation of witnesses to the veracity of those Spirit-enabled "time travel" accounts.

TIME TRAVELERS

Let's take a look at several biblical "time travelers." What follows is only a partial list. Serious students of the Word can certainly add many other examples to the list. This is especially true now that we know what we are bumping into when we read these accounts and others like them:

- **The Apostle John** was "warped" into the throne room of God (Revelation 4). Then he was shown the future, right up to the very last days at the restoration of all things. Much of what John spoke of in the book of Revelation is now coming to pass in our day, more than two thousand years from when he received it.

- **The Apostle Paul** had a very similar experience of being "transported" into the presence of the throne of God (2 Corinthians 12:2–4). There, he too received numerous detailed glimpses into the last days. Paul saw the Rapture of the Church (1 Corinthians 15:51ff) and the time of the Antichrist (2 Thessalonians 2). He also witnessed specific details concerning the physical return of Jesus Christ (1 Corinthians 15).

- **The prophet Isaiah** was taken to the scene of the life, ministry, persecution, beating, crucifixion, burial with criminals, and the resurrection of Jesus Christ (Isaiah 53). Isaiah wrote this prophecy seven hundred years before it came to pass.

- **Likewise, King David** was taken to the foot of the cross of Jesus, witnessing the piercing of Messiah's hands and feet and hearing the very words of mocking that were, indeed, spoken on the day of crucifixion (Psalm 22:6–8). David saw the soldiers gambling for Jesus' clothing under His feet (Psalm 22:16–18), as well as many more details of that day. Psalm 22 was written a thousand years before the actual crucifixion event.

- **The prophet Ezekiel** witnessed the geographical return of the nation of Israel in the last days. Furthermore, he was shown the nations that would ultimately form a coalition to unite in war against the revenant Israel. He saw these things more than twenty-seven hundred years before they came to pass (Ezekiel 37–39).
- **The prophet Daniel** was also warped into the presence of the throne of God, the divine council, the heavenly host, and the coronation of the Son of God—and while there he also got a glimpse of the antichrist and his ultimate defeat. Not only that, but Daniel also witnessed the manifestation of global travel technology during the last days, as well as instantaneous communication and information exchange (Daniel 12:4)—and the days of the Great Tribulation and the Rapture in the very end. (Daniel 7–9, 12:1)

There are still other amazing revelations along these same lines throughout the Word of God.

INTERDIMENSIONAL PORTALS

- **The prophet Elijah** was instantaneously taken to heaven, into another dimension, in a chariot of fire (2 Kings 2:11).
- **Enoch was also taken up** to heaven without experiencing human death. He entered another dimension *instantly* (Genesis 5:21–24).
- **Jacob had a vision** of a ladder, or stairway, to the dimension of heaven itself (Genesis 28:12). *Ellicott's Commentary* describes the "ladder" as: "The Bridge of union between the material and spiritual world." In other words, Jacob saw two different dimensions connected to each other through a specific portal.[241]

- **Isaiah had a vision** (Isaiah 6) in which the "veil" was pulled back and he was suddenly at the throne of God. Several scholars describe this event as interdimensional–similar to Paul's in 2 Corinthians 12:3.[242]
- **Jesus presented Himself** alive at the resurrection event, proving interdimensional existence. He is shown to "walk through walls" (John 20:19–20) and to be ascending into the sky in front of witnesses (Acts 1). Of course, each of his miracles demonstrated not only his divinity, but also his absolute power over the quantum world of physics (Matthew 8:23–27, 14:23–33, John 6:1–14, etc.).
- **Jesus spoke of Himself** as being a "portal" or "door" to other dimensions: "I am the door: by me if any man enter in, he shall be saved, and shall go in and out, and find pasture" (John 10:9, ESV).
- **The evangelist Philip** was *instantly* transported from the presence of the Ethiopian eunuch on the road from Jerusalem to Gaza—to Azotus. This would normally have been at least a two-day trip to that destination (Acts 8:39–40).
- **In the opening pages of Genesis,** we are told of the "real" Garden of Eden being sealed off (Genesis 3). Jesus later tells us that it still exists—and always has (Revelation 2:7).
- **The book of Hebrews** speaks of the reality of another dimension—in paradise—behind the veil that separates this world from that one (Hebrews 8:5).
- **John the Baptist**, as we have already discussed and demonstrated, had heaven's portal opened to him (Matthew 3, Luke 3).
- **Stephen** had heaven's dimensional gates opened to him as well (Acts 7:55–56).
- **Jesus** promised the **thief on the cross** that on that very day of His crucifixion, the two would enter another dimension, *paradise,* together in bodily form (Luke 23:39–43).

- **Peter, James, and John** had heaven's door opened to them at the transfiguration event, and they met and fellowshipped with the three prophets who came out of that interdimensional portal (Matthew 17:1–8, Mark 9:2–8, Luke 9:28–36, 2 Peter 1:16–18).
- **Daniel** was visited by the archangel Michael. That divine being was bringing a message to the prophet Daniel from the throne of God as a result of the prophet's fervent prayers. Michael confided in Daniel that he would have been with him sooner, except that he had been engaged in warfare in other dimensions, with other-dimensional "princes" of evil that were behind the thrones of earthly kingdoms—specifically, the princes of Persia and of Greece (Daniel 10).

We now have a much better idea of just how complex the cosmic war is. It is between the heavenly throne of Elohim and the earthly established and demonically manipulated thrones of Satan. Very real dimensions. Very real, and living, entities. And a very real war.

But had we gone straight to the next chapters without laying the foundation of what we've just examined, you might have closed this book, shaking your head in bewilderment.

But you didn't…you're still here!

As you read the next chapters, you'll be glad you came this far!

PART SEVEN

The Pursuit

*Woe to the earth and the sea, because the devil has gone down to
you! He is filled with fury, because he knows that his time is short.
When the dragon saw that he had been hurled to the earth, he
pursued the woman who had given birth to the male child.*
—Revelation 12:12–14

43

THE FOUNTAINHEAD

He will crush your head, and you will strike his heel.
—Genesis 3:15

As we move forward, let's first go all the way back to the Garden of Eden. It was in that primordial paradise where the very first prophecy of the coming Messiah was spoken—and it was declared from the mouth of Elohim Himself. This is the foundational pivot point of the entire Bible, for it is here where Satan first learns of his ultimate demise.

From the time of the Garden forward, Satan will launch a desperate, multigenerational expedition, searching for this *One* who is coming to crush his head. If he can find *the Seed* in time, Satan plans on destroying him. Satan determines that *he* will become the hunter; he is determined that *he* will be the one who rules the ultimate final kingdom.

THE JUDGMENT

Let's look at the death sentence pronounced upon Satan in the Garden of Eden, right after the depredating perversion that occurred there:

[Elohim said to Satan] And I will put enmity between *you* and the woman, and between your offspring [seed] and hers; *he* [a singular person] will **crush *your* head**, and **you will strike *his*** [a singular person] heel. (Genesis 3:15, emphasis and brackets added)

There is very little disagreement among scholars, both classical and modern, as to the message this passage conveys.

Benson's Commentary

Her seed—That is, her offspring, **first and principally Christ**, who, with respect to this promise, is termed, by way of eminence, **her seed**, (see Galatians 3:16; Galatians 3:19) **whose alone work** it is to bruise the serpent's head, to **destroy the policy and power of the devil**.[243] (Emphasis added)

Pulpit Commentary

The seed of the woman signifying...**in particular** the Lord Jesus Christ, who is styled by preeminence **"the Seed"** (**Galatians 3:16, 19**), and who came "to destroy the works of the devil" (Hebrews 2:4, 1 John 3:8).[244] (Emphasis added)

Dr. Lehman Strauss, former professor of Old Testament history at Philadelphia Bible Institute, asserts the following:

[Genesis 3:15] *is the fountainhead of all prophecy* from which flows the ever-increasing stream of testimony to the promised Deliverer. One great promise respecting the Redeemer is that He **should be of the human race**, but peculiarly of the woman's "seed," not the man's. To fulfill this promise, Jesus Christ cannot, therefore, be begotten by any man. He must be born of a virgin.

This is **precisely what Isaiah prophesied more than 3000 years after the promise was first given:** Therefore the Lord Himself shall give you a sign: Behold, a virgin shall conceive, and bear a son, and shall call His name Immanuel (Isaiah 7:14).[245] (Emphasis added)

Bob Deffinbaugh, ThD, contributes extensive commentary material for the online biblical research source *Bible.org*. In an article titled "The Anticipation of Israel's Messiah," Dr. Deffinbaugh affirms the following regarding Genesis 3:15:

God began **by addressing Satan** and spelling out the punishment for his sin. This is appropriate in light of the fact that Satan was the instigator, the tempter.... As the promoter of sin, his punishment rightly comes first. *The first promise of a coming Messiah in the Bible* **comes in God's rebuke of Satan in Genesis 3:15.** The Messiah was to come, then, both **to destroy Satan** and to deliver men from his dominion, a theme which continues on into the New Testament.[246] (Emphasis added)

Similarly, Dr. Don Stewart, who provides scholarly material for the online source, *Blue Letter Bible*, declares of Genesis 3:15:

The ultimate seed of the woman would be Jesus Himself.

Therefore, we have in Genesis 3:15, *the first promise of a Redeemer.* It is the beginning of a long line of prophecies concerning the coming Messiah. The Promised One would be from the woman's seed an indication of the eventual virgin birth of Christ.[247] (Emphasis added)

REVELATION 12

Satan's cosmic search for the Seed was one of the primary reasons for the presentation of the information found in Revelation 12. That chapter is a scriptural and historical panoramic, written using several metaphorical terms, to express the deepest reality of the viciousness of Satan's hunt for the messianic Seed. The passage vividly highlights Satan's psychopathic desire to destroy Yeshua while He was in the flesh and dwelling among humanity, beginning with Yeshua's *birth*.

Revelation 12 also methodically sets up the disclosures found in Revelation 13. That chapter reveals how the culmination of Satan's blunder, in exposing himself through Calvary's cross and the resurrection event, will eventually result in Satan once again inhabiting a man, similar to what he did with Judas. This time, however, that demonically inhabited human and his global seat of power will be known as *the beast*, the *lawless one*, or *the Antichrist*.

The *Cambridge Bible for Schools and Colleges* says of Revelation 12:

[Rev. 12:2] Here is probably a **reminiscence of Genesis 3:16**...
[Rev. 12:3] **Here is an undoubted reference to the Fall** in this picture of the woman, the man, and the serpent. In Psalm 74:13–14 (14, 15); Job 26:13; Isaiah 27:1; Isaiah 51:9, we seem to find **references to a "war in heaven,"** either past or future, like that which follows here.[248] (Emphasis and brackets added)

Likewise, *Ellicott's Commentary for English Readers* asserts:

All life dawns in anguish, **according to the ancient fiat (Genesis 3:16)**. There is an anguish of **the Church** which Christ laid upon her; it is the law of her life that **she must bring forth Christ to the world.**[249] (Emphasis added)

Meyer's New Testament Commentary also states:

> The idea of **the devil (cf. Revelation 12:9) as a serpent** is **based upon Genesis 3** to which the connection of Revelation 12:9, and the interchange of the expressions found in Revelation 12:13; Revelation 12:15, clearly refers.[250] (Emphasis added)

So, we discover, from the opening pages of Genesis to the last book of the Bible, the message is about the celestial pursuit. The serpent—Satan—is searching for *the Seed* that will crush his kingdom. But, more importantly, it's also about Yeshua's mission concerning the destruction of that ancient serpent.

That mission was to pursue Nachash, on his own stolen turf, to call him out and to coax him into exposing his profane arrogance to all the powers of the universe, proving himself to be the obscene liar and ravenous murderer that he truly is.

More than that, Satan would be utterly defeated at his own game. This divine feat would be achieved before the rulers of three different, but very real, dimensions: the divine council of heaven, the thrones of earth, and Satan's own earthly jurisdiction of loathsome evil. That jurisdiction, for the time being, belongs to the *prince of this world*, the *prince of the power of the air.*[251]

This is where the interdimensional hunt began.

44

THE *SSS*ERPENT'S DILEMMA

**He imagined that if he could figure out the details
of Elohim's plan, he could eventually thwart heaven's agenda.**

essianic Rabbi Eric Walker is the executive director of the Igniting a Nation ministries and television program headquartered in Birmingham, Alabama. Rabbi Walker comes from a long line of deep Jewish heritage, and fluently reads and speaks the Hebrew language.[252] On numerous occasions, I have discussed the theology of Satan's intergenerational hunt for the Seed with Rabbi Walker.[253]

The following is Rabbi Walker's personal commentary concerning Satan's dilemma, and how that diabolical search for the coming Messiah began.

When Elohim announced the judgment upon Satan in the Garden of Eden, as it is found in Genesis 3:15, He planted in the serpent's heart a great challenge. It would haunt Satan throughout history, and the Bible records the resulting psychotic journey of the *evil one*.

The problem was this—Elohim had pronounced the ultimate destruction of Satan for what He had so vilely accomplished in the Garden. In so doing, Elohim assured him that his head would one day be "crushed," and that the deed would be accomplished through a specific "seed." That seed would eventually come through the womb of a certain woman.

With that pronouncement, Satan knew the "why" of the verdict (he had profaned the Garden), and he knew the "what" (he eventually would be destroyed).

But, Satan didn't know the "how" or the "when" of the matter. Nor did he know through exactly "whom" it would actually take place. Without those missing pieces of crucial information, Satan would forever be in the dark. He would always be looking over his shoulder.

Satan set off on his mission of discovery. He became the cosmic "stalker." In his thoroughly arrogance-soaked delusion, he imagined that if he could figure out the details of Elohim's plan that he could eventually thwart heaven's agenda. Satan also supposed that if he could somehow gain victory over Elohim in this matter, then he himself could rule in Elohim's place—*as God.*" (Isaiah 14: 12–14)

With this scenario in place, the Word of God records, from Genesis to Revelation, Satan's merciless and relentless attack upon human civilization. And eventually, once Satan had collected the bulk of the Intel he needed, he focused in on a very specific group of people—*the line of Abraham*—the Hebrew people.

Once he had traced the lineage of the promised Seed to the nation of Israel, he continually sought to destroy that *One* by destroying the people through whom He would come.

But once the Seed had been victorious in his mission, through the cross and the resurrection, Satan refocused his revengeful attack upon the "offspring" of the Christ—the *called out ones.* (Revelation 12, Ephesians 6:10ff).[254]

FINDING THE SEED

There certainly must be more to the specific details of the entire story than what we find in the pages of Scripture. However, through the biblical account we are at least given the foundation of what we need to know as to just how obsessed Satan was with finding the *One* who would eventually crush his head. Satan still needed more information than what he had been given in the Garden judgment. Most importantly, he first needed to know through what lineage this Seed would ultimately appear.

The first clue we get in Scripture concerning the promise of a specific "seed" emanating from a particular bloodline, comes from Genesis chapter 12. This is where Yahweh drops the first hint:

I will make you [Abraham] into a great nation [through your offspring/seed], and I will bless you; I will make your name great, and you will be a blessing. I will bless those who bless you, and whoever curses you I will curse; and all peoples on earth will be blessed through you [your seed]. (Genesis 12:2–3, brackets added)

If Satan or any of his demonic emissaries had been watching and listening at that time, he would have known that God was singling out the genetic lineage of a man called Abraham. This man was the one whom God was now planting right in the middle of what would later be known as the Promised Land.

But the biggest clue that would cause Satan to zero in on Abraham's "seed" would be Yahweh's next declaration to Abraham. This occurred right after Abraham was put to the test concerning the potential sacrifice of his son Isaac. The test would take place in the region of Moriah, the locale where Abraham's descendants would eventually settle and become the nation of Israel. And, it would also be the very site where the Temple of the Lord would ultimately be built.[255]

Yahweh's promise to Abraham on that auspicious day was given as follows:

> And the angel of the LORD called to Abraham out of heaven the second time, And said, By myself have I sworn, said the LORD, for because you have done this thing, and have not withheld your son, your only son: That in blessing I will bless you, and in multiplying **I will multiply your seed** as the stars of the heaven, and as the sand which is on the sea shore; and *your seed shall possess the gate of his enemies*; And *in your seed* shall *all the nations* **of the earth be blessed**; because you have obeyed my voice. (Genesis 22:15–18, KJV, emphasis added)

Consider the comments of *Barnes' Notes on the Bible* concerning this promise to Abraham:

> In hearing this transcendent blessing repeated on this momentous occasion, Abraham truly saw **the day of the seed of the woman, the seed of Abraham, the Son of man....** The **seed that was threatened to bruise the serpent's head** is here **the seed that is promised** to bless all the families of the earth.[256] (Emphasis added)

Gill likewise affirms the greater context of Yahweh's promise to Abraham. Notice what it says about a specific element of that promise:

> **Thy seed shall possess the gate of his enemies:** [This promise] was literally fulfilled...spiritually in **Christ, Abraham's principal seed,** when he **destroyed Satan** and his principalities and powers; overcame the world; made an end of sin and abolished death....

In his one and **principal seed, the Messiah,** that should **spring from him**, Galatians 3:16.[257] (Emphasis and brackets added)

By the time we get to the New Testament, we are told the Seed, first promised to Abraham, was none other than Jesus Christ Himself:

The promises were spoken to Abraham and to his seed. Scripture does not say "and to seeds," meaning many people, but "and to your seed," meaning one person, who is Christ.... Why, then, was the law given at all? It was added because of transgressions until the Seed to whom the promise referred had come. (Galatians 3:16, 19)

Of course, we now have the advantage of looking back upon the entire picture of God's redemptive plan through Jesus Christ. But at the time of the promise given to Abraham, Satan was still trying to decipher the entirety of that heavenly design. He was still trying to discern the future—specifically his own impending fate.

Hearing God promise Abraham that his "seed" would one day "possess the gates of his enemies" certainly had to perk up the ears of Satan. He knew *he* was "the enemy." And he knew from the Garden pronouncement that one day a very specific Seed would appear that would destroy his gates of power.

Therefore, at that juncture, Satan may have rightly figured that the promised Seed would come from the line of Abraham—later known as the Children of Israel. But he still didn't know when that Seed would arrive, nor did he know the identity of the person through whom the promise would enter the earthly realm. Furthermore, he didn't yet understand where "the coming" of this Seed would occur. But at least for now he had a place to start.

The outpouring of his rage would begin with the Children of Israel—those who would come through the lineage of Abraham.

45

A TRIP TO EGYPT

**There can be little doubt that Satan was now
the power behind the throne of this particular Pharaoh.**

As we move through the biblical saga, a striking pattern emerges. The next episode where we observe Satan's hunt for the delivering Seed is in the eventual enslavement of Abraham's lineage—in Egypt. After the Genesis account disclosing how the "children" of Abraham wound up in Egypt through Joseph and his brothers, we're told that a particular pharaoh eventually came to power who "knew not" Joseph. This is our first clue that something evil was about to happen.

In the first chapter of Exodus, we find the doleful beginning of the account:

Now Joseph and all his brothers and all that generation died, **but the Israelites were exceedingly fruitful; they multiplied greatly, increased in numbers and became so numerous that the land was filled with them.**

Then a new king, to whom Joseph meant nothing, came to power in Egypt. "Look," he said to his people, "the Israelites have become far too numerous for us. Come, we must deal shrewdly with them **or they will become even more numerous** and, if war breaks out, will join our enemies, fight against us and leave the country."

...so the Egyptians came to dread the Israelites and worked them ruthlessly. They made their lives bitter with harsh labor in brick and mortar and with all kinds of work in the fields; in all their harsh labor the Egyptians worked them ruthlessly. (Exodus 1:6–14, emphasis added)

There can be little doubt that Satan was now the power behind the throne of this pharaoh. Not only would God's people be kept in slavery—a sort of presumed "checkmate" upon God's moving forward with his plan—but what happens next can only be described as Satan's first direct attack on the Seed.

The king of Egypt said to the Hebrew midwives, whose names were Shiphrah and Puah, "When you are helping the Hebrew women during childbirth on the delivery stool, **if you see that the baby is a boy, kill him; but if it is a girl, let her live.**" The midwives, however, feared God and did not do what the king of Egypt had told them to do; they let the boys live…. **Then Pharaoh gave this order to all his people: *"Every Hebrew boy that is born you must throw into the Nile*, but let every girl live."** (Exodus 1:15–22, emphasis added)

THE FOCUS NARROWS

Satan thought he had the Israelites corralled into one place where he could control them and perhaps destroy any "threatening seed" that might come forth from them.

Even the classical commentator Matthew Henry saw what Satan really had in mind:

The enemy [Satan] who, **by Pharaoh,** attempted **to destroy the church in this its infant state,** is busy to stifle the rise of serious reflections in the heart of man.[258] (Emphasis added)

Likewise, the *Pulpit Commentary* says:

The devil...through Pharaoh...**endeavors to crush** the chosen people of God, **through whom the Messiah** was to bless all the earth.[259] (Emphasis added)

Also note that in the following commentary examples, Satan is directly linked to the human personage of Egypt's Pharaoh:

Ellicott's Commentary for English Readers

The devil, the old spirit whose malignity wrought **through the fears of Pharaoh**...is **on the watch to destroy** every token of good and **every resemblance to Christ in the world.**[260] (Emphasis added)

Jamieson-Fausset-Brown Bible Commentary

So the dragon, **represented by his agent Pharaoh** (a name common to all the Egyptian kings, **and meaning,** according to some, crocodile, *a reptile like the dragon*, and made an Egyptian idol), was ready **to devour Israel's males** at the birth of the nation.[261] (Emphasis added)

Vincent's Word Studies

In these words we have **the dragon doing what Pharaoh did** to Israel (Exodus 1:15-22), and again and again, in the Psalms and the Prophets, **Pharaoh is spoken of as the dragon** (Psalm 74:13; Isaiah 27:1; Isaiah 51:9; Ezekiel 29:3). Nor is it without interest to remember that **Pharaoh's crown was wreathed with a dragon.**[262] (Emphasis added)

And of course, we know Revelation 12 unquestionably identifies Satan himself as the "dragon," or that "ancient [all the way back to the Garden] serpent."

> **The dragon stood in front of the woman** [Israel] who was about to give birth, **so that it *might devour her child*** the moment he was born....The **great dragon** was hurled down—**that *ancient serpent* called the devil, or Satan**, who leads the whole world astray. He was hurled to the earth, and his angels with him. (Revelation 12:4, 9, emphasis added)

The Satan/Pharaoh plan ultimately failed. Even though many of the male children of Israel's offspring were indeed destroyed, the lineage of the coming Seed lived on. A particular male child was divinely preserved in the midst of the massacre. His name was Moses. But God had a plan. Through that plan, He would take his people to a specific place wherein his divine purpose would ultimately be fulfilled.

Satan still didn't have a clue where all this was headed.

But what he finally figured out would enrage him.

46

BACK TO THE GARDEN

**He was taking them right back to the place
where Satan's judgment had first been delivered.**

Let's now move forward in time…to the Exodus event. When God brought the Israelites out of Egyptian captivity, He told them He was going to eventually deliver them to a very special place. It would be the place where He had "put his Name." That place would, in due course, become the capital city of the nation of Israel. That city was Jerusalem.

- …Jerusalem, the city where I chose **to put my Name.** (1 Kings 11:36, emphasis added)
- This is what the Sovereign LORD says: This is Jerusalem, **which I have set** *in the center of the nations*, with countries all around her. (Ezekiel 5:50, emphasis added)

God's transportation of the formerly enslaved Israelites directly into the Land of Promise, then settling them in and around the location of Jerusalem, had to absolutely floor Satan. *Why might that be?*

Satan knew exactly why that place was so significant. If you've never been made aware of this next revelation, prepare to be shocked.

JERUSALEM'S REAL SIGNIFICANCE

There is a monumental reason Jerusalem is called the center of the planet or the center of the nations (Ezekiel 5:5). There is also a very good reason God says, "This is where I have put my Name." It's because Jerusalem is the place where the Garden of Eden was originally located.[263]

Jesus gives us a huge clue about all this in the book of Revelation:

To him who overcomes, I [Jesus] will give the right to eat from **the tree of life**, which *is in the paradise of God*. (Revelation 2:7, emphasis added)

The Greek word for "paradise" means "the Garden of Eden." In fact, the Hebrew equivalent word for "paradise" (as it refers to heaven) is *Gan Eden*—"Garden of Eden."[264]

Jesus declared in Revelation 2 that the Tree of Life has always been, and still is, in the Garden of Eden. The original Garden of Eden—*paradise*—has never disappeared from existence. It has only been temporarily veiled from the earthly realm (Genesis 3:23–24).

To the one who is victorious, I will give the right to eat from the tree of life, ***which is in*** the paradise [Garden of Eden] of God. (Revelation 2:7, emphasis added, brackets added)

Note the commentary of the *Geneva Study Bible*, concerning the Apostle Paul being "caught up into paradise," as he related in 2 Corinthians 12:2–4:

How that [Paul] was caught up into paradise, and heard unspeakable words, which it is not lawful for a man to utter.... **Those that translated the Old Testament out of Hebrew into Greek,** *called the garden of Eden by this name* [**paradise**], into which *Adam was put* immediately after his creation, as a most delicate and pleasant place. And from this it occurred that *the blessed seat of the glory of God is called by that name.*[265] (Emphasis and brackets added)

When the Apostle John was shown the ultimate "restitution of all things" that will occur in the very last days, he described it in the following manner:

I saw the Holy City, *the New Jerusalem*, coming **down out of heaven** from God, prepared as a bride beautifully dressed for her husband. (Revelation 21:2, emphasis added)

At this point in our study, we now understand that the "coming down out of heaven" most likely signifies the peeling back of another dimensional reality. The sky is being "rolled up like a scroll" and the new dimension is being revealed, appearing to "come down" from the "new sky"—and it's all centered in Jerusalem (Galatians 4:26; Hebrews 11:10, 12:22, 13:14; Revelation 3:12).

Cambridge Bible for Schools and Colleges

This is the New Jerusalem of which the earthly city is an imperfect copy; see on Revelation 4:6, Revelation 6:9 for the heavenly Temple. While this world lasts, this true Jerusalem is above (Galatians 4:26); and **we only know its nature from the earthly copy of it**, before Christ came, and the spiritual approach to it (Hebrews 12:22) since. But in the days here described, *it will be realized on earth* in all its perfection.[266] (Emphasis added)

Barnes' Notes on the Bible

It is here represented as "coming down from God out of heaven." *This, of course, does not mean that this great city was "literally" to descend upon the earth*, and to occupy any one part *of the renovated* world.[267] (Emphasis added)

Commentary Critical and Explanatory on the Whole Bible

The Vulgate reads, "out of the throne." ...the tabernacle—alluding to the tabernacle of God in the wilderness (wherein many signs of His presence were given): of which this is the antitype, **having previously been in heaven:** Revelation 11:19:15:5, "the temple of the tabernacle of the testimony in heaven"; also Revelation 13:6. Compare the contrast in Hebrews 9:23 Hebrews 9:14, between "the patterns" and "the heavenly things themselves," between "the figures" and "the true."[268] (Emphasis added)

Regardless of the particulars of interpretation, we can at least settle the biblical fact that Jerusalem has always been the center of God's earthly throne; it is the locale of the original Garden of Eden. Genesis 3 tells us the Tree of Life was in the middle of the Garden of Eden. Jesus tells us that it is still there (Revelation 2:7). And now, John's vision assures us that the Tree of Life, which has *always been* in the Garden of Eden, is in the *New* Jerusalem:

Then the angel showed me **the river of the water of life**, as clear as crystal, **flowing from the throne of God** and of the Lamb down the middle of the great street of the city. On each side of the river **stood the tree of life**. (Revelation 22:1–2, emphasis added)

There can be no doubt. Elohim was taking His children—*the ones through whom He would deliver the Seed that would crush Satan's kingdom*—right back to the area where the Garden Fall originally occurred. He was taking them to the earthly place where Satan's judgment was first delivered.

He was taking them to Jerusalem.

God's reason for moving His people to this particular destination would thoroughly unnerve the ancient serpent.

APPLE OF GOD'S EYE

For thus said the LORD of hosts…he who touches
[Israel/Jerusalem] touches the apple of his eye.
—ZECHARIAH 2:8

Dr. Keith Krell holds a PhD from the University of Bristol and is an associate professor of biblical exposition at the Moody Bible Institute in Spokane, Washington. Dr. Krell asserts that the Garden's original location was specific to the *region* of the Promised Land:

> The Tigris and Euphrates are now in Babylonia. Eden (meaning delight, pleasure, or perhaps place of abundant waters) therefore appears to have lain in the general area of the Promised Land.
>
> It can hardly be coincidence that two of these rivers are exactly the ones that God uses to explain to Abraham where the Promised Land will be (15:18).[269]

Of course, we know the Garden of Genesis 3 was indeed located *within* the region of Eden.

Now the Lord God had planted a garden in the east, in Eden; and there he put the man he had formed. (Genesis 2:8)

Rabbi Avraham Arieh Trugman, director of Ohr Chadash Torah Institute, confirms the ancient Jewish scholar's understanding of the truth we are examining. Those early Hebrew authorities understood that the Garden of Eden was, indeed, located in what we now know as the ancient land of Israel:

The Garden of Eden is associated with the Land of Israel, according to the big borders—from the river of Egypt to the Euphrates.[270]

The *Benson's Commentary*, commenting upon Genesis 2:8, agrees:

A place peculiarly pleasant, a paradise, separated, it seems, from the rest of the earth, and enclosed, but in what way, we are not informed; eastward—from the place where Moses wrote, and from the place where the Israelites afterward dwelt—In Eden.[271]

Likewise, the *Pulpit Commentary* declares the original location of the region of Eden to have been in the Promised Land:

Israel, **like Adam**, had been **settled by God in Palestine**, the **glory of all lands**; but, ungrateful for God's great bounty and gracious gift, they broke the covenant of their God, the condition of which, as in the case of the Adamic covenant, was obedience.[272] (Emphasis added)

Another attestation of the Garden of Eden having been located in Jerusalem is expressed in an article at the Israel Bible website:

Eden and its rivers may signify the real Jerusalem, the Temple of Solomon, or the Promised Land. It may **also represent the divine garden on Zion**, and the mountain of God, which was also Jerusalem.[273] (Emphasis added)

But that's not all. Have a look at the following additional scholarly sources that also insist Jerusalem was the location of the original Garden of Eden.

Dr. Jim Sibley is the director of the Pasche Institute of Jewish Studies. He is also a faculty member and editor of Mishkan, an international journal dealing with the gospel and the Jewish people. Dr. Sibley has taught courses related to Judaism and Jewish evangelism as a guest professor at seminaries and Bible colleges across North America. His articles have been published in Israel, England, and the United States.[274]

Consider Dr. Sibley's position on the matter of the location of the Garden of Eden. Notice that he ties together many of the theological assertions already made in the preceding chapters of this book.

"Scripture equates Satan's presence in the Garden with his presence in Jerusalem." In Ezekiel 28:12–15, Ezekiel describes Lucifer as the power behind the king of Tyre and the description is given to Satan that he was "in Eden, the garden of God" (v. 13). In verse fourteen **God seems to equate Eden with "the holy mountain of God,"** which is identified in Scripture as Mount **Moriah, the Temple Mount in Jerusalem.**

If **Jerusalem is the site of the Garden of Eden,** then where Abraham was told to offer Isaac (Gen. 22), [and where] Solomon was told to build the house of the Lord (2 Chron. 3:1), [and] where oceans of blood were spilled in the centuries of sacrifice," is where Jesus, the second Adam—the faithful one—died on

the cross. And it's where Jesus will reign as the King of kings and Lord of lords when he comes back to establish his Kingdom.[275] (Emphasis added)

Additionally, in the graduate research project of Dr. Eric Baker titled "The Eschatological Role of the Jerusalem Temple: An Examination of Jewish Writings Dating from 586 BCE to 70 CE," we find the following observation:

> **The Garden of Eden, the tabernacle, the first Jerusalem temple,** the second Jerusalem temple, and Ezekiel's temple vision (Ezek. 40–48) are depicted as places for God to dwell. The Garden of Eden is the garden of God and the place where human and divine first coexisted (at least for a time). This original coexistence has been interpreted as the original dwelling of God…
>
> The cherubim in the Holy of Holies **connect the most holy place [of the Temple at Jerusalem] to Eden**…. In biblical texts, **the Jerusalem temple is depicted as a dwelling place of God equivalent to Eden.**[276] (Emphasis and brackets added)

Dr. Margaret Barker is the author of seventeen scholarly books on this topic. She has developed an approach to biblical studies known as "Temple Theology." Concerning the Garden of Eden being located in Jerusalem, she writes:

> But **the temple was also built in accordance with a heavenly plan to represent on earth the garden of God…. The Garden of Eden** was the first dry land created in the midst of the primeval waters and so the temple was the center of the created order.
>
> There is, however, a great deal [of biblical and scholarly evidence] which suggests that the Garden of Eden and the temple

had at one time been one and the same.[277] (Emphasis added; brackets added to accurately express the context of the entire article.)

Even the International Mission Board of the world's largest evangelical denomination recognizes that the prevailing Jewish worldview has always been that Jerusalem is the earthly site of the Garden of Eden:

The Temple and the mount on which it was placed has significance that reaches back to *the moment when history began.* **In the Jewish worldview, the Temple Mount was the site of the Garden of Eden.**[278] (Emphasis added)

WRITTEN IN STONE

Ancient Jewish tradition also asserts the Temple Mount in Jerusalem to be the location of the foundation stone upon which God created the world. That tradition does not point to just any stone; rather, it has identified a specific one.

In Hebrew, that rock is called the *Even HaShtiya,* translating to "the foundational stone." The Jews claim this rock is at the center of the original Garden of Eden. It was also the place, they attest, of Abraham's intended sacrifice of Isaac (Genesis 22). According to Scripture, this spot is also where Solomon built the first Temple and is the sacred place where the "Lord appeared" to King David (2 Chronicles 3:1). That stone is now the centerpiece of the Islamic Dome of the Rock.[279]

Think of the biblical symbolism. The foundation stone of the Garden of Eden is now enshrined within the Dome of the Rock, an Islamic symbol of subjugation over a conquered area.[280]

On the western facade of the Dome of the Rock, Zev Vilnay (1900–1988), a renowned Israeli geographer, author, and lecturer has documented that the following inscription is written in Arabic, "The Rock of the Temple from the Garden of Eden." The northern gate of the mosque, facing the foundation stone, is named the Gate of Paradise, *Bab ej-Jinah.* On the floor in front of this gate is a stone of green jasper about half a meter square, which the Muslims call "the Stone of Eden."[281]

Not only do the Jews believe this location is where the Garden of Eden was established "in the beginning," but apparently Satan has now marked it as belonging solely to him. He has written his claim in stone.

When we consider that the "real" Garden of Eden still exists, interdimensionally, in this same location, today's geopolitical turmoil and its laser focus on Jerusalem take on a completely new meaning.

Blue Letter Bible (paradise)

According to the early church Fathers, **the paradise in which our first parents dwelt** before the fall *still exists,* neither on the earth nor in the heavens, **but above and beyond the world.**[282] (Emphasis added)

In other words, Eden is still there. It has always been there, but in another dimension. Its original location, however, was right in the center of the planet: Jerusalem (Ezekiel 5:5).

Does the world's anxiety over the 2018 legal establishment of Jerusalem as the original and rightful capital of Israel make more sense to you now?[283]

SATAN PANICS

The Exodus event from Egypt eventually resulted in God's people settling in the Promised Land, where its center of government and worship was ultimately located in Jerusalem. But it was also the place where Abraham was directed by Elohim to take Isaac for the sacrifice of his "only son" unto the LORD. This was where Elohim had put his Name, and this was where He had formed the first humans by His own hand.

Of course, Jerusalem is also the place where Jesus spent the last week of his earthly ministry and where He was crucified, resurrected, and ascended into heaven. Further, it's the place—the Mt. of Olives—to which He will return to rule and reign over His restored kingdom (Zechariah 14:4, Acts 1:11, 12).

We also understand that this locale was the spot where Satan's judgment and final destruction were first pronounced. It was right there, on the earthly soil of where the heavenly Garden had originally existed—*and still exists*—but in another dimension.

- They serve **at a sanctuary** [the Temple in Jerusalem] that is **a copy and shadow** of **what is in heaven**. This is why Moses was warned when he was about to build the tabernacle: "See to it that you make everything according to the pattern shown you on the mountain." (Hebrews 8:5, emphasis and brackets added)
- It was necessary, then, for **the copies of the heavenly things** to be purified with these sacrifices, but **the heavenly things** themselves with better sacrifices than these. For Christ did not enter a sanctuary made with human hands **that was only a copy** of the true one; **he entered heaven itself**, now to appear for us in God's presence. (Hebrews 9:23–24, emphasis added)

And now, God's people, who were carrying within their lineage the Seed that would destroy Satan, were back in the Garden of Eden! At this point, surely Satan had to wonder: *Would Jerusalem be the place where the coming Seed of retribution would carry out the divine crushing of my head?*

So the ancient serpent went to work on Israel while they were dwelling in the land of Promise. But the bulk of Satan's demonic work against the people of God would first filter through the thrones of the surrounding nations and empires. These were the thrones the serpent had long ago learned to supernaturally manipulate to his advantage.

Now, once again, they would bend to his desires...

48

THE NATIONS

This was Satan's obsession.

Have you ever heard the old adage that the word "history" could be more accurately labeled as "His Story"? There's a good reason why that play on words is considered so true.

From the Egyptian Empire and forward, Israelites were constantly under attack by the surrounding kingdoms, and on several occasions they were utterly destroyed and subsequently enslaved by them.

Satan's continual targeting of the nation of Israel was to accomplish one major goal: to destroy the coming Seed and unleash his rebellious vengeance upon the people of Yahweh, through whom that Seed would arrive. This was Satan's obsession. He knew if he couldn't stop the prophecy of Genesis 3 from coming to fruition, his own kingdom dreams would eventually be obliterated. So he used the human powers he had at his disposal—the thrones and the kings who would do his bidding.

This fact is not lost on those who truly know and understand the contextual historical connections. In March 2019, Fox News personality Judge Jeanine Pirro summarized this truth on a news broadcast:

Jews have been persecuted almost from the beginning of time when they were forced out of Egypt to the six million killed in the Holocaust and now, we are witnessing the rise of anti-Semitism in Europe where incidents are up 74% in the last year alone in France, where Jewish cemeteries are regularly desecrated with swastikas and people relay the common tropes of Jews with too much money and influence.[284]

THE PLAYERS

The major empires of world history, especially those that directly affected the Middle East, Europe, and parts of Asia and Africa, tell the story in regard to Israel's history and Satan's agenda as they unfolded through those nations.

Even though the following synopsis of major world empires is a simple and admittedly abbreviated version of the complex saga of history's unfolding, what is presented here is an accurate assessment of the details as they pertain to our current examination.

The Egyptian Empire was intermittently friend and foe to the children of Israel once they were in the Promised Land. On several occasions, ancient Egypt conspired with other empires for the purpose of destroying God's people and their new nation.

Egypt's rulers continued these kinds of conspiratorial arrangements and attacks right up to the Six Day War in 1967. However, prior to the times of the New Testament, it can be biblically asserted that much of Egypt's animosity toward Israel was fueled by Satan's never-ending desire to find and destroy that coming Seed.

The Assyrian Empire was one of Israel's most ruthless enemies. By 722 BC, Assyria had finally succeeded in becoming the ancient world's newest superpower. It also succeeded in conquering the Northern Kingdom of the civil-war-divided Israel. As a result, ten of Israel's twelve tribes were eventually taken into captivity by Assyria.

Assyria attempted, several times, to conquer the Southern Kingdom of Judah in order to capture Jerusalem, the ultimate prize, along with the two remaining tribes. They were never successful and eventually had to turn their attention to another rising world superpower. The brutal Assyrian Empire would soon be conquered by the blood-thirsty beast that was on the rise—the Babylonian Empire.

The Babylonian Empire under King Nebuchadnezzar was finally able to conquer the Southern Kingdom of Judah around 597 BC. In so doing, it destroyed the city of Jerusalem as well as the Temple of Yahweh that had been built by King Solomon. In addition to carting off the Temple treasures, Babylon also took the surviving Israelites into captivity. The best and brightest of them, especially the male children, were schooled in the ways of paganism and the Babylonian language and customs (Daniel 1–6).

The Persian Empire came to fruition around 560 BC. It came to possess what the Babylonians and the Assyrians before them had conquered. By default, that Persian inheritance included what used to be the land of Israel and the capital city of Jerusalem.

The Jews were hated by certain factions within the Persian Empire, including a particularly influential government official by the name of Haman. Haman plotted to have all the Jews in Persia destroyed by a decree of the emperor. Once again, Satan filled a singular man of power to carry out his plan of destroying "the Seed" and those who were carrying it. The plot nearly succeeded, except for the hand of Elohim working through the Jewish queen of Persia named Hadassah or, as she is often known by her Persian name, *Esther.*

Under the Persian Empire, the Jews were allowed to return to Jerusalem to rebuild the city walls and the Temple. Even then, the satanically inspired enemies of God's people persistently plotted the ruin of the Jews and their plans to revive their Temple-centered worship of Yahweh (Nehemiah).

The Greek Empire, by 449 BC—after a series of long and brutal wars with the Persian Empire—finally prevailed, and a treaty was signed with Persia. Within one hundred years of that date, the Persian Empire ceased to exist altogether. The Greeks were firmly entrenched as the world's new superpower and would go on to conquer the "known world" under Alexander the Great.

After Alexander's death in 323 BC, the land of Judea, including Jerusalem, fell under the power of the resulting Greek Seleucid Empire. The process of *hellenization*, the infusion of the pervasive customs and culture of the Greeks, was brutally enforced upon the Jews, including their pagan religious practices.

Consequently, by 167 BC, Jewish religious sacrifices were forbidden, among numerous other distinctly Jewish religious and cultural practices. Altars to Greek gods were set up and animals considered "unclean" by the Jews were sacrificed upon those altars. The Olympian Zeus was set up in the Temple. Possession of Jewish sacred texts was outlawed and enforced by a sentence of death.

By 166 BC, the Jews had violently revolted, protesting the heavy hand of their Greek overlords. The war became known as the Maccabean Revolt and eventually resulted in the liberation of Jerusalem and the surrounding area. That Jewish emancipation lasted for about a hundred years.

However, this "freedom"—politically speaking—was largely due to an alliance the Jewish leaders had struck with a fledgling empire that was quickly gaining prominence...*and massive power*.

It was a power Satan would eventually mark as his own.

49

THE DRACO STANDARD

**Satan had relentlessly labored over the
discovery of the meanings of those prophecies.**

By 63 BC, the Roman general Pompey had sailed across the Mediter-
ranean with his devastating naval supremacy. Rome's final grip upon
the throat of the collapsing empire of Greece had commenced.

It was into this new and history-altering world that God implanted
the beginnings of his strategy to deconstruct Satan's empire. Heaven's
divine insertion began in a lowly manger in a tiny hamlet just a little over
five miles outside of Jerusalem. This is where Elohim would discreetly
slip into His own creation—in the little village of Bethlehem.

At the same time, Caesar Augustus mercilessly ruled from Rome.
Just before Yeshua's earthly birth, Caesar issued an empire-wide decree
of census and taxation, requiring every head of household to register in
the town of their birth. Caesar could not have known that in issuing
such an executive order, his desire for ever-burgeoning government cof-
fers would play a pivotal part in bringing about the most monumental
prophecy ever fulfilled. Rome's decree would assure that the promised

Seed would be born in the exact spot heaven had pronounced—750 years before it happened.

> But as for you, Bethlehem Ephrathah, too little to be among the clans of Judah, from you One will go forth for me to be ruler in Israel. His goings forth are from long ago, from the days of eternity. (Micah 5:2, NASB)

During those same days, a Roman appointed puppet-king, Herod the Great, had been assigned to manage the religious and civil affairs of the Jews living within the Roman province of Judea. When word finally arrived at Herod's palace that the new "king of the Jews" had most likely been born in Bethlehem, Herod issued his own decree.

Satan pulled his interdimensional puppet strings. Similar to what Pharaoh had done in Egypt more than fifteen hundred years earlier, Herod ordered the killing of all the boys in Bethlehem who were age two years and younger. As shocking as Herod's edict sounds when we first read it in the pages of Scripture, the act was not that out of the ordinary for this egocentric psychopath. Herod was known far and wide as being a sociopathic madman who notoriously murdered several of his immediate family members—and anyone else who dared to get in his way.[285]

Expositor's Greek Testament

> Anything is credible of the man who murdered his own wife and sons. This deed shocks Christians; but it was a small affair in Herod's career, and in contemporary history.[286]

Once again, the specific biblical connections of Satan's insatiable quest for the divine Seed were also obvious to the classical scholars.

Ellicott's Commentary for English Readers

> Our minds go back to the hatred and fear of Pharaoh, setting a watch for the offspring of Israel and ordering their destruction; and even more are we reminded of the jealous hatred of Herod seeking the life of the infant Christ. It shows us that evermore, as Herod waited to destroy Christ, the devil, the old spirit whose malignity wrought through the fears of Pharaoh and of Herod, is on the watch to destroy every token of good and every resemblance to Christ in the world.[287]

Cambridge Bible for Schools and Colleges

> [This] symbolizes the enmity of the serpent against the seed of the woman, beginning with the intended treachery of Herod, and massacre of the Innocents; but including also the malice that pursued Him through life, the temptation, and at last the Cross.[288] (Brackets added)

Gill's Exposition also connects Pharaoh of the Exodus event with the similar atrocities of Herod. And it connects both of those historical figures with being interdimensionally manipulated by the power of Satan's sway over the thrones of the earth.

> Just as the dragon Pharaoh lay in the midst of his rivers, in the river Nile, Ezekiel 29:3; to slay the male children of Israel as soon as born; and as the dragon Herod sought to take away the life of Jesus quickly after his birth; and as Satan is like a roaring lion, seeking whom he may devour, so the Pagan empire, or the Pagan emperors, took every opportunity to stifle the kingdom of Christ in embryo.[289]

THE SERPENT'S FLAG

By the time of the pervasive spreading of the early Church, the symbol of the dragon had become a common emblem of the Roman cavalry. Satan was boldly marking his territory and embedding his symbol into the breastplates and standards of the empire he manipulated.

Barnes' Notes on the Bible

> Now it so happens that [at the time of the hurch] the "dragon" had become a common standard in the Roman armies, and had in some measure superseded the eagle.[290] (Brackets added)

THE DRACO, THE LATE ROMAN MILITARY STANDARD

The Draco ("dragon" or "serpent," plural "Dracones") was a military standard of the Roman cavalry. Carried by the draconarius, the Draco was the standard of the cohort as the eagle (*aquila*) was that of the legion.[291]

ROMAN MILITARY STANDARDS

The Draco was usually carried by the cavalry units. A Draco was created by shaping metal to form a hollow head that resembled a toothed dragon. A cloth tube tail was also attached to the neck of the head, so it would expand when the wind passed through it as the standard was being carried high in the air. If the Draco was carried at the correct speed, a subtle hissing noise would be created by the air-stream passing through the dragon's mouth.[292]

However, heaven's ultimate plan was intricately complex from the outset. In fact, it was so multifaceted that as Satan tried to unravel its initial mystery, as it existed in the person of Jesus Christ, he would make one blunder after another. And each of those blunders turned out to be the threads that would weave together the serpent's ultimate undoing.

In the meantime, as we've traced the serpent's winding path through the dusty trails of time and history, we have also discovered an eternally important truth: history is not *history*—until it's over. Satan's psychotic war rages on. It will, in fact, all be over soon. But not quite yet.

Like dancing the Native American Ghost Dance,[293] Nachash continues to beat his war drums and plots to pour out his vengeance. It is his final act of desperation. He is vainly hoping for the revival and subsequent salvation of his collapsing empire…

…because he knows his time is short.

50

THE DRAGON'S FURY

**Satan's destructive quest will continue
to mount right up to the end.**

The divine strategy of finally bringing forth the full force of the Seed would prove to be such an enigma that neither the prophets, the teachers of Scripture, nor the angels of heaven fully understood the gravity of the details until the prophecies blossomed into fulfilment. Satan had relentlessly labored over the meanings of those prophecies as well—though, by the time he understood them, it was far too late to save his kingdom.

The divine decree was finally unfurled in all of its grand significance at an empty tomb, and it was further punctuated by the subsequent birth of the Church. But when the Church was born, the great dragon, as prophesied in Revelation 12, determined to rip it asunder. If he couldn't defeat the ultimate Seed, then Satan would be resolute in his plans to destroy the offspring of the Seed.

GLOBAL PERSECUTION

That demonic rage is now evidenced in our daily personal battle with the serpent, and the advanced outpouring of Satan's fury that is so poignantly expressed in our ever-pervasive news cycles.

> Then the dragon was enraged at the woman and went off to wage war against the rest of her offspring—those who keep God's commands and hold fast their testimony about Jesus. (Revelation 12:17)

Jamieson-Fausset-Brown Bible Commentary

Satan's first effort was to root out the Christian Church, so that there should be no visible profession of Christianity. Foiled in this, he wars (Re 11:7; 13:7) against the invisible Church, namely, "those who keep the commandments of God, and have the testimony of Jesus." These are "the remnant," or rest of her seed, as distinguished from her seed, "the man-child" (Re 12:5), on one hand, and from mere professors on the other.

The Church, in her beauty and unity is now not manifested, but awaiting the manifestations of the sons of God at Christ's coming. Unable to destroy Christianity and the Church as a whole, Satan directs his enmity against true Christians, the elect remnant: the others he leaves unmolested.[294]

The prophecy from Revelation 12:17 is now more than two thousand years old. Yet, we alone are the first generation to experience the worst levels of global Christian persecution in the history of humanity.

The Christian Post—October 14, 2017

The persecution of Christians is now *"worse than at any time in history"*… not only are Christians more persecuted than any other faith group, they are also experiencing the worst forms of persecution.[295] (Emphasis added)

As 2018 opened, the Orthodox Christian Network announced:

The outlook for Christians in countries around the world is looking *worse than ever before* according to a new report from Aid to the Church in Need. According to the report **persecution against Christians is** *at an all-time high.* "In 2016, estimates for the number of Christians worldwide who have suffered some form of persecution for their faith range from 200,000 to 600,000. *These numbers have grown exponentially since."*[296] (Emphasis added)

By the close of 2018 a Catholic NGO *Aid to the Church in Need* report asserted:

Respect for *religious freedom is on the decline worldwide.*
More than 60 percent of the world's population of more than 7.5 billion reside in countries where the right to religious freedom is obstructed or denied. **An estimated 505 million Christians face persecution for following their faith.**[297] (Emphasis added)

In the opening months of 2019, the world was faced with this headline, "11 Christians Killed Every Day for Their Decision to Follow Jesus."

Today, in the 21st century, we are living in a time when persecution against *Christian believers is the highest in modern history*. Christian persecution…is increasing at an alarming rate…. *Each day, a staggering 11 Christians are killed* for their faith.[298] (Emphasis added)

And this, "Report: 245 Million Christians Facing 'Extreme' Persecution Worldwide."

North Korea remains at the top of a list of 50 countries where at least 245 million Christians are facing "extreme persecution" this year, up 14 percent from 215 million at the beginning of 2018, the World Wide Watch List (WWL) released on Wednesday by Open Doors, a group that monitors the mistreatment of Christ followers, revealed….

"Radical Islam is the driver behind eight of the top 10 on the World Watch List this year, four of which are from Africa," the Open Doors chief proclaimed.[299] (Emphasis added)

And of course, Islam is the religious system that has erected its monument of occupation squarely on top of the Temple Mount in the city that sits in the center of the nations (Ezekiel 5:5)—in the place where God has put His Name.

As I have demonstrated, Satan's goals of targeting God's people and establishing his claims upon the original earthly location of the Garden of Eden have been his primary objectives since the very beginning. We are the first generation to be living in at least the leading edges of the fulfillment of what Jesus declared would happen shortly before his return.

For then there will be great distress, unequaled from the beginning of the world until now—and never to be equaled again. (Matthew 24:21)

There has never been a generation before us that has come even close to the current global conditions that precisely match Jesus' prophecies of the last days. Like it or not, we are the generation of those "unequaled" times that Jesus warned us about.

The process of Satan's outrage, at least in the geopolitical realm, most fervently began with Israel's enslavement in the land of Egypt. The pursuit continued through the thrones of the empires of antiquity, and they still march on through the geopolitical wrangling of today's world. From the eventual rise of the Ottoman Empire and its conquest of Jerusalem to the Crusades, the Inquisitions, Stalin's agenda of outrageous human slaughter, and the Nazi ovens of Hitler's maniacal delusion—and right up to the time of Arab Spring and the Organization of Islamic Cooperation and beyond…Satan's bloodbath of God's people marches on.

EPIDEMIC SCOURGES

The preceding truths don't even take into account Satan's perpetual war on children. *The seed of the woman* is still the primary target of Satan's realm. The holiest and most sacred of all of God's human components of creation is the womb (Psalm 139:13). Is there any wonder, then, why the killing of the "little ones" plods forward in a murderous rampage of demonic rage?

We are the first historical generation to witness the killing of the unborn child in the womb to be labeled by the World Health Organization as the *leading cause of global death*.[300]

In 2018 alone, more than forty-two million children among the nations of the world were destroyed in their mothers' own wombs. This is almost equivalent to the globe having once again experienced a devastation on the scale of World War I or World War II—*in a single year*. And the butchery continues, year after year. This is an especially accurate comparison when we consider that an enormous proportion of abortions around the globe—perhaps the majority of them—are never even reported.[301]

Added to the global abortion holocaust is the current international epidemic of sex crimes against children, physical abuse of children, and every form of exploitation imaginable committed against the most innocent and vulnerable among us. The atrocities against children number into the billions each year. No other species of animal life treats its offspring in a more hideously cruel manner.[302]

The seed of the womb of the woman is squarely in Satan's crosshairs. He knows his end is imminent. He is filled with indignation. His destruction of the institutions of marriage, home, family, childhood, and gender identity is the result of his petulant temper tantrum. His outrage is aimed at thumbing his nose at Elohim, as Nachash—the ancient homicidal serpent—prepares to take his final bow.

But woe to the earth and the sea, because the devil has gone down to you! He is filled with fury, because he knows that his time is short....

Then the dragon was enraged at the woman and went off to wage war against the rest of her offspring—those who keep God's commands and hold fast their testimony about Jesus.

The dragon stood on the shore of the sea.... The dragon gave the beast his power and his throne and great authority.... People worshiped the dragon because he had given authority to the beast, and they also worshiped the beast and asked, "Who is like the beast? Who can wage war against it?"

It opened its mouth to blaspheme God, and to slander his name and his dwelling place and those who live in heaven. It was given power to wage war against God's holy people and to conquer them. And it was given authority over every tribe, people, language and nation.

Whoever has ears, let them hear. (Revelation 12:12, 17; 13:1–2, 4, 6–7)

Regardless of what Satan imagines or how viciously he unleashes his unthinkable scourges of death and destruction upon this planet, he does not get to have the last word in the matter. The *final* word is still coming.

In the meantime, there's still this little matter of being "reduced to ashes."

That singular divine declaration still, to this very day, haunts the ancient dragon to the very core of his being.

PART EIGHT

The Pathway

There is a way which seemeth right unto a man,
but the end thereof are the ways of death.
—PROVERBS 14:12

Enter through the narrow gate.
For wide is the gate and broad is the road that
leads to destruction, and many enter through it.
—MATTHEW 7:13–14

51

RETHINKING DEATH

**What does the Bible really say regarding our
departure from this earthly realm?**

Not long after writing *Gods of Ground Zero: The Truth of Eden's Iniquity*, I received the following question on one of my social media sites:

> If the fallen angels are to be judged as mortals and they lose their immortality, then could it stand to reason that judgment and the lake of fire are the obliteration of the un-repented? Eternity in hell is still immortality. If an angel is cursed to die like a human and a human is eternal after death, then what is death?

What is death? What a brilliant and truly elemental question!

In *Gods of Ground Zero*, I made the scriptural point that not only will Satan be completely defeated in the end, but that he would be utterly destroyed. I zeroed in on the fact that, throughout the Bible, God pronounced several pointed death sentences upon that ancient serpent.[303]

However, I did not expand upon what being "utterly destroyed" meant. So, in the pages that follow, I will fill in that gap. It is a fair question, and important to address.

The question actually covers two areas of concern, yet the two are inextricably related. We will begin with an understanding of "death" in general. There is so much conjecture and out-and-out misinterpretation of Scripture regarding death that I believe it is monumentally important to take a deeper look at what God's Word actually reveals. Once we have achieved that fundamental understanding, we'll next answer the question concerning Satan's ultimate demise—*his own death*.

You might be surprised by some of the things you're getting ready to discover.

52

THE GREAT DELUSION

*I have been told by very wise people that I have
to make friends with Death.
I believe they are right. But I have not yet been able.*
—Dr. Judith Acosta[304]

Judith Acosta is a licensed psychotherapist and crisis counselor who has been engaged for presentations by some of the country's leading corporations, hospitals, and international conferences, including the New York City Police Department and the National Association for Missing & Exploited Children. She is the author of numerous articles and several books on mental health and cultural issues.[305]

Ms. Acosta wrote an article titled "Why Do We Dread Being Dead?" Her treatise was carried by a major media website. In that article, Ms. Acosta offered the following analysis of America's "death fear" culture:

> My observation is that we don't just fear death, nor do we just ignore it by housing our dying in group homes or hospitals. Out of unprecedented decades of comfort in this country, we simply refuse it. **It is the most systematic—and systemic—delusion in world history.**[306] (Emphasis added)

I'm not certain of Ms. Acosta's faith life. Regardless, I agree with her assessment. The dread of death truly is the most systemic aberration leveled upon the human race—and it began way back in the Garden of Eden.

As a pastor and a former law enforcement officer, I have been surrounded by, immersed in, and at times almost suffocated by the specter of death. In the midst of dealing with the ever-recurring aftermath of the most prevalent fear universally common to the human race, I have continually heard people say, "Death just doesn't seem natural. It ought not to be this way. It seems like there should be something more. Life is vastly too important to merely end in death. The whole process of life—anticlimactically ending in death—is utterly meaningless."

There's a reason for that almost-global reaction to death. It's because dying is not *natural*. It truly was not supposed to be this way. And, there actually is something *more*. Everything within our soul screams it, and practically everyone in the world feels it—to their very core. Again, I appeal to Ms. Acosta as an example of the virtually universal human internalization of the phenomenon of death.

In yet another *Huffington Post* article, one in which Ms. Acosta related a poignantly heart-tugging saga about the death of her beloved pet dog, she opined:

> When I told my mother about Bugsy's passing, I started crying again. And as soon as I wept, she did, too. In between our sniffing and sobbing, I somehow managed to rail at the universe again, to be shocked again, to wonder again—how, why, *what the heck was all this about*, anyway? I told her, "*I'm so sick of death.*"
>
> And she said to me, "You know, that's the problem. **You can't stop it.** You're not eternal. **No one's eternal.**"
>
> And I remembered what Peter Kreeft had to say about that:

Maybe the problem is actually the other way. *Maybe we are eternal.* **Maybe we are continually shocked by death because it represents the antithesis to our highest natures, to our spirits.**[307] (Emphasis added)

Exactly! The problem really is "the other way." As it turns out, there's no "maybe" to it. We really are eternal. But the mechanics of what really happens after death still appear to be one of the greatest mysteries of the ages—especially to those who are unfamiliar with God's Word. The sad thing is that the understanding of this mystery is one of the Bible's greatest gifts to the fallen human race, yet the depth of that revelation is largely unknown, or even ignored. Answering humanity's collective question about death is one of the reasons the resurrection of Jesus Christ is so important. The foundation of the gospel message is predicated upon the truth that life on "the other side" is real—and available to all.

In May 2019, while we were still in the editing process of the final words of this book, Fox News posted an article at its website titled, "What Happens in Hours before Death? Many Don't Know." Here's a brief excerpt from that article:

A new survey of nearly 1,000 people in the U.K. found that a majority of people are clueless about the realities of death and dying…respondents admitted they knew little or nothing about what happens in the final hours before death…. According to a statement from the academy, death and dying have become such taboo subjects in Western cultures that many people resist talking about them…. This reticence has resulted in widespread cultural ignorance about death, the survey found.[308]

So, what does the Bible truly reveal about this great mystery called *death*? Let's begin with the death of a believer.

From everything we have discovered thus far, we can say with certainty that there truly is a "dimensional shift" at the moment of death for the one who is born again. We don't "cease to exist"[309] and we don't "sleep" in the grave until some future date.[310] We walk through a veil—a dimensional portal is opened—and we are in paradise. As we have already learned, this "paradise" is also known as the actual, presently veiled Garden of Eden—the place where Yahweh dwells with redeemed humanity. That place is also called heaven.

AT THE TOMB OF LAZARUS

Just a short while before He would offer Himself upon the cross, Jesus raised Lazarus from the "dead."[311] At that ominous resurrection miracle, in the tiny village of Bethany, Jesus used the event as a teachable moment to rectify Martha's apparent misconception about the process of death for the believer.

> Jesus said to her, "Your brother will rise again." Martha answered, **"I know he will rise again in the resurrection** at the last day." Jesus said to her, "I am the resurrection and the life. **The one who believes in me *will live*, even *though they die*; and whoever lives** by believing in me **will never die.** Do you believe this?" (John 11:23–25, emphasis added)

The context of each of these declarations, from the mouth of Jesus himself, is that when a born-again believer closes his or her eyes in death, that person immediately enters the physical realm of God's presence… *paradise*. Those who die in Christ pass through dimensional doors into a real and glorified existence.

Ellicott's Commentary for English Readers

> [Martha] thinks and speaks of Lazarus as dead. [Jesus] asserts that in the true thought of the spiritual life **the fact of physical *death does not interrupt* that life.**[312] (Emphasis and brackets added)

Pulpit Commentary

> In these words [spoken to Martha] [Jesus] identifies the "life" with the transfiguration of the bodily life.... **So-called "death" is veritable "life."** There are multitudes now believing (*and therefore living*) in him.[313] (Emphasis and brackets added)

Meyer's New Testament Commentary

> Whoso believeth in me, even if he shall have died (physically), **will live** (be a partaker of life **uninterruptedly**).[314] (Emphasis added)

THE UPPER ROOM

Jesus promised His disciples they, too, would share in that same paradise. On that night, in the upper room of His last Passover celebration, Jesus guaranteed that they would, indeed, live in His "Father's house" with Him. The clear implication of His promise was that passing from this earthly existence meant an immediate entrance into eternal life:

> My Father's house has many rooms; if that were not so, would I have told you that I am going there to prepare a place for you?

And if I go and prepare a place for you, I will come back and take you to be with me that you also may be where I am.… if that were not so, would I have told you that I am going there to prepare a place for you? (John 14:2–3, 8)

There can be little doubt that one of the aspects of Jesus' promise— "I will come back" was a reference to his *Second Coming*. However, the specific wording and the context of the original biblical language also speak of the ongoing process of God's children leaving this world in death until the day when He ultimately returns in all His glory:

Expositor's Greek Testament

Its **completion** is effected **by his coming again** and receiving them to himself, or "to his own home"… **The present is used in [I am coming] as if the coming were so certain as to be already begun,** cf. John 5:25. **The promise is fulfilled in the death of the Christian**, and it has changed the aspect of death.[315] (Emphasis added)

Pulpit Commentary

Not until **He comes in all his glory** will the words be perfectly fulfilled; **but the early Church**, on the basis of communion with Christ himself in the power of his Spirit, **expected that Christ had come and** *taken to himself one by one those who died in the faith* (1 Thessalonians 4:14).

Thus Stephen expected the Lord to receive his spirit (Acts 7:59); and **the dying thief** was to be **with him**, in paradise; **and Paul knew** that to be away from home, so far as body is concerned, was to be "at home or **present with the Lord**" (2 Corinthians 5:8). "**To be with Christ**" was "far better" than to labor on in the flesh (Philippians 1:23).[316] (Emphasis added)

Vincent's Word Studies

The present tense; I come.... **Not to be limited to the Lord's second** and glorious coming at the last day.

Here the future tense, **will receive**. I come again and will receive you. The change of tense is intentional, **the future pointing to the future personal** *reception of the believer through death.* Christ is **with the disciple always, continually "coming" to him,** unto the end of the world.[317] (Emphasis added)

Jamieson-Fausset-Brown Bible Commentary

I will come again and receive you unto myself—**at his Personal appearing;** but in a secondary and comforting sense, *to each individually.*[318] (Emphasis added)

However, these instances are certainly not the only times that Jesus uttered distinct promises concerning the immediacy of an actual physical *and other-dimensional* life after death.

53

FAMOUS LAST WORDS

**The fact that Jesus meant an immediate entrance
into the dimension of paradise is well established.**

Not long after those historically iconic hours spent with His disciples in the Upper Room had passed, Jesus promised a place in the Father's house to yet another person—and by merely human standards, a very unlikely person. Additionally, the promise was made from a very unlikely location.

Jesus promised one of the thieves on the crosses to either side of His own: "Today, you will be with me in paradise"[319] (Luke 23:43).

With these words, Jesus assured the repentant thief that soon he would experience an immediate entry into another dimensional reality. The promise of this continuation of life was described as "paradise." It was a physical existence beyond mortal contemplation and description.[320]

Furthermore, Jesus assured the thief that *on that very day* he would begin his new life in that dimensional shift of reality. This is what we earlier illustrated with the parable of Eddie Red.

The fact that Jesus meant an *immediate* entrance into the dimension of paradise is well-established, both by the original language in which it was written, as well as by classical commentators' exegesis.

Benson's Commentary

Christ here lets us know, 1st, that he was going, not only to...*the invisible world*, but to **that part of it termed *paradise*. his human soul was removing to *the place of separate souls*; not to the place of the damned, but to **the place of the blessed**.... As if he had said, I will not only remember thee when I come into my kingdom, *but this very day;* and will confer upon thee more than thou hast asked.[321] (Emphasis added)

Gill's Exposition of the Entire Bible unveils the same stunning truth. Jesus could not have been any plainer in his speech. They were going back to the Garden of Eden that very day:

Verily I say unto thee, today thou shall be with me in **paradise;** **"in the garden of Eden"**; ...the state of the happiness of the saints, **even heaven**, and eternal glory, which the Jews frequently call by this name;...and is so called, because, as the earthly paradise, **or Eden's garden...and this he was to enter upon that very day.**[322] (Emphasis added)

Expositor's Greek Testament

Luke 23:43. To be connected with what follows, *as opposed to* a boon expected at some future time.[323] (Emphasis added)

Jamieson-Fausset-Brown Bible Commentary

Today—"Thou art prepared for a long delay before I come into My kingdom, **but *not a day's delay* shall there be** for thee; thou **shalt not be parted from Me even for a moment,** but **together we shall go,** and with Me, *ere this day expire, shalt thou be in paradise.*"[324] (Emphasis added)

WORD BY WORD

Breaking down Jesus' actual words to the thief into each of their prominent meanings helps us grasp the gravity of His promise.

"I tell you the truth": *I am not lying.* This is exactly what Jesus had told His disciples in the upper room just a few hours earlier (John 14:2).

"Today": *This very day.* Not later. Not in the future. But *today* "you will be there with Me."

"You": *The essence of who you are. Your very being.* Your physical reality (although glorified). Not a wispy shadow of you. Not a ghostly image of you—but *you.*

"Will be": *The essence of life and reality.* Breathing. Laughing. Physically living. The state of "being." "You will *be…*"

"With Me": *In another dimension.* But only through the singular portal that leads there—Jesus Himself. And, you will be *with* Jesus. "To be absent from the body is to be present *with the Lord*" (2 Corinthians 5:8, emphasis added).

"In paradise": *In the Garden of Eden.* A real place. Another realm, and a physical reality. Behind the veil. In the Father's house. Indescribable. Eternal. Perfect. Without sin, pain, or death.

That breakdown of Jesus' promise is based upon the preponderance of scholarly understanding of the Greek language and its proper punctuation context. In fact, out of several dozen of the most used and reliable versions of the Bible, each one translates this sentence to read exactly as we have parsed it here.[325]

Once we examine Jesus' words the way in which they were actually spoken, the meaning leaves no room for argument. The promise is for all believers—everyone who is truly born again. The promise is of *immediate* life in the dimension of paradise.

And…not that we necessarily needed it, but there's still more. We have the testimony of yet another person who went into paradise then returned to tell about it.

His life and his view of death were forever altered.

54

TESTIMONY FROM THE OTHER SIDE

He had, in fact, been through those dimensional doors of the "other side" and actually entered paradise.

The Apostle Paul, writing to the Church in Corinth, also spoke of an immediate promise of the paradise that awaits the believer who passes from this earthly existence:

> For we know that if the earthly tent we live in is destroyed, **we have a building from God**, an eternal house **in heaven**, not built by human hands. Meanwhile we groan, **longing to be clothed instead with our heavenly dwelling**, because when we are clothed, we will not be found naked.
>
> For while we are in this tent, we groan and are burdened, because we do not wish to be unclothed but to be clothed instead with **our heavenly dwelling, so that what is mortal may be swallowed up by life.** Now the one who has fashioned us for this very purpose is God, who has given us the Spirit as a deposit, guaranteeing what is to come.

Therefore we are always confident and know that as long as we are at home in the body we are away from the Lord. For we live by faith, not by sight. **We are confident, I say, and would prefer to** *be away from the body* **and** *at home with the Lord.* (2 Corinthians 5:1–8, emphasis added)

Just how did the Apostle Paul know these things with such certainty? He had been through those dimensional doors of the "other side" and had entered *paradise*—the other-dimensional and true Garden of Eden. Read his words to the Church at Corinth:

I know a man in Christ who fourteen years ago was caught up *to the third heaven.* Whether it was **in the body or out of the body I do not know**—God knows. And I know that this man—**whether in the body or apart from the body** I do not know, but God knows—was *caught up to paradise* and heard inexpressible things, things that no one is permitted to tell. (2 Corinthians 12:2–4, emphasis added)[326]

Geneva Study Bible

Those that translated the Old Testament out of Hebrew into Greek, called the Garden of Eden by this name [paradise].[327] (Brackets added for context of entire commentary)

Cambridge Bible for Schools and Colleges:

Paul was not only caught up to the highest heaven, and there saw visions of God like those of Isaiah and St John, but that he was transported among the saints departed to that particular region of heaven called paradise.[328]

Barnes' Notes on the Bible

Paul meant to say that he could not attempt by words to do justice to what he saw and heard.... It would not have been possible for language to convey clearly the ideas connected with the things which Paul was then permitted to see.[329]

Even though he could not adequately describe the rapturous wonder he had experienced, Paul knew firsthand what awaited those who departed from this earth in a believer's death. Because of what he had experienced, he would later boldly declare:

For to me, **to live is Christ and to die is gain**. If I am to go on living in the body, this will mean fruitful labor for me. Yet what shall I choose? I do not know! I am torn between the two: **I desire to depart *and be with Christ*,** which is better by far; but it is more necessary for you that I remain in the body. (Philippians 1:21–24, emphasis added)

Barnes' Notes on the Bible

Paul believed that the soul of the Christian *would be immediately* with the Saviour at death. It was evidently his expectation that he would at once pass to his presence, and *not* that he would remain in an intermediate state to some far distant period.[330] (Emphasis added)

Jamieson-Fausset-Brown Bible Commentary

This *refutes the notion of the soul being dormant* during its separation from the body. To depart is better than to remain in the flesh; *to be with Christ* is far, far better.[331] (Emphasis added)

Bengel's Gnomen

> Paul takes it for granted as a certainty, that, after his martyrdom, **he *will be immediately* with Christ**, and that his condition will be greatly superior to what it was in the flesh.[332] (Emphasis added)

PASSING THROUGH PORTALS

Furthermore, just a short time before Paul's final passing from his earthly life, he penned these famous last words of assurance to his young protégé—a pastor named Timothy:

> For I am already being poured out like a drink offering, and **the time for my departure is near**. I have fought the good fight, I have finished the race, I have kept the faith. ***Now*** **there is in store for me** the crown of righteousness, which the Lord, the righteous Judge, will award to me **on that day—and not only to me, but also to all** who have longed for his appearing. (2 Timothy 4:6–8, emphasis added)

From everything else the Apostle Paul told the church through his writings in the years before his death, we can certainly assume that when he finally spoke of his earthly departure, he was certain of his immediate entry into the promised paradise. It was a physical existence that occurred at the moment of death, and it was just behind the veil.

Meyer's New Testament Commentary

> [The meaning] **cannot be "future in sense"**, for the signification of **the word forbids it.** At the end of his life-course, when he has

faithfully played out his part, *there remains nothing more* for the apostle—**than to** [immediately] *receive the reward* which is already prepared for him.[333] (Emphasis added)

Expositor's Greek Commentary

The notion of duration of *future time is not in the word* [*now*]. Paul means here "I have nothing more to do than to receive the crown."[334] (Emphasis added)

Gill's Exposition of the Entire Bible

Death is **not an annihilation of man**, neither of his body, nor of his soul…. it is a *removing of persons from one place and state to another;* from an house of clay, from this earthly house of our tabernacle, to an house not made with hands, eternal in the heavens, to everlasting habitations, and mansions in Christ's Father's house. **This phrase, "a departure", is an easy representation of death, and** *supposes an existence after it.*[335] (Emphasis added)

THE PROMISE

Each of the foregoing biblical attestations underscores the reality of a guaranteed, instantaneous, physical life beyond the veil of death. The born-again believer in Jesus Christ passes from this earthly realm to what is merely, from our earthly perspective, *an unseen realm*. Again, the illustration of Eddie Red and the fish tank is a useful analogy when attempting to conceptualize this amazing truth of interdimensional realities.

This is why Paul assured us that anything we might now suffer for the kingdom's sake will have been deemed worthy in eternity—and in that day, we will glory in it:

I consider that our present sufferings are not worth comparing with the glory that will be revealed in us. (Romans 8:18)

However, the next logical questions would have to be:

"If passing from one dimensional reality directly into paradise is the promise for the believer, what about the one who has had no use for God's salvation offered in Jesus Christ?"

"What about the one who has mocked or ignored God's offer of grace and mercy?"

"What happens to the 'lost' at death?"

55

RETHINKING HELL

There simply are no "second chances." *Ever.*

Biblically answering the question of what happens to the unbeliever at death is not that difficult even though the facts have certainly been muddied and, down through the ages, riddled with false notions.

The reason it's not that difficult to answer is because Scripture gives us a direct glimpse into that dimensional reality. Jesus Himself pulled back the veil for all the world to see.

The surface reading of Luke 16 is certainly interesting enough. But when the original languages and the appropriate Hebrew concepts are dissected, several startling revelations are brought to light. Of course, I am speaking of the account of the rich man and Lazarus.

Scholars have debated for centuries as to whether this passage is a parable. To me, it matters not. Its point is to reveal the answers to several deep mysteries regarding death, specific details Jesus wanted to make certain we understood.

Have a look at the most pertinent part of this narrative.

The time came when the beggar died and the angels carried him to Abraham's side. The rich man also died and was buried. In Hades, where he was in torment, he looked up and saw Abraham far away, with Lazarus by his side. So he called to him, "Father Abraham, have pity on me and send Lazarus to dip the tip of his finger in water and cool my tongue, because I am in agony in this fire." (Luke 16:22–24)

Let's examine the main concepts of this passage.

HADES

Meyer's New Testament Commentary

Hades corresponds to the Hebrew Sheol, which in the [Septuagint—the Greek translation of the Hebrew Scriptures] is translated by [Hades], and hence denotes **the whole *subterranean*[336] *place of abode*** of departed souls until the resurrection, divided into paradise (Luke 23:43) for the pious, and Gehenna for the godless.[337] (Emphasis and brackets added)

Expositor's Greek Testament

Luke 16:23–26. ***In the other world.***— [Sheol]: from the O.T. point of view **Hades means simply the state of the dead. Thus *both the dead men* would be in Hades.** But here Hades seems = hell, the place of torment, and of course Lazarus is not there, but in paradise.[338] (Emphasis and brackets added)

Helps Word Studies

> Hádēs—properly, *the "unseen place,"* referring to *the (invisible) realm* in which *all the dead* reside, i.e. the present dwelling place of all the departed (deceased); Hades.[339] (Emphasis added)

In other words, the term "Hades" speaks of another dimension, one entirely separate from this earthly existence, yet vividly real. It is the dimension of those who have departed their bodies of flesh and earthly life. Upon their "death," they are *immediately* alive and aware. Furthermore, we learn that Hades consists of two distinct and further separated realms—paradise and Gehenna.

Another translation for Gehenna would be "hell." The words are synonymous and denote the prison or holding place of the unbelieving realm until the day of the final judgment.[340]

Those who are unfamiliar with these truths and the nuances of the word meaning may find this a bit confusing. Because of this, even some biblical teachers have used these words incorrectly. The terms have even been mistranslated in various biblical versions. But once we properly understand them, Scripture begins to make much more sense.[341]

IN TORMENT

Twice in this passage, we are told that the rich man was "in torment." That idea often carries in our minds a picture of a person being "tortured" and physically punished and brutalized. This is perhaps one of the most debated and misunderstood concepts in the entire passage. After all, could it really be that those who reject God's offer of salvation in Jesus Christ are relegated to some sort of torture chamber, where all manner of sadistic horrors are brutally inflicted upon them? And if that is so, *who* does the torturing? You'll soon discover, after looking at the etymology of the original Greek word, that this is not likely the most accurate interpretation.

However, you'll also learn that simply because the word doesn't always *contextually* mean a "chamber of literal physical horrors inflicted by sadistic torture masters," the reality might be even more heartbreaking than that, especially when we understand there is no coming back from that place, or state of being. There simply are no "second chances." *Ever.*

THE MEANING

Let's start with what we know about the state of the rich man. We know he was in a literal, physical state of existence—even on the other side of "death." He experienced the sensation of thirst, and he spoke of heat. He was conscious of his surroundings; he knew where he was and where Lazarus was. He was in great agony. He was very much alive and experiencing deep, emotional anguish. He spoke, pleaded, and reasoned with Abraham. So we know that he could think, analyze, and communicate. But what does the word "torment" contextually indicate? This is usually the focus of the curious student of this passage.

Our English word "torment" in this passage, comes from the Greek word *basanos.* That word is NT #931 in *Strong's Concordance.*[342]

Although *basanos* came into our language from the Greek, it originated in the Latin. It literally means a "touchstone," which is a dark stone used in testing precious metals, especially gold. Hence, *basanos* first meant "an intense process of examination."[343]

This meaning evolved to indicate any act of testing, trying, or investigating. To be sure, the word ultimately included "an examination process conducted through the means of torture" at the hands of an examiner. However, in every instance of its use in the New Testament, it is translated as some sort of gut-wrenching anguish, even physical pain—but never by the hands of a literal and sadistic torturer.

Besides, what could be "beaten out" of the rich man at this point? There was no need to discern his guilt. He was already deemed guilty of rejecting God's offer of salvation. There was no need to extract a confession from him. Nothing is unknown to God. It's all in the "books."

NEW TESTAMENT USAGE

The word *basanos* is used in the New Testament to denote: "straining or struggling" against the oars (Mark 6:48), to be "battered or tossed" by the wind and waves (Matthew 14:24), the "pains of childbirth" (Revelation 12:12), or to be in a "state of emotional vexation" (2 Peter 2:8). It can also mean "to be in severe pain," usually brought about by the environment in which one is dwelling, or because of the specific condition of one's body (Revelation 9:5, 11:10, 12:2, 14:10, 20:10).[344]

Consider the context of the passage in Matthew 4 where the word *basanos* first appears in the New Testament:

> News about him spread all over Syria, and people brought to him all who were ill with various diseases, those *suffering severe pain*, [*basanos*] the demon-possessed, those having seizures, and the paralyzed; and he healed them. (Matthew 4:24, emphasis and brackets added)

These New Testament uses of the word *basanos* and their English translations are telling indeed. They give context to the translation of Jesus' account of the rich man in Hades and the "fire" of his suffering.

So, what type of *basanos* was the rich man truly experiencing? In reality, it was worse than what you might be thinking.

56

ALONE WITH HIMSELF

**The "trial" had been the substance of
the living of his earthly life.**

In relating the account of the rich man and Lazarus, Jesus at least intended to convey the truth that the condition of being separated from paradise and the presence of God *for eternity* was a torment itself, beyond imagination. It was utter isolation. Unbearably claustrophobic. Suffocating. Miserable beyond description. Absolutely horrifying.

Pulpit Commentary

> ***What picture of a hell*** was ever painted by man comparable to this vision ***of eternal solitude***, peopled ***alone by remorseful memories***, described by Jesus?[345] (Emphasis added)

Barnes' Notes on the Bible

> In what that suffering will consist it is probably ***beyond the power of any living mortal to imagine.***[346] (Emphasis added)

The crux of the rich man's *torment* was that he was so vividly and consciously aware of his eternal fate. He knew he had rejected the Lord's kindness and offer of salvation. He knew he had lived a life of godlessness and selfishness. If he had ever doubted it before, he now knew there truly *was* life after death. He also was aware that he was in prison. He could "see" Lazarus. And the sight of that former, poor beggar in paradise—now in a state of unspeakable bliss—was indescribably tortuous to the unrepentant, innately selfish rich man.

The rich man, in his prison of regret, was also awaiting the final judgment of the ages, and he knew it. There was no second chance for salvation.

And as it is appointed unto men once to die, but after this the judgment. (Hebrews 9:27, KJV)

There was absolutely no way out for the rich man. No bargaining. No sweet talking. No bribery. His vast earthly wealth was of no consequence here. He had amassed riches and fame, but had lost his soul.

For what shall it profit a man, if he shall gain the whole world, and lose his own soul? (Mark 8:36, KJV)

In this place, all he had was time—time to "examine" the condition of his lost humanity, his horrible and godless choices, and his selfish character. He had squandered the gift of earthly life God had given him. And now, the touchstone of *basanos* had rubbed against him, and he was found utterly wanting. His daily existence was an ordeal of distress beyond description. It was a torment that plunged to the very depths of his doomed soul.

IN THIS FIRE

All of this, and more, is why the rich man finally cried out to Abraham, "I am in agony in this fire!" He would get no relief from the misery of his circumstances. He was in the "fire of examination" that could never be quenched—a concept that mere earthly minds can't even begin to imagine.

Ellicott's Commentary for English Readers

> What is meant is that there shall be for the soul of the evil-doer, **when brought face to face with that holiness of God which is as *a consuming fire*** (Hebrews 12:29), an anguish as intolerable *as the touch of earthly flame* is to the nerves of the mortal body.[347] (Emphasis added)

Pulpit Commentary

> **What were the torments? Men with hushed voices ask.** A little further on the doomed one speaks of a flame and of his tongue apparently burning, owing to the scorching heat; but **it would be a mistake to think of a material flame being intended here.** There is nothing in the description of the situation to suggest this; it is rather *the burning never to be satisfied,* **longing for something utterly beyond his reach** that the unhappy man describes as an inextinguishable flame.[348] (Emphasis added)

Gill's Exposition of the Entire Scripture

> ***The wrath of God poured into the conscience,*** and the bitter remorse of that for speaking against the Messiah; and which are still greater in hell.[349] (Emphasis added)

Whedon's Commentary on the Bible

That tongue which had so often been pampered with sensual gratifications, is now parched with the terrible deprivation. **Those licentious passions** which had heated his blood **will now, in the atmosphere of the new world,** *kindle to a flame*. Are the damned tormented by **a real material fire?** We might, perhaps, answer—**the visible fire may be but** *a material emblem of an immaterial power*.[350] (Emphasis added)

In Mark 9:48, which is a partial quote of Isaiah 66:24, Jesus uses a similar image of hell, regarding fire: "Where their worm dies not, and the fire is not quenched."

Barnes' Notes says of this passage:

It is not to be supposed that there will be any "real" worm in hell—*perhaps no material fire*; nor can it be told what was particularly intended by the undying worm. *It is an image* of loathsome, dreadful, and *"eternal" suffering*.[351] (Emphasis added)

The imagery of a "fire" that tests, refines, or even punishes (yet, it is not a literal flame) is a common theme in Scripture. Have a look at few examples:

- See, I have refined you, though not as silver; I have tested you in the furnace of affliction. (Isaiah 48:10)
- If anyone builds on this foundation using gold, silver, costly stones, wood, hay or straw, their work will be shown for what it is, because the Day will bring it to light. It will be revealed with fire, and the fire will test the quality of each person's work. If what has been built survives, the builder will receive a reward. If it is burned up, the builder will suffer loss but yet will be

saved—even though only as one escaping through the flames. (1 Corinthians 3:12–15)

- Dear friends, do not be surprised at the fiery ordeal that has come on you to test you, as though something strange were happening to you. (1 Peter 4:12)
- But who can endure the day of his coming? Who can stand when he appears? For he will be like a refiner's fire or a launderer's soap. (Malachi 3:2)
- Therefore, as tongues of fire lick up straw and as dry grass sinks down in the flames, so their roots will decay and their flowers blow away like dust; for they have rejected the law of the LORD Almighty and spurned the word of the Holy One of Israel. (Isaiah 5:24)
- Neither their silver nor their gold will be able to save them on the day of the LORD's wrath. In the fire of his jealousy the whole earth will be consumed, for he will make a sudden end of all who live on the earth. (Zephaniah 1:18)

THE BOTTOM LINE

Whether these horrifying descriptions in Luke 16 are to be taken figuratively or in fiery literalness doesn't really matter in the final analysis. There certainly is a torturous "fire" of solitude, physical pain, and unrelenting regret that will burn eternally within the lost soul. And, if there is a *literal fire* involved in the matter as well, then the horror of that lost condition is only further intensified.

Regardless of how we approach the passage, the image of it should ultimately leave us in a state of spiritual shock. The reality of life in Gehenna will be whatever the Lord of Glory says it will be, regardless of our attempts to interpret the matter otherwise.

Suffice it to say this certainly is not the eternal fate anyone should hope for or even one with which they should take a chance. God's mercy and grace are held out to all. This state of everlasting, separate existence can be avoided by accepting the offer of salvation in Jesus Christ.

> If you declare with your mouth, "Jesus is Lord," and believe in your heart that God raised him from the dead, you will be saved.... For, "Everyone who calls on the name of the Lord will be saved." (Romans 10: 9, 13)

The point is, we will live forever, regardless of what we do with God's offer of life in Jesus Christ. But *where* we spend a thoroughly conscious eternity is our own choice. It belongs to no one else. Only pride stands in the way of the decision. This eternal truth is the bottom line of what Jesus was presenting that day as He spoke of the rich man and Lazarus.

But we're still not at the end of our look at this account.

THE GREAT DIVIDE

And besides all this, between us and you a great chasm has been
set in place, so that those who want to go from here to you cannot,
nor can anyone cross over from there to us.

—LUKE 16:26

Besides all this.

What ominous words.

With those words, Jesus was asserting: *If all these before-mentioned*
horrors were not enough...there's still something else. There truly is no way
out.

The matter is set in stone. Once a person is in hell/prison through
rejection of God's Word of salvation, there are no second chances. Any
sort of reprieve is an impossible proposition.

As Jesus related the account of the rich man and Lazarus in Luke 16,
He was in the process of wrapping up a day of teaching. The narrative
of that begins in Luke 15:

> Now the tax collectors and sinners were all gathering around to
> hear Jesus. But the Pharisees and the teachers of the law mut-
> tered, "This man welcomes sinners and eats with them." (Luke
> 15:1)

From there, Luke 15 through Luke 17 relates another massive preaching and teaching event. But the account of the rich man seemed to be the focal point of everything else He revealed that day.

Here was the problem: The indignant, religious ruling class of the day could not fathom that this Jesus, who was supposedly the "son of God," would sully Himself by rubbing elbows with so many "sinners." After all, they reasoned, if He really was the true Messiah of heaven, shouldn't He be hanging out with *them* instead of these *deplorable ones*?

The teaching about the rich man and Lazarus was designed to straighten out the religious leaders' mistaken ideas regarding the true economy of God's genuine kingdom work. The idea of a rich man suffering while a common, worthless beggar is in ecstasy shocked their self-righteous sensibilities. As Jesus went on to describe the horror of eternal separation for those who ultimately spurn God's gracious offer of restoration, the indignation of the religious ruling class only intensified.

THE CHASM

Jesus also spoke of a "dimensional divide." This was a dire warning to His listeners that their earthly decisions would follow them throughout eternity. There would never be a possibility of "crossing over" from one dimension to the other.

Besides all this…there is a great chasm…it is set in place…it cannot be crossed.

Nearly every classic scholar and commentator, including the ancient rabbinical teachers, speak of this ominous dimensional gulf between the blessed and the damned at death.[352] It is defined in various ways among the scholars, but none are able to deny its ultimate existence, for it is revealed throughout the teachings of God's Word in both the Old and New Testaments.

Whether or not there might be actual conversations between people existing in various dimensions has been a subject of extensive debate as well. But, in my opinion, it also is a topic that matters little in the final analysis. The point of Jesus' teaching is to make certain that His audience understood the gravity of rejecting God's offer of salvation.

This is a crucial concept, and it gives us further biblical evidence of the reality of multiple dimensions and the portals between those dimensions.

AN ILLUSTRATION

Students of the Bible sometimes question how it was that Abraham could have had a conversation with the rich man, since there is an uncrossable chasm between the two dimensions. It might help to conceptualize how something of this nature could have taken place.

I liken the scenario to that of a huge, foreboding, and inescapable prison (1 Peter 3:19), one situated at the very brink of the abyss. Outside the walls of the prison there is nothing but complete "outer darkness." That gloom, in and of itself, is an ever-present, suffocating element of torment (Matthew 25:30).

But from the rich man's cell window overlooking the edge of the chasm, he could see across it. There was no darkness "on the other side." Instead, he saw utter bliss. He could make out the forms of some of those who were dwelling in that paradise, but he couldn't communicate with them. He saw one person he recognized, the poor beggar Lazarus. But no matter how loudly he screamed, the chasm swallowed his cries.

He was isolated.

Powerless.

In torment.

Barnes' Notes on the Bible

> **One of the first things** that occurred in hell **was to look up, and see the poor man** that lay at his gate completely happy.... These circumstances mean that there will be "a separation," and that **the wicked in hell will be conscious** that the righteous, though on earth they were poor or despised, will be in heaven. heaven and hell will be far from each other, and **it will be no small part of the misery of the one that it is far and forever removed from the other.**[353] (Emphasis added)

Ellicott's Commentary for English Readers

> There **is a great gulf fixed.**—literally, a chasm, the opening or gaping of the earth. The scene brought before us is like...the fair garden of paradise and the kingly palace, and the banquet at which Abraham presides. And **those that are bearing the penalty,** or reaping the reward, of their life **are within sight** [of it all].[354] (Emphasis and brackets added)

Scripture does not tell us by what means the condemned man was able to finally communicate with Abraham. If it was a literal event, obviously Abraham was given the divine privilege of interdimensional travel. The "keys of hell" (prison) would have been afforded to him by Jesus himself (Revelation 1:18, Revelation 20). Abraham was permitted to pass temporarily through that dimensional portal and the great *chasm of division.*

However, only *after* the rich man engaged in that conversation with Abraham did the condemned man finally become aware of the hopelessness of his circumstances. Of all the factors of torment Jesus related in that account, perhaps none was as doleful to the rich man as the revelation of the uncrossable chasm and the paradise he had eternally forfeited…one he could now behold with his own eyes.

By the way, as you are reading these words, the rich man is still there—to this very day—immersed in unrelenting and fiery torment. Let that thought sink in for a moment before moving on.

THE DEATH OF NACHASH

We are now ready to examine what the Word of God contextually asserts concerning the final demise of Satan. If the things Jesus disclosed in the account of the rich man and Lazarus are true of humans, then what of Satan and the angels that rebelled with him against the throne of God? Is their ultimate fate the same as that of lost humans? Or is their "death" something different?

As you might imagine, the Word of God reveals the answers to those questions as well.

PART NINE

The Purge

*You were in Eden, the garden of God.... You were anointed as
a guardian cherub, for so I ordained you. You were on the holy
mount of God; you walked among the fiery stones.*

*You were blameless in your ways from the day you were created
till wickedness was found in you. Your heart became proud
on account of your beauty, and you corrupted your wisdom
because of your splendor. So I threw you to the earth;
I made a spectacle of you before kings.*

*...I made a fire come out from you, and it consumed you, and
I reduced you to ashes on the ground in the sight of all who were
watching. All the nations who knew you are appalled at you...*

You have come to a horrible end and will be no more.

—Ezekiel 28:13–15, 17–19

58

KILLING THE *SSS*ERPENT

Not too long ago, I came across a book wherein the authors insisted that the "overwhelming" evidence of the Old Testament asserts the "total destruction" or annihilation of the wicked. They insisted that the Old Testament "never affirms or even hints at anything resembling conscious unending torment."[355]

In truth, what we really deal with concerning this issue is a matter of misinterpretation of the biblical subject of multidimensional realities, a topic with which you are now thoroughly familiar. That unfortunate oversight has produced a sizeable body of believers who have simply misconstrued the biblical concept of the fullest meaning of the word "death." And that misunderstanding has created a lot of theological confusion among believers. Let's unravel the mystery of the realm of death.

DEATH IS DIMENSIONAL

We now know that *death*, according to Jesus Himself, means a very real and conscious existence, yet in another dimension. It is a dimension that is altogether separated from the earthly one, as well as all others. This separation between realms occurs at *the moment* of our leaving the earthly dimension concurrent with the exiting of our mortal bodies. From that point on, there is no "coming back" for those who are lost. So, in that sense, the unrepentant ones are truly "annihilated" from the presence of the saved. They will never again be seen or remembered after the final judgment. It will eventually be as though they never existed.

If this state of eternal affairs is true of humans, then what about Satan and the demonic realm? What will be their ultimate demise? We know the Bible says they will be "thrown into the lake of fire," but what exactly does that mean?

First, let's address the question: *Does the Bible really say that Satan will die?* Secondly, we'll examine what all of this really means concerning Satan's ultimate fate.

DEATH OF AN ANGEL

Both the Old and New Testaments contain rather pointed declarations about Satan's *death*. Of this fact there can be no contextual denial.

In fact, out of the mouth of Jesus Himself we are told that Satan and the demonic horde that accompanies Him will ultimately suffer the same fate.

> Then he will say to those on his left, "Depart from me, you cursed, into **the eternal fire prepared for the devil and his angels.**" (Matthew 25:42, ESV, emphasis added)

Armed with the biblical understanding of interdimensional banishment and "torment," let's now have a look at several examples of Satan's death sentence. We'll start at the beginning.

THE CRUSHING

We've already seen that the very first pronouncement of Satan's demise was from the mouth of Elohim in the Garden of Eden. In Genesis 3:15, Satan is told that the seed from the woman would "crush" his head. Of course, the New Testament unequivocally assures us this Seed was, indeed, Jesus Christ and that the crushing process started at the cross, continued through the resurrection, and will ultimately culminate in the lake of fire (Revelation 20).

Additionally, common sense informs us that when one's head is "crushed"—*he or she is dead.* This fact has not escaped the attention of the scholars, both classical and recent:

Jamieson-Fausset-Brown Bible Commentary

The serpent's poison is lodged in its head; and a bruise on that part *is fatal.* Thus, *fatal shall be the stroke* which Satan shall receive from Christ, though it is probable *he did not at first understand* the nature and **extent of *his doom.***[356] (Emphasis added)

Dr. Richard T. Ritenbaugh—Forerunner Commentary

God will see the curse through to its end, the total humiliation *and imprisonment* of the Adversary.... **God says plainly** that *Satan would be put down;* the woman's Seed—Messiah— would "bruise his head." The Hebrew word for "bruise," qâmal, means "to slay, kill." When a person's head is "bruised" in this way—**given a killing blow**—*he dies*, while the same blow on the heel causes pain and damage, but not death. **God's curse on the serpent signals what the *ultimate end* of Satan will be.**[357] (Emphasis added)

Dr. Volkmer, Biola University, Talbot School of Theology

In the midst of God pronouncing a number of effects that result from Adam and Eve's decision to eat from the tree of the knowledge of good and evil...**God promises** that there is **a particular child** to come who will deal **the *death blow* to the serpent.**[358] (Emphasis added)

Lange's Commentary on the Holy Scriptures: Critical, Doctrinal, and Homiletical

There is a difference between the fallen man and the fallen angel; the former is lyingly seduced, the latter is the lying seducer; the one becomes evil from without; the other is the author of evil from himself. The fiend has struck us only on the heel; **therefore shall *his head be crushed*:** the wounds which he inflicts are curable; **the wounds inflicted on him must bring him *unto death*.**[359] (Emphasis added)

Keil & Delitzsch Commentary on the Old Testament

However pernicious may be the bite of a serpent in the heel when the poison circulates throughout the body (Genesis 49:17), it is not immediately *fatal and utterly incurable*, **like the cursing of a serpent's head.**[360] (Emphasis added)

There seems to be little scholarly doubt that "crushing Satan's head" was certainly the declaration of a death sentence. That judgment was put into motion by the earthly appearance of the *Seed*. It will be brought to its finality in the Revelation 20 account of Satan's final sentencing, at the Great White Throne judgment. More on that later.

First, let's examine three other places in the Old Testament where Satan's death sentence is spelled out.

59

THE LOWEST DEPTHS

How fitting it is that the one who affected humanity's demise, in the first place, will also share that same end.

Two of the most illustrative Old Testament passages that ultimately expose the magnitude of Satan's evil designs are found in Isaiah 14 and Ezekiel 28.

These two chapters are what Bible scholars call compound prophecies.[361] That is to say, the passages begin by first speaking of an earthly situation, occurrence, or national ruler, then morph, eventually, into a hidden glimpse behind the veil of what is happening in future multiple fulfillments (Ephesians 6:10–12).

For example, in Isaiah 14, the prophet is first told to "take up a taunt" against the king of Babylon. The Hebrew word for "taunt" is *mashal,* and is *Strongs'* OT #4912. That Hebrew word means "a proverb, or a metaphorical illustration—a parable."[362]

In other words, while some of this passage would most certainly apply directly to the description of the literal, human king of Babylon, another underlying purpose of the depiction was to metaphorically compare that earthly king to someone else—namely, Satan, the chief architect of the heavenly rebellion.

The Bible Exposition Commentary: Old Testament

The prophet saw in this event **something far deeper** than the defeat of an empire. **In the fall of the king of Babylon, he saw** *the defeat of Satan,* **the** "prince of this world," who seeks to energize and motivate the leaders of nations (John 12:31, Ephesians 2:1–3).[363] (Emphasis added)

Delitzsch's Biblical Commentary on the Prophecies of Isaiah

A retrospective glance is now cast at the self-deification of the king of Babylon, in which he was **the antitype of the devil** and the **type of Antichrist.** The passage transcends anything that can be said of an earthly king and *has been understood from earliest times to also refer to Satan's fall* as described in Luke 10:18.[364] (Emphasis added)

Guzik Commentary

Isaiah 14 tells us *Satan's fall* had to do with his desire to be equal to or greater than God, to set his will against God's will.[365] (Emphasis added)

ISAIAH 14—THE TEXT

Here is that portion of Isaiah 14. Note the reference to God's sentence of death upon Satan.

How you have fallen from heaven, morning star, son of the dawn! **You have been cast down to the earth,** [compare the distinct similarity with Revelation 12:10–12] you who once laid low the nations!

You said in your heart, "I will ascend to the heavens; I will raise my throne above the stars of God; I will sit enthroned on the mount of assembly, on the utmost heights of Mount Zaphon.

I will ascend above the tops of the clouds; I will make myself like the Most High."

But you are brought down to *the realm of the dead*, to the *depths of the pit*.

Those who see you stare at you, they ponder your fate: "Is this the man who shook the earth and made kingdoms tremble." (Isaiah 14:12–16, emphasis and brackets added)

How fitting it is that the one who affected humanity's demise, in the first place, will also share that same end.

Benson's Commentary

Yet thou shalt be brought **down to hell**—*to the grave*, and *the state of the dead*; to the sides of the pit—and lodged there **in the lowest state of misery** and degradation.[366] (Emphasis added)

Keil and Delitzsch Biblical Commentary on the Old Testament

This psychical image, to which **the dead body bears the same relation as the shattered mold** to a cast, is the shade-like corporeality of the inhabitants of Hades, in which they appear essentially, though spiritually, just as they were on this side the grave. **This is the deep root of what the prophet has here expressed.**[367] (Emphasis added)

Barnes' Notes on the Bible

> The "sides of the pit" here stand opposed to the "sides of the north." **He had sought to "ascend" to the one; he should be "brought down" to the other.** The reference here is, doubtless, to the land of shades; to the dark and dismal **regions where *the departed dead* dwell—to "Sheol."**[368] (Emphasis added)

PRISON OR LAKE OF FIRE?

However, some might ask, "If Satan is ultimately to be cast into the lake of fire, to be tormented forever, as Revelation 20:10 declares, then when is Satan actually imprisoned in Hell, Gehenna, or 'the grave,' as Isaiah 14 seems to indicate?" The question comes to mind because the place of imprisonment mentioned in Isaiah 14 sounds exactly like the place where the rich man was held in Luke 16.

The answer is found in Revelation 20:13. It appears this is that period in the future when Satan is bound for a thousand years. His "binding" is his term of imprisonment in Gehenna. It seems Satan will not "skip" any portion of the multistage sentencing process the rebellious ones are destined to face.

Although it is beyond the scope of this chapter to examine the various interpretations of the subject of the thousand-year binding, Scripture plainly states the matter. And it is during this thousand-year period (however one wishes to interpret this truth) when, apparently, Satan suffers the same fate as the rich man (Luke 16) along with a certain class of outrageously rebellious angels that have been there since ages past.

- For if God did not spare angels when they sinned, but sent them to hell, putting them in chains of darkness to be held for judgment. (2 Peter 2:4)

- And the angels who did not keep their positions of authority but abandoned their proper dwelling—these he has kept in darkness, bound with everlasting chains for judgment on the great Day. (Jude 1:6)

Following are several commentary entries regarding Satan's double portion of imprisonment and eternal punishment.

Barnes' Notes on the Bible

In Revelation 19:20, it is said of the beast and the false prophet that they were "cast alive into a lake of fire, burning with brimstone." **Satan, on the other hand, instead of being doomed at once to that final ruin,** *was confined for a season in a dark abyss,* Revelation 20:1–3.[369] (Emphasis added)

Jamieson-Fausset-Brown Bible Commentary (Revelation 20:10)

Lake of fire—**Satan's final doom: as "the bottomless pit"** (Revelation 20:1) was his **temporary** prison.[370] (Emphasis added)

Jamieson-Fausset-Brown Bible Commentary (Revelation 20:3)

Here, Satan himself is **shut up for a thousand years in the "abyss"** (Greek for "bottomless pit"), *the preparatory prison* to the **"lake of fire,"** *his final doom.*[371] (Emphasis added)

We now understand from our previous study that "death" certainly does not mean a "cessation of existence" or an annihilation of a person, an angel, or even of Satan. "Death" means a very physical and conscious awareness of where one is and why he or she is there. It is banishment to a dimensional reality that is forever separated by a chasmic gulf—a portal that can never again be opened. Only Jesus holds the keys to these doorways.

This is the pronouncement God leveled against Satan in Isaiah 14: "The lowest depths of hell are preserved for you and for what you have done."

But this is not the only place in the Old Testament that speaks of Satan's ultimate death sentence. The prophet Ezekiel was also made privy to Satan's demise—more than once.

60

REDUCED TO ASHES

*And the devil, who deceived them, was thrown
into the lake of burning sulfur…*
—REVELATION 20:10

Ezekiel 28 is a close companion to that of Isaiah 14. It is also a compound-reference prophecy. And like Isaiah 14, it pronounces the death penalty upon Satan, after *first* speaking of an earthly king. In this case, the earthly regent is the king of Tyre.

Before we examine the passage, let's have a look at several scholarly attestations of what I've just said.

Guzik Commentary

> **Ezekiel 28** tells us *Satan, before his fall,* was an **angel of the highest rank** and prominence, even **something of a leader of worship** in heaven.[372] (Emphasis added)

Bible scholar Dr. Merrill F. Unger held a PhD from Johns Hopkins University and a ThD from Dallas Theological Seminary, where he was a professor of Old Testament Studies. Dr. Unger wrote *Unger's Bible*

Dictionary, numerous books on theology, and several academic level commentaries. He sums up the message of Ezekiel 28 and the lament against the king of Tyre, with these words:

> That the career of *Satan is here reflected* under the person of the king of Tyre is **true because of *eleven reasons.***[373] (Emphasis added)

Thomas L. Constable, ThD, Senior Professor Emeritus of Bible exposition at Dallas Theological Seminary, explains Ezekiel 28 like this:

> **Eden, the garden of God**, is probably a figurative way of describing the blessing that this ruler [King of Tyre] had enjoyed at God's hand (cf31:9; Genesis 13:10). If we take the statement literally, *this must refer to someone who was in the Garden of Eden, probably Satan.*[374] (Emphasis added)

Dr. E. W. Bullinger states the certainty of the Ezekiel 28:13 declaration with this pointed affirmation:

> *Satan,* the *Nachash* or shining one, was there.... This is added to leave us in no doubt as to **what is meant by Eden**, and to show that it was no mere "summer residence" of the "prince" of Tyre, but, *the "garden" of Genesis 2:8–15.*[375] (Emphasis added)

The acclaimed work of Robert Jamieson, A. R. Fausset, and David Brown, *Commentary Critical and Explanatory on the Whole Bible*, explains Ezekiel 28 and its connection to Satan in this manner:

> The language, **though primarily here applied to the king of Tyre**, as similar language is to the king of Babylon *(Isaiah 14:13, Isaiah 14:14)*, yet has an ulterior and fuller accomplishment *in*

Satan **and his embodiment** in Antichrist (Daniel 7:25, Daniel 11:36, Daniel 11:37, 2 Thessalonians 2:4, Revelation 13:6).[376] (Emphasis added)

Coffman's Commentaries on the Bible

Thus, we find that the narrative here is not merely **founded upon the Genesis account of** *Satan's having been in Eden,* but it *anticipates portions of Revelation 12* in the fact of a cherub having cast Satan out of heaven. In Revelation, the name of that cherub was revealed as that of the archangel himself, namely, Michael! Thus, as F. F. Bruce noted, *"This passage in Ezekiel has contributed some details to the picture of the fall of Satan."*[377] (Emphasis added)

THE PRONOUNCEMENT OF EZEKIEL 28

Now have a look at the pertinent portion of the prophecy against Satan in Ezekiel 28:

You were **the seal of perfection**, full of wisdom and perfect in beauty. *You were in Eden, the garden of God....* You were **anointed as a guardian cherub**, for so I ordained you. You were on the holy mount of God; you walked among the fiery stones.... So I drove you in disgrace from the mount of God, and I expelled you, guardian cherub, from among the fiery stones....

So I made a fire come out from you, and it consumed you, and *I reduced you to ashes* **on the ground** in the sight of all who were watching.... All the nations who knew you are appalled at you; *you have come to a horrible end and will be no more.* (Ezekiel 28:12–19, emphasis added)

It is as though Elohim is telling the reader, "When I say I am reducing Satan to ashes, I mean just that. Just in case there is any confusion, I also declare that Satan will, in the end, *be no more.*"

Where might this "reducing to ashes" finally take place? Some of the closing words of the book of Revelation give us the answer:

> And the devil, who deceived them, was ***thrown into the lake of burning sulfur***, where the beast and the false prophet had been thrown. They will be tormented day and night for ever and ever. (Revelation 20:10, emphasis added)

I would think that a lake of fire—especially one consisting of burning sulfur—could reduce even old *smutface* to ashes, wouldn't you? However, we also see here that Satan is not annihilated by this "burning." Rather, like the rich man of Luke 16, he now suffers *basanos,* "torment," for eternity. Again, the argument of whether the burning fire and a "reducing to ashes" is literal or figurative of something equally horrifying really doesn't matter.

YOU WILL BE "NO MORE"

What do we do with God's words, "You will be no more?" Doesn't this mean that Satan simply ceases to exist?

Actually, it doesn't mean that at all. To "be no more," in this context, means Satan will be banished from every dimensional realm of existence he has previously roamed. And, he will be locked down in another dimension altogether—*forever*. Therefore, he shall literally "be no more," never to be seen again.

In the closing of the preceding chapter, I mentioned that the prophet Ezekiel spoke of Satan's death sentence more than once.

The next chapter reveals that second instance.

61

THE TREES OF THE GARDEN

**Here, the "Satan-tree" is told that he will eventually
be brought down to the pit—in the realm of the dead.**

The compound prophecy of Ezekiel 31 is strikingly similar to that of
Ezekiel 28. Only three chapters later, in the Ezekiel 31 prophecy,
the focus is upon yet another powerful earthly ruler before it ultimately
shifts into a depiction of Satan, the real power behind the throne of that
mere earthly king.

In this passage, Egypt's Pharaoh is compared to a tree standing in
the midst of other trees. This Pharaoh/tree arrogantly exalts itself above
all the others.

Additionally, the Assyrian/tree is presented as "succumbing" to the
evil persuasion of the Pharaoh/tree. The other trees are presented as sym-
bols of literal living entities as well, as nations and/or leaders. However,
the most shocking feature of Ezekiel 31 is that the entire story is placed
in the Garden of Eden—by name. These are not just any trees; they are
said to be the "trees of Eden," and specifically those located in the "garden of God."

THE SCHOLARS AND EZEKIEL 31

Before we examine the passage, especially the words that speak of the death sentence upon Satan, let's have a look at what the scholars say about Ezekiel 31.

The *Jamieson-Fausset-Brown Bible Commentary* connects the King of Assyria as a type of "Adam" in the Garden of Eden. This commentary also connects Ezekiel 28 with chapter 31.

> *The lesson on a gigantic scale of Eden-like privileges* abused to pride and sin by *the Assyrian, as in the case of the first man in Eden*, ending in ruin, was to be repeated in Egypt's case.... **As in the case of Tyre (Ezekiel 28:13)**, the imagery that is applied to the Assyrian king [in Ezekiel 31], is **taken from Eden.** [378] (Emphasis added)

The *Pulpit Commentary* ties Ezekiel 28 with Ezekiel 31 as well:

> The cedars in the garden of God. **As in Ezekiel 28:13**, the thoughts of the prophet [in Ezekiel 31], dwell on **the picture of Eden in Genesis 2:8.** [379] (Emphasis and brackets added)

Also see the *Encyclopedia Judaica: The Garden of Eden*:

> Ezekiel (28:11–19; 31:8–9, 16–18) in his description introduces **new and variant details** not present in the Genesis narrative of the Garden of Eden.... While **Genesis speaks only in general terms about the trees in the garden (2:9), Ezekiel describes them in detail (31:8–9, 18).** [380] (Emphasis added)

EZEKIEL 31—TEXT

I urge you to read the entire chapter of Ezekiel 31 on your own; it's quite eye-opening.[381] That chapter is far too lengthy to quote in its entirety here.

However, I will reproduce the pertinent portions for our focus:

> The cedars **in the garden of God** could not rival it, nor could the junipers equal its boughs, nor could the plane trees compare with its branches—no tree in the garden of God could match its beauty.
>
> I made it beautiful with abundant branches, the envy of all **the trees of Eden in the garden of God.**
>
> I made the nations tremble *at the sound of its fall when I brought it down to the realm of the dead to be with those who go down to the pit....*
>
> Which of the trees of Eden can be compared with you in splendor and majesty? Yet you, too, *will be brought down with the trees of Eden to the earth below;* you will lie among the uncircumcised, with those killed by the sword. (Ezekiel 31:8–9, 16, 18, emphasis added)

THE SATAN TREE

Here, the "Satan tree" is told that he will eventually be brought down to the pit—in the realm of the dead—along with all the other rulers who have rebelled against the Lord of creation. This particular "cedar" is tied directly to Satan, through the imagery. To clinch the intended compound message of Ezekiel 31, the passage ends with these words:

This [tree] *is Pharaoh* and *all his hordes*, declares the Sovereign Lord. (Ezekiel 31:18, emphasis and brackets added)

In regard to this, almost every scholarly commentary presents Pharaoh as *a type of Satan,* especially when commenting upon Pharaoh of the Exodus event, or other pharaohs who, down through the ages, stood as unmitigated enemies of Israel.

Dr. John W. Ritenbaugh, writing in the *Forerunner Commentary,* gives an example of this:

We know that we are not completely free from **Satan and this world.… We see this pictured in the children of Israel in the wilderness.…** Slavery in Egypt, where they faced certain, ignominious death, represents the world, **and Pharaoh represents Satan.** [382] (Emphasis added)

Certainly, Ezekiel 31 follows this same typecasting of the Pharaoh of Egypt with Satan himself. In keeping with this symbolic contrast, the phrase "all his hordes" would most likely symbolize the demonic realm of the fallen angels who followed in Satan's blasphemous rebellion (Matthew 25:41, Revelation 12:7–9).

Of course, the overarching point of our examination of Ezekiel 31 is to discover that, once again, mystically buried in the heart of a compound prophecy, we find the death sentence pronounced upon Satan from the mouth of Yahweh Himself.

62

HOLDING THE KEYS

And the devil, who deceived them, was thrown into the lake of burning sulfur, where the beast and the false prophet had been thrown. They will be tormented day and night for ever and ever.
—REVELATION 20:10

It should be apparent by now that the "eternal death" spoken of throughout Scripture is the final condition that is fulfilled in an interdimensional banishment. It is a cosmic deportation process from which there is no return. *Ever.*

Jesus holds the keys to death and hell (Revelation 1:18). He has never "lost" them. He was never required to "go into hell" in order to "steal" them back, as some are fond of insisting.

Jesus created hell, or prison, in the same way humans build prisons to segregate the disobedient and lawless within our own fallen society (Colossians 1:16–17). Gehenna, Hades, or hell have *never* been under the control of Satan. Neither are they Satan's haunt or domain, this is yet another misconception. It is true that Satan is temporarily the "prince of the power of the air" (Ephesians 2:2) and is the "god of this world" (2 Corinthians 4:4), but it is equally true that he has never been in possession of the keys to death and Hades.

Ellicott's Commentary for the English Reader

> **"I have the keys of death and of Hades."** Our risen Lord has both under his power. The keys are the emblems of his right and authority.[383] (Emphasis added)

Barnes' Notes on the Bible

> And have the keys of hell and of death—**To hold the key of this, was to hold** *the power over the invisible world.* It was the more appropriate that the Saviour should represent himself as having this authority, as he had himself been raised from the dead by his own power thus showing that the *dominion over this dark world* **was entrusted to him.**[384] (Emphasis added)

Pulpit Commentary

> **The keys,** as so often, are **the sign of authority** (Revelation 3:7; Revelation 9:1; Revelation 20:1; Matthew 16:19). **Christ,** as the absolutely Living One, **who "has life in himself"** and is the Source of life in others, **has control, not merely over the passage** *from this world to the other,* **but over** *the other world* **itself.**[385] (Emphasis added)

Some might argue that only *after* the resurrection did Jesus claim to hold the keys to the authority of the domain of the dead. But that is not biblically accurate. Even before the crucifixion and resurrection, Jesus publicly exercised his authority over those realms. Jesus raised Lazarus (John 11:38ff), Jairus' daughter (Mark 5:21–43, Matthew 9:18–26, Luke 8:40–56), and the widow of Nain's son (Luke 7:11–17)—not to mention that He raised his own physically dead body from the grave.

No one takes [my life] from me, but I lay it down of my own accord. *I have* authority to lay it down and ***authority to take it up again.*** (John 10:18, emphasis added)

BY THE POWER VESTED IN ME...

Jesus has fated Satan and all those who follow him—*human or angelic*—into an existence of everlasting separation from the soon-coming, reinstated paradise. In this way, all things will be restored to their beginning state in the Garden of Eden.

In that day, there will be no more pain, no more crying, and—most important—no more *death.* The old order of things will have passed away. Everything will be made new (Isaiah 65:17, Revelation 21–22).

The making of "all things new" will also encompass the eternal and unredeemable, interdimensional banishment of Satan from the domain of God's reconstituted paradise. Even the Apostle Paul confirms that the term "eternal destruction" is synonymous with being banished to another dimensional realm, one from which there is no return.

They will suffer the punishment of ***eternal*** **destruction,** ***away from the presence of the Lord*** and from the glory of his might. (2 Thessalonians 1:9, ESV, emphasis added)

When examining this New Testament declaration and others like it, the scholars agree: There truly is a dimensional shift of realms that occurs at "death." The believer is alive in paradise. The unbeliever is ultimately doomed to the same fate as Satan and his demonic horde. They are alive—and in torment:

Ellicott's Commentary for English Readers

> **The word "destruction" does not stand** absolutely and alone *as a synonym for "annihilation."* This passage, in itself, gives us no reason to suppose that the lost will be "destroyed" in the ordinary sense of the word. *They are to be "destroyed from the presence of the Lord,* and from the glory of his power"—i.e., *cut off from it forever.*[386] (Emphasis added)

The *Benson's Commentary*, its writer obviously without knowledge of the modern terms for the condition, even speaks of death as being associated with a "parallel" universe:

> *Not the annihilation,* but the perversion and **utter ruin of all their powers of body and mind,** so that those powers become *instruments of torment and sources of misery* to them in all possible ways. As there can be no end of their sins, (the same enmity against God continuing,) so neither of their punishment: *sin and its punishment running parallel through eternity* itself.[387] (Emphasis added)

Additionally, the *Cambridge Bible for Schools and Colleges* speaks of the phenomenon of the death of the wicked, couching the description in terms of a type of time warp:

> "Eternal destruction" is the antithesis of eternal life." **There is no sufficient reason for interpreting the destruction of the reprobate as signifying their annihilation, or extinction of being;** they will be lost forever—lost to God and goodness. Nor can we limit the range of **the word eternal** in its relation to this fearful doom; it *removes all limits of time,* **and is the express opposite of temporary** (2 Corinthians 4:18).[388] (Emphasis added)

Barnes' Notes on the Bible

> ***The meaning then must be, that the soul…will not be annihilated, but will live and linger on in destruction.*** It seems difficult to conceive how anyone can profess to hold that this passage is a part of the Word of God, and yet deny the doctrine of future eternal punishment. It would not be possible to state that doctrine in clearer language than this.[389] (Emphasis added)

Matthew Poole's Commentary

> ***Not an annihilation, and cessation of being…***elsewhere called **death**, Romans 6:23, ***and the second death***, Revelation 20:6, which imports also not all ceasing of life, but all comfort of life. ***And it is not the body alone, nor the soul alone, but their persons.***[390] (Emphasis added)

As we've discovered, there simply is no obliteration of the body and/or soul. The lost, along with Satan and his angels, will forever possess a very genuine consciousness of their physical being. They are able to feel and think. They are thoroughly aware of their fate and understand their doom will last throughout eternity…never, *ever*, to end.

That eternal state of being will be the *fire of their torment*.

63

THE DEVIL AND HIS ANGELS

It is our own wilderness of temptation.
Satan is before us each day with the same lies and deceptions.

What about the argument that the "eternal fire" of the final judgment was made only for Satan and his angels? After all, didn't Jesus teach this truth?

> Then he will say to those on his left, "Depart from me, you who are cursed, into the eternal fire prepared for the devil and his angels." (Matthew 25:41)

Those somber words of Jesus appear to be very clear. However, in the English translations, we often miss a crucial factor. The word translated as "angel" from both the Greek and Hebrew languages also means a "messenger" or "emissary"—in general. Therefore, an "angel"—in proper context—can be either a fallen, divine being or an *unrepentant human* who rejects Jesus Christ and spends his or her life doing the bidding of Satan, whether or not it's a conscious choice.

Just as humans can willfully decide to be an ambassador of Jesus Christ and His coming kingdom (2 Corinthians 5:11–21), alternatively, they can choose to become an ambassador, emissary, or *messenger* (angel) of the domain of darkness (Matthew 23:15). We either serve the kingdom of God as born-again believers in Jesus Christ or we work for the soon-to-be obliterated kingdom of the devil. It's our choice. But, in the final analysis, every single human who has ever lived belongs to one kingdom or the other.

HELPS Word-studies

> Greek: ággelos—properly, a *messenger or delegate—either human* (Mt 11:10; Lk 7:24, 9:52; Gal 4:14; James 2:25) *or heavenly* (a celestial angel); someone sent.... only **the context determines** whether *a human or celestial messenger* is intended. For example, 32 (ággelos) in Rev 1:20 can refer to *heavenly angels or key leaders* (perhaps pastors) of the seven churches.[391] (Emphasis added)

Not only do the Greek lexicons bear out this truth, but classical scholars have long recognized that Jesus is speaking here of *any and all* who have followed Satan's voice and rejected God's offer of salvation (Romans 10:9).

Pulpit Commentary

> Prepared for the devil and his angels. *This region or sphere* [Note that this commentary also speaks of other dimensions] of torment.... **What it is to the devil it must be to those who share it with him.** It is *man's own doing* that he is unfit for the company of saints and angels, and, **having *made himself like unto the evil spirits*** by rebellion and hatred of good, he must consort with them and *share their doom.* ...the wicked *fall into the society of demons.*[392] (Emphasis and brackets added)

Benson's Commentary

But the fire of hell was prepared for the devil and his angels, namely, after their fall: and **because wicked men partake with devils** in their sin of rebellion against God. [393] (Emphasis added)

Barnes' Notes on the Bible

His angels—his messengers, his servants, or those angels that he drew off from heaven by his rebellion, and whom he has employed as his "messengers" to do evil. The word may extend also *to all his followers—fallen angels or people....* They will inherit it because **they have the same character** "as the devil," **and are therefore suited to the same place—not because it was originally "prepared for them."**[394] (Emphasis added)

Meyer's New Testament Commentary

But *as men became partakers in the guilt of demons*, so now are they also condemned to *share in their punishment.*[395] (Emphasis added)

In addition to those scholarly attestations, don't forget that Jesus Himself confirmed the matter as well—on several occasions:

Woe to you, teachers of the law and Pharisees, you hypocrites! *You travel over land and sea* to win a single convert, and when you have succeeded, you make them *twice as much a child of hell as you are.* (Matthew 23:15, emphasis added)

You belong to your father, the devil, *and you want to carry out your father's desires.* (John 8:44, emphasis added)

In other words, rebellious humans can certainly be called "Satan's angels." The eternal choice of who our true "father" will be has always been laid at the feet of humanity. No one can make the decision for us. We each live in our own Garden of Eden decision-time scenario, our own wilderness of temptation. Satan is before us each day with the same lies and deceptions. We can choose the Tree of Life, or we can choose the Tree of Death.

From the Garden of Eden and right up to this very day of your own life, God's hand of salvation through grace has always been held out to humanity.

> But if serving the LORD seems undesirable to you.... Then choose for yourselves this day whom you will serve.... Whether the gods your ancestors served beyond the Euphrates, or the gods of the Amorites, in whose land you are living. But as for me and my household, we will serve the LORD. (Joshua 24:15)

However, the ability for us to make that choice was purchased at a horrific price.

PART TEN

The Passion

*But he was pierced for our transgressions;
he was crushed for our iniquities; upon him
was the chastisement that brought us peace,
and with his wounds we are healed.*

—Isaiah 53:5

64

ONE MORE GARDEN

Jerusalem—circa AD 33
Just outside the East Gate
The Garden of Gethsemane

He knelt beside a huge rock, not far from the base of an ancient olive tree.

The weight of thousands of years of rebellious degradation was now strapped to his shoulders. If there was ever a time when He actually thought He might be tempted to give up, it was here, in the Garden of Gethsemane.

Jesus knew exactly what awaited Him. Within the next few hours, all of the horrors of the kingdom of darkness would be unleashed upon Him. But He had to submit to it. This, after all, was why He had come. *Wasn't it?*

Maybe there's still some other way to accomplish this mission?

He already knew the answer. But the question continually raced through His mind—tormenting him. Yet another temptation.

Deliver yourself from here! You have the power to do so…just say the word.

No! It has to be this way. This was the plan from the beginning.

And, so far, the divine plan had worked. That old serpent was already in the trap, and the door had fallen softly behind him…his pride and arrogance had sealed his ultimate defeat. He just didn't know it yet. In three days from now, he would.

Judas should be coming soon. It won't be long…

There it is again! Why do these seductive thoughts keep filling my head like a raging flood? Of course—there can be no other way…Father…please **help me!**

He fell back to his face—and prayed. He clawed at the earth as He agonized, filling His hands with great scoops of dirt, and then releasing it back to the ground.

My soul is overwhelmed with sorrow. Give me strength…

His closest friends were in the Garden with Him. They were supposed to be praying with Him. They were about a stone's throw away at this moment, somewhere in the deep recesses of the shadows behind Him.

But they were asleep. It seems they just couldn't hold out any longer. Even now, He could hear their snoring.

Snoring? So soon?

Peter? John? You too?

They had eaten their fill just a few hours earlier in that secreted Upper Room in downtown Jerusalem. Another Passover celebration. Another feast. How He had loved to take those meals with His disciples!

But this one had been different. Ominously so. He had explained to them what this distinctive celebration was really about—what this night was about—what all of this would mean to them in the years to come. But, had they really understood? *Not entirely.* It would eventually hit them like the stunning shock of a boulder crashing into their midst. But not yet.

Hot, salty tears spilled from His eyes—the overflow of His broken heart streaming down His cheeks and splattering onto the garden soil beneath Him.

He moaned, and looked up into the deep night sky. The beauty of what He beheld was breathtaking. But it was nothing compared to what would one day be revealed—after the rolling up of the dimensional scrolls…the unveiling of what had been there all along.

But there was so much yet to be done. The hardest part would begin, just moments from now.

He ached for the luxury of a little sleep. His eyelids had grown heavy with grief, weighted down with a cosmic burden that no human had ever carried.

Could He allow Himself the treat of a short nap…only for a moment? Just then, His eyes slammed shut, startling Him. His neck quickly stiffened, catching His head as it tried to drop to His chest.

So…here was yet another enticement? Even the modest thought of the delightful bliss of a little respite—only a simple resting of His eyes and soul—had now become an unrelenting fleshly allurement. But, He *must* not.

He looked back over His shoulder at the slumbering disciples. They slept like children—without a care in the world. His lips trembled as He fought back even more tears. He was alone. But not for long.

If they only knew what lay ahead for them and their families. How I love them, Father! I know that you will not yet remove them from the tribulation of this world, but, please…Father… protect them in the midst of the coming calamities.

He wiped more sweat from his forehead and continued to agonize before the throne of heaven. It was a grief that ripped at his soul, torturing His mind beyond any hope of immediate relief. In His body of earthly human flesh, He had never felt anything like this before.

Why is it so hard to pray tonight? Is the darkness of the night actually growing even dimmer? Or, am I just imagining it?

He looked down at His hand. He had just pulled it away from His face after wiping the sweat from His brow.

The dampness on His hand was bright red.

Under the traumatic stress of what He knew awaited Him, the microscopic capillaries in His temples had burst. Great drops of bloody sweat trickled down His face.[396]

Where were His dearest friends when He needed them?

Couldn't you stay awake for just awhile? He uttered the question aloud, knowing that no one actually heard His words.

An overwhelming flood of sheer loneliness engulfed Him now, something He had not felt since the Judean wilderness. It ached to the depth of His heart. It was as if a huge millstone had been laid upon His chest. He struggled for a proper breath.

But, He forced Himself on, remembering how far He had come. *The strong man's house will soon be plundered and destroyed. Paradise will be restored, and Satan and his emissaries... will be banished forever.*

He allowed Himself a brief smile, in spite of the fact that the terrorizing flashes of what was yet to come continued to pummel His thoughts.

If I can only hold out. Help me Father! **Strengthen me**...

These words were the focus of His tortured prayers on this shadowy, dark night. He knew the words were true. Of that, there was never a doubt. But to live them out—*in human flesh*—that was a different matter altogether. Those words, that goal, no matter how beautiful, would come with an enormous...indescribable...agonizing price. He knew that, too.

He also knew that all of what lay ahead would require the spilling of blood.

Lots of blood.

65

DRACO

**He was somewhere slightly behind Him,
in the shadows of the night.**

The serpent's appearance was accompanied by an atmospheric spark, and then a popping noise, like the quick crack of a whip. A dark presence had just entered earth's domain. It had come from the *other side.*[397]

He's here. In the Garden.

He was somewhere slightly behind him, in the shadows of the night.

Jesus knew he would eventually show up. In fact, He was counting on it.

The sulfuric odor of Nachash's vileness permeated the night air—a suffocating presence. It was then that Jesus heard the familiar voice.

"*Hmm.* So, we are together again? At last."

The words were silky. Hypnotizing. Musical. Almost irresistible.

"I tried to tell you. I tried to warn you, didn't I? I figured it would eventually come to this." He clucked his tongue several times, as though he actually empathized with Jesus.

A slight groan was Jesus' only response.

Nachash continued. "You have to admit, I actually gave you the chance to *ssskip* all thi*sss*… Did I not? But you wouldn't listen… You could have saved your*sss*elf from this dreadful me*sss*."

Jesus felt the ground tremble beneath Him. Even creation groaned and creaked as it struggled to bear up under the burden of the serpent's perversion.

Jesus simply lowered His head…in prayer.

The ancient serpent continued his taunt. *"But… no…* You had to try and make your point, didn't you? Well, you've taken your *ssstand* now! You've had your *sssay.* Yes—*yesss,* your power is from heaven's throne. Everyone knows it now. Everyone has *ssseen* it… They're all talking about it!"

Nachash persisted, "If that's all the validation you require, I can easily arrange it for you. Why, I'll have everyone bowing and *sssraping* at your feet…if that's what you want. What *sssay* you?"

Just like that day in the wilderness three years back, Jesus still refused to acknowledge Satan's presence. The challenges were vile. They deserved no response. There would be no banter with this profanely rebellious cherub.

Jesus didn't turn to look, even though He could feel, down the back of His own neck, the heat of the serpent's presence. Satan was standing right over Him, just behind Him. His breath was rancid, drowning in the stench of death.

Nachash hissed… *"Once more,* but this*s* is the last time. *Here…*I'll hold out my hand of undeserved mercy."

Jesus saw the hand. It slowly stretched out and appeared from just over His right shoulder. Even the movement of the hand and arm was like that of a serpent.

Heaven's Son turned his head away from the vile thing.

Father! If it is possible! Please…take this cup from me!

"Oh, come now! Don't be ridiculous*s!* You won't even take my hand? *Who* are you anyway? *What* are you? Where is your *Father* now?"

There was an awkward silence. Jesus looked straight ahead. He still had not uttered a word to Nachash.

"Okay. *Okay.* I'll offer it just one more time. Simply acknowledge me as the prince of this world and I'll give you all the kingdoms of earth! After all, they are *mine* to give. Isn't that ultimately what you want, anyway? A kingdom of your own? We can rule together! No co*sss*t to you! No ludicrou*ss* price to pay. No 'cup' to drink. No one has to 'lay down their life' for anything—or for *anyone*. What do you say? What will it be?"

Nevertheless Father…

Not my will…

But yours.

More tears spilled into the dirt.

Satan growled, "*You fool!* Have it your way then! You have no idea what you've just given up!"

Satan positioned himself in front of Jesus, glaring at Him through slatted, serpent-like pupils. His face was just inches away from Jesus'.

"If this is the road you choose, then I *do* have a very special cup prepared for you at the end of it…and you *will* drink from it—deeply! I'll personally see to it. I'll be there the whole time. *Watching. Enjoying.* Relishing each long and dreadful moment of it! It's already been arranged. Just in case you were to refuse my gracious and merciful offer. You will rue the day you refused my hand!"

The air popped. The ground rumbled again. There was a slight folding of the atmosphere—barely discernible to the human eye. Golden sparkles of a glitter-like substance fell into the dirt in front of Jesus, and melted into the earth.

Nachash was gone.

For now.

RESOLVE

This was it. No turning back. No more struggling. No more doubt.

He wiped His brow again…His sweat was bloodier than ever. But there was still much more blood to be spilled.

He stood to His feet from His place of tormented prayer and made His way back to the sleeping disciples. His face was set like flint as He steeled His heart for the gruesome mission ahead.

Jesus stood directly over John. He stooped and placed is hand gently upon the beloved disciple's shoulder. He nudged the young man until he finally stirred. John opened his eyes as though he was awakening from an all-night drinking binge, both fists twisting in his eye sockets, trying to clear the haze of sleep.

"John, why are you sleeping? Why *now*, of all times?"

Jesus' countenance startled the youthful disciple. There was a directness and firmness in His intonation that was uncharacteristic. What had happened while Jesus was praying? What had He seen?

"Get up, John. Wake the others, *and pray*—so that you will not fall into temptation."

"What do you mean, Lord? What *temptation*?"

Jesus nodded toward Jerusalem, "The betrayer draws near. Satan now comes—in the body of a man."[398]

John snapped his head around.

He could see the approaching torches bobbing in the darkness like gigantic fireflies flittering in the night, and he could now begin to make out the temple guards who carried them.

There were dozens of them.

And Judas was leading the way.

66

THE LAST TEMPTATION

They were waiting for something to die.

The vultures always showed up first.

The feathered ones, as well as the black-robed ones.

The men in black robes taunted, "If you are truly the Son of God, show us your authority from heaven! Look at Him! He claimed to save others, but He can't even save Himself? Come down from that cross! Deliver yourself!"

The heat of the afternoon sun unmercifully drilled down upon Jesus. Like a worm under a magnifying glass, He squirmed under its scorching blaze…with nowhere to escape. Sweat and blood streamed down His face in rivulets, pouring their salty-fiery torment into His eyes. It was impossible to wipe Himself free of the tiny liquid flames.

A few hours back, His hands and feet had been pinioned with iron spikes to a thick, wooden crossbeam. That bar was then suspended from another vertically driven beam, also hewn of rough-cut lumber. It took a specialized team of Roman soldiers to accomplish the feat. But they were highly skilled at what they did. They should have been. They had done this a thousand times before now.

Jesus hung before the heavens like a prized trophy, crucified between two common thieves. Every nerve in His body screamed at Him in white-hot agony, and the day had only begun. The torture would only grow worse as the hours cruelly slithered along.

Just now, Jesus spotted him…

The interdimensional hunter—*the prince of this fallen world*—moved among the crowd, a dark, foul figure. He was unseen by the people. But Jesus caught glimpses of him when His eyes occasionally refocused through the glaze of the searing pain.

When their gazes met, Nachash merely leered at Him. He intended for Jesus to have to look upon his visage. Satan glanced up at the circling vultures, then looked back down at Jesus and smiled. His diabolical plan was coming together just as he had calculated. He had personally arranged to put Jesus on the cross as a way of taunting the throne of heaven. Satan rubbed his hands together and mumbled, "Look what I have done to you! If this really is your 'Son'—well …*You failed!* His life is now in my hands—and now I will snatch it from Him! And, there's nothing you can do about it! Soon, your very throne will be mine, mark my words!"

Nachash appeared to float across the ground, invisibly arriving behind a particular man standing in the crowd, a member of the Jewish ruling class. The ancient serpent laid his hand upon the esteemed priest's shoulder. The elderly cleric had no idea what had just happened to him.

Instantly, like a marionette having its strings pulled, the priest cried out, "Save yourself! Come down from that cross—*if you are the Son of God!* Work a miracle for us now!" his arms flung upwards, his fists balled toward the heavens in an irrational rage.

Others in the crowd joined the cacophony, directed by the unseen maestro, arrogantly hooting in agreement. *Mocking. Cajoling. Cursing.* "Yes! Come down from the cross!"

At that moment of triumph, Nachash eased back through a brief folding shimmer in the atmosphere—and he was gone, again. No one had seen his arrival. No one saw his exit. No one…except Jesus.

The foul one would be back though. He had been loitering in the crowd's midst for hours. Jesus had seen him at Gethsemane, with his hand upon the shoulder of Judas as he arrived with the Temple guards. He had seen him again at the proceedings of the Sanhedrin Council. He saw him skimming the edges of the on looking crowd, lustfully gloating at the blood fest of His scourging. And He had observed the vile serpent frequently—throughout the remainder of the day—as He dangled here on this rough beam of wood.

The two criminals, condemned to die on the same day—hanging on crosses to His left and to His right—were squealing in wretched agony. All morning long, they had made pain-filled yelping sounds that resembled those of pitiful, dying animals more than of human beings. It was an unnerving noise—otherworldly—profane and demonic in intonation. Some of those in the crowd actually seemed invigorated by the pathetic shrieking.

EARLIER

The temple guards, led by Judas Iscariot, had snatched Jesus out of the Garden of Gethsemane in the wee hours of that same morning. After every single one of His disciples had fled in terror, Jesus had been rushed away to an illegal mockery of a trial at the home of Caiaphas, the High Priest, in downtown Jerusalem.[399]

While Jesus stood alone in that mockery of a hearing, most of Jerusalem slept in peace. No one came to His defense. He remained silent before his accusers—like a lamb being helplessly led to slaughter.[400]

But, Jesus wasn't helpless. Far from it. Actually, He was purposely submissive—for the time being. He was right where He wanted to be. This is why He had come from heaven's throne in the first place.[401] Unbeknownst to those who surrounded Him, Jesus was working *the plan*.[402]

All of eternity's forward motion hung upon one profound question—and one *longed-for* answer.

An exasperated Caiaphas screeched that question at Jesus, "Tell us plainly! Are you the Christ—the Son of the Most High God?" Caiaphas took a deep breath, waiting for the response.

There it was again. How many times had Jesus heard that same question out of the mouths of so many different people? *If you are the Son of God—tell us!* In the past, He had refused to give the answer. Today—right now—all that would change. *Now* was the time to make it happen…finally, the moment had arrived.

Jesus paused. Then He raised His head to look Caiaphas in the eyes, and answered, "It is as you say. And from now on you will see the Son of Man sitting at the right hand of the Mighty One and returning with the clouds of heaven."[403]

There was a brief sparkle of folding light behind the throne of Caiaphas. Jesus saw Nachash, with his gnarled hand upon the High Priest's shoulder, grinning. *Taunting. Arrogant.*

Jesus heard Satan whisper: "*At long last! The pitiful and delusional 'Son of God' has played right into my hands! If nothing else could be used to bring about your death—this one particular idiotic claim surely will. Thank you, for being ssso utterly ridiculousss!*"

This was the so-called blasphemous statement from Jesus that Caiaphas had hoped for as well. Upon Jesus' claim of equality with God, the Sanhedrin could now appeal to the Roman officials for the death penalty. After all, if Rome didn't kill Him quickly, this one, who could attract crowds of over ten thousand in one place, might soon start a national insurrection. The Roman officials shouldn't be too hard to convince, now that they had this confession from Jesus' own lips. The Jewish elite could finally be rid of this troublemaker once and for all. Only then could they could begin to regain their quickly waning prominence among the people.

Early that morning, when the Council delivered Jesus before a hastily arranged hearing with the Roman governor, Pontius Pilate, the frenzied crowd practically demanded His death. They had been encouraged into that frenzy by well-positioned agents of the Sanhedrin. Over and over again they had screamed…*Crucify Him! Crucify Him!*

Pilate acted as though he had no choice in the matter, even making a public spectacle of washing his hands as a feigned act of innocence. Little did he know, in the bigger scheme of things, he truly didn't have a choice by the time the ordeal had arrived to this point, because this very moment had been preordained from heaven's throne. And everyone involved had made their own free choices. Now those choices had converged.

But no human being—nor any demonic creature—knew that particularly important piece of information.

Not yet.

67

FINISHED

A bloodied smile engulfed Jesus' battered face.

The circling vultures screeched non-stop. Their cries pierced the atmosphere with squawking vulgarities. They were waiting for something to die. *Anything.*

It had been hours. Yet, the crowd continued to grow. Practically everyone in Jerusalem had heard that the Romans, at the urging of the Jewish elders, were in the process of killing the miracle worker from Galilee. But few protested the thing, lest their own lives be put in danger as well.

The mockers started up again, "Look at Him! He says He's the King of Israel! Can you believe it?"

Others joined in, "Well then, let Him come down from the cross!"

Additional onlookers became tangled in the demonically induced frenzy of the moment as well, "If the Galilean would just deliver Himself, maybe then we would believe in Him! He claims to trust in God. So...let God rescue Him! Show us a miracle!"

By now, they merely echoed the expected jeer. They had heard the mantra for the better part of the day. It was as if they were being enticed to repeat the words by some unseen power, some cosmic conductor.

In truth, their mocking words had actually been prophesied one thousand years before this day. King David had seen this day in a vision, and had faithfully recorded what he saw and what he heard.[404]

In that vision David had seen the Holy One, "pierced" through His hands and feet, suspended above the derisive throngs below.[405] He saw the soldiers gambling for His clothing. David saw the circling animalistic crowds.

And David heard the taunting aimed directly at the crucified one: "He trusts in the Lord, let the Lord rescue Him. Let Him deliver Him, since He delights in Him."[406]

Jesus knew it would not be long now. To reinforce their precisely foretold actions and words, Jesus cried out to the taunting horde below. In so doing, He recited the first line of David's prophetic psalm:[407] "*My God, My God, why have you forsaken me!*"

After shouting the line, His head fell to His chest. He was still alive. Barely.

At His anguished outburst, an instant hush fell over the stunned crowd.

Many were familiar with that passage of Scripture. Now, the words of it whipped through their brains, searing their souls. Even the centurion, the one in charge of the crucifixion, succumbed to the spirit of the moment. Could this really be? Why had he not seen this before?

Look! There they were! There were his own men gambling for Jesus' clothing—*just as the prophecy foretold!*

Furthermore, *he* was the one who had overseen the piercing of Jesus' hands and feet. The words the people were using to mock this man... why *were they using those exact words?* Did they not know that their words concerning this very moment actually echoed the prophetic utterances of their own revered King David?

When the centurion and those around him felt the earthquake and saw everything else happening before their eyes, the dread of the moment's revelation welled up within them.[408]

What had they done? What was the nature of this event in which they were participating? Surely, this was no "ordinary" crucifixion. There was something deeply spiritual about this moment. He could feel it in the air. Something evil lurked among them. There was a growing sense of dread that some dark power was behind the profanity of this day. Never before had he felt such a thing in the routine exercise of carrying out a crucifixion.

Was the God of the Jews going to lash out in vengeful outrage? The centurion and his entourage began to mutter amongst themselves, "Could this really be the *Son of God* that we have crucified?"

Then, as though it had been choreographed and rehearsed, Jesus pushed up on the spike that had been hammered into the tops of his feet. He took the deepest breath He could muster, and cried out again.

"Father! Into Your hands I commend my spirit!"

The exclamation from the Suffering One startled the onlookers.

But Jesus had not quite yet completed His proclamation…

As He let out his very last words, He slowly pushed Himself up one more time. He sucked in His last huge breath, filling His tortured lungs to capacity. It was obvious to everyone that He was going to speak once more. The crowd moved closer, as one huge mass.

A bloodied smile engulfed Jesus' battered face. He lifted His swollen eyes to the heavens, peering through the tiny slits of flesh that enclosed them. He exhaled with an otherworldly power as He screamed out His final decree.

It. Is. Now. Finished!

Instantly, Jesus' head fell to His chest. He had taken His last breath. His heart refused to offer another beat.

How could this be, the centurion thought. *How could a dying man ordain the exact second of His very last breath?*

The centurion was convinced. He didn't care what anyone else thought of him. Overcome with grief, he removed his helmet, steeled himself, and turned to face the now-silent mob of stunned onlookers.

Pointing to the bloodied, lifeless body of Jesus, he accusingly shouted to the crowd, "Surely this man was the Son of God!"

Most of the throng stood dumbfounded.

How should they respond to this heartfelt charge leveled against them by a Roman military officer, one who could easily place any one of *them* upon a similar wooden beam of death and torture?

The Sanhedrin gaggle responded by storming from among their midst, unspoken indignation oozing from their countenances. The black line of robes leaving the crowd formed a serpentine shape as it threaded its way through the mob. *That arrogant, Gentile pig! How dare he proclaim this delusional blasphemer to be the Son of God!*

Nachash was there, too. He had never left. *This was his day.* At least that was what he imagined it to be…until this precise moment.

Now, however, for the first time, the ancient serpent wasn't quite so certain. Had this event actually been preordained by Elohim? If that was true, just how could he have missed the clues? Had the truth of it, the whole plan, been right before him all along? *A crucified savior*—How could that be? A cold shiver coursed through his body.

This doesn't make any sense, Nachash thought. After all, *he* had orchestrated this event himself—hadn't he? The scourging, the mocking, the hammer, the nails—*his idea!*

But, if this was not really *his* doing…then whose was it? *What would happen next?* What did this mean for his plans of securing the throne of Elohim for his very own? There were at least a dozen unanswered questions churning through his twisted mind. But, thus far, the most obvious answers to each of his questions only pointed to his potential demise.

As the creeping sense of dread finally caught up with itself, Nachash balled his fists and fumed. His fury grew into a consuming rage. He would *not* be defeated! This was *his* kingdom!

The atmosphere fizzled, then folded in on itself—right where Nachash had been standing.

And darkness closed in upon the land.

PART ELEVEN

Paradise

After three full nights, early on the morning of the third day, the ancient serpent finally had his answer. Jesus had actually given life *to Himself.* No one could pull off a feat like that except Elohim. At that moment Satan finally knew what the title "Son of God" really meant. Nachash had been duped. He had gambled it all…and he had lost.

Throughout the four Gospels—from the time of Jesus' resurrection on—we never hear Satan's name mentioned again. In those eyewitness accounts, we never see or hear of Satan launching a direct attack upon the divine Son of God, not even during the forty days after the resurrection.[409]

Instead, Satan would eventually focus his attack upon the believers—*the Church*—the army that Jesus was raising up against the serpent's stolen valor (Revelation 12).

But, perhaps there is still time. Maybe, Satan thought…*just maybe… my kingdom can yet be salvaged.*

If history has proven anything at all, it is that Satan's conceit knows no boundaries.

68

THE VISION

Circa AD 100
John, the beloved disciple, is ninety-four years old

John, the son of Zebedee, one of the *Sons of Thunder,* was slipping away.
His breathing was noticeably labored—even more so than just an
hour ago. And his chest felt like it had one of Alexander the Great's
famed war elephants standing upon it. *So...this is what it feels like to die?*

But why shouldn't it be this way? John chuckled to himself. After all,
he was now in his mid-nineties and it was almost the turn of another
century.

He was surrounded by loved ones, though he could barely see them
through his dimming eyes. Even though he could not always make out
their specific words, he could still hear them speaking and laughing.
That was enough for him at the moment, just to know they were there.

Warm blankets had been snuggled around him and a crackling fire
in the fireplace created a ballet of dancing shadows across the room. A
familiar warmth enveloped him. It was calming, peaceful, and penetrating to the depths of his soul. What more could a dying man ask for?

He had experienced this same presence of serenity several times before, even in his darkest moments of despair and grief. Especially when he had survived being thrown into a vat of boiling oil, then banished to Patmos for refusing to offer an altar-sacrifice in honor of Emperor Domitian.[410] Mercifully, those horrifying days had finally ended, and he had been allowed to return home.[411]

But for now, John was fairly comfortable. It wouldn't be long. He could feel it. He was more certain of that truth than of life itself.

In fact, for the vast majority of his existence upon this earth, this was the moment he had been living for—his moment of passing back into the divine realm and back into the presence of his Creator. He would soon be in that hidden dimension, eating the fruits of its joy and bliss, feasting upon the tree of life. He already knew what he was going to see when he arrived, and he couldn't wait to get there…

Please, Lord, take me soon…bring me home.

CAUGHT UP

Some thirty to forty years earlier, his friend and fellow minister, the Apostle Paul, had also witnessed the reality of paradise. He too had been caught up to the throne of Elohim. From that day forward, Paul had longed to be "absent from the body and present with the Lord." Yes, Brother Paul *knew*.

John smiled when he thought of these wondrous things. Even though he had faithfully preached the great truths that the risen Yeshua had given to Paul as a result of his *catching up*, John had no idea that before his own life was over, he too would be caught up. He could not have dreamed that he also would enter paradise and that he would return to the earthly realm to tell of his experience, just like Paul did.

Not only would John return, but he would also come back with a scroll—the scroll of the *Revelation*. And at the command of Yeshua Himself, John would faithfully disperse that scroll among seven very specific churches. Those churches were located in a region that would prove to be central to the very last days before Yeshua's return.[412]

THE PORTAL

During his foray into that unseen realm, John had been whisked into the distant future, thousands of years from his own day. Dimension after dimension of the progression of time had flown before his eyes. He had been taken to a "high mountain" and shown things that were beyond his comprehension, yet he was told: *Write what you have seen.*

He had obediently written. The indescribable imagery had, letter-by-letter, flowed from his pen, guided by the hand of the Holy Spirit. There was no other way to define the phenomenon. Not only had he somehow traveled through time deep into the future, but to this very day he could often smell the air of the eras through which he traveled. He could hear the sounds of each passing age of humanity, growing more clamorous and metallic as the pages of the calendar flipped by, like leaves blowing on a blustery fall afternoon.

John had not experienced a mere vision. No—it had not been a dream. He had actually been there, in the flesh, from the throne of God, all the way into the halls of the Antichrist's kingdom lair.

John now understood what Jesus meant when He assured the disciples that He alone was the door, the gate, and the only portal through which the believer could enter. John had been through that portal, into the future. He had traversed time itself. There had been no dimensional barriers standing in his way after entering through the "door" of Jesus.

But, even in the midst of the tumult of those final days, John had also witnessed the amazing patience and endurance on the part of the saints who were faithfully advancing the gospel of Jesus Christ. They were the only ones who understood what life was really all about, and where everything was ultimately heading. In the end, he had seen them greatly rewarded for their faith and for their witness, advancing the kingdom work, even in the midst of global chaos.

THE LAWLESS ONE

Most terrifying of all was when John beheld the rise of the appalling beast that was to come. He saw the son of perdition finally seated upon the throne of his lustful desire. He was high and lifted up, and blindly worshipped by the inhabitants of the earth. The world had no idea this mesmerizing man was actually possessed by Satan. This was the dragon's "Christ," his diabolical counterfeit of heaven's Son. For a brief while, this fallen elohim would finally have his coveted kingdom.

Then John foresaw the final days of the wrath of Yahweh. He saw, in an instant, the sky rolled up like a scroll and the dimension of the divine realm of Elohim exposed to the planet. The stars of the heavens appeared to shoot toward the earth at supersonic speed. The entire spectacle had burst into global view at the sound of celestial trumpets.

The ominous, blood-curdling blasts of those angelic shofars had filled the heavens, echoing throughout the cosmos. People who had formerly cursed the God of heaven now scattered like panicked insects. The inhabitants of the earth cried out for the mountains to fall upon them. John heard their anguished pleas for mercy. But their entreaties came far too late. The wrath of the Lamb was upon them, and there was no place to hide (Revelation 6:12–17).

THE GREAT WHITE THRONE

After this, John saw the gleaming white throne of Yahweh's final judgment upon Satan's doomed kingdom and all that belonged to it. The prisons of death and hell had been opened. The condemned of the ages were brought forward. The former inhabitants of Gehenna, both the ancient and the recent, stood as a multitude, as far as the eye could see. John had watched as the books were opened. And he heard the collective groans of humanity as the pages were read aloud. There was no escape from the condemnation of their purposed rejection of the Lamb of God (Revelation 20).

John saw Satan, along with the beast, the false prophet, and the disobedient angels as they were thrown into the lake of fire. The kings of the earth were appalled to see the final end of Nachash, the one who, for eons, had so easily controlled and manipulated them. He was gone from their midst forever; cast into an impenetrable dimension of alternative existence. Never to return. Never to be remembered again.[413]

John saw the new earth—as the old and sin-fallen dimensional layer of reality supernaturally morphed into a thing of sublime perfection and unspeakable beauty. From this point forward, there would be no more pain, no more crying, no more death. The old order of things instantly passed away at the command of Yahweh. Paradise, for eons hidden from fallen humanity, but *there* all along, was now revealed as the eternal dwelling place of redeemed humanity. The restitution of all things had finally come, just as Jesus had promised. Everything had finally been made new.

John saw it all. He saw it in real time and in the flesh. He had been physically present—there, in the future. He had effortlessly traveled through time—by the will of Elohim.

However, there had been a price to pay for what he had been shown. Much of what he witnessed ceaselessly haunted him from that day forward, vexing his righteous soul, just like so many of the prophets before him.[414]

Until now. Now he was getting ready to walk through that portal again.

Soon, John would be by Jesus' side once more…

69

THE GLORY

Great drops of salty tears streamed down his face…

The old man shivered as a sudden chill coursed through his body. Alexander's elephant grew heavier upon his breast. John's breathing became shallower, more labored.

He groaned aloud, in an ever-weakening whisper… *How much longer, Lord?*

His thoughts were interrupted as someone placed another log in the fireplace. The flames sputtered back to life and spewed forth a rush of heavenly warmth. The room once again filled with a lovely aureate glow, punctuated by a soothing, crackling sound. A cool rag was placed on his forehead. The tears were wiped from his cheeks by a gentle hand.

John flipped through the pages of his memory, and pondered once more the amazing days of Messiah.

Those sweet memories ambulated through the creases of his mind and into the depths of his soul. *God had actually been with us in those days! What a thought! Our Creator! In the flesh…walking with us…like it must have been in the Garden!*

How could it be that he, John, had been born for such a time as this? How could it be that the Creator of the universe had actually chosen *him* to walk by His side during those stunningly prophetic days? But those days had truly been the substance of *real* life—the way it was meant to be from the beginning. If the world could only understand this boundless, liberating, and wonderful truth.

Yeshua would, in time, tap a small group to be His inner circle. But how could John have known, on that day at the Jordon River, what the rest of his days would eventually entail? Emanating from the collective faithfulness of that small group, however, the world would never again be the same. From them the church would be born! And now, John had become the last of Jesus' inner circle to inhabit this earthly realm. The rest had been martyred for their faith. They had stepped through the veil and into *genuine* life. Soon it would be John's turn. But not soon enough.

He wondered: *Why was he the only one who would leave this world lying upon the bed of old age?* But then, John remembered what Yeshua had said to Peter, after the resurrection event, as they had walked the shores of Galilee, "If I want John to remain until I return, what is that to you, Peter? You follow me!"[415] Yes. John had remained. And Peter was already with the Lord. *If we had only known, way back then, the glory of what we know now!*

Great drops of salty tears streamed down John's face as those memories flooded his mind. A slight smile formed on his lips. He opened his eyes wide as he glanced about the room—as though he had unexpectedly beheld something spectacular. The room grew silent, as its occupants noticed the sudden change in John's demeanor.

As his family and friends gathered around him, John announced in a raspy whisper, *"The music! The singing! It's magnificent! It must be my time! Finally! I see them! I... I..."* His whispers faintly drifted into nothingness.

John exhaled a great sigh as his eyelids gently fluttered together, finally shuttering out the sights of his former earthly existence. And then...he was gone. But he did not cease to "live."

PARADISE

In that very next moment, in the twinkling of an eye, and in a spontaneous burst of an intensely dazzling white light…a shimmering golden curtain was lifted. Only John could see it. The room and everything that filled it were left behind him. He was presently enveloped in a cocoon of divine luminance, bathing him in unspeakable ecstasy.

He held out his hands and marveled at what he saw. His entire body was transforming right before his eyes! His very being was enveloped in renewal and vigor. His eyes and ears worked as though his youth had been instantly returned to him. It was happening! It all seemed so natural—so *rapturous!*

Just then he heard a familiar voice. It was the very voice he had so desired to hear. *"John! Come here! Well done my friend! Here—take my hand…"*

John walked through the open veil. He took hold of the strong and outstretched hand. A blast of air hit him in the face, like a cool, utterly delightful ocean breeze. Indescribably beautiful music accompanied the moment. He felt more alive than he had ever been! He was vibrant, and at complete peace—and he was whole. He was on *the other side.*

The light instantly separated, as if a great and magnificent door had been flung open before him. Behind the folds of brilliance, John beheld a face…a familiar and welcomed face. He fell to his knees and wept.

He felt that strong and wonderful hand in his as the other hand firmly gripped his shoulder, gently squeezing, in the same way a father would comfort his child. Then…he felt the embrace for which he had been longing. The embrace of the Master—his dearest friend. *His life.*

John—*the disciple whom Jesus loved*—was finally in paradise.

He was home at last.

Forever.

70

PRESSING ON

The prophets have already spoken...

This one thing I know...

We, dear reader, are living in the midst of the most prophetic days since the first coming of Jesus Christ. We are at least in the front edges of that foretold cosmic battle of the ages. If there was ever a time for the Church to come to grips with this glaring biblical fact, it's now. We are not in darkness. We are children of the light. This day should not overwhelm us, like a thief in the night (1 Thessalonians 5:2).

To be certain, the war against Nachash has already been won at Calvary's cross. And he knows it. Consequently, his unmitigated rage knows no shame or remorse. He is determined to inflict his scorched-earth policy upon God's people, the Church, the returned nation of Israel, and humanity as a whole. We are witnessing Satan's petulant tantrum of retaliation, brought about because of his humiliating defeat through heaven's eternal plan. His kingdom dream will soon come to naught.

Consequently, the biblically predicted demonic outpouring of the last days is here. The unmitigated flood of perversion and profanity that continually pours out upon humanity is spreading across the globe at lightning speed. You are not imagining it. It is really happening, while most of the world slumbers through it, believing everything is "normal."

CARL GALLUPS

I do not claim to be a prophet. The way I see it, the prophets have already spoken; their words concerning the last days are found within the pages of Scripture. Those declarations have been there throughout countless generations. My ministry goal is to contextually unveil what the prophets have already said—and what many of the scholars who have been poring over their words for ages have already seen.

I look forward to the moment when the atmosphere will crack and sparkle, and the days of fallen humanity's blasphemous outrage will be rolled up like a scroll, and time shall be no more. I relish the day when all things will be made new—including the planet, our minds, our hearts, and our bodies. On that day, everything that was so desperately wrong with this sin-diseased existence will finally be made right (Isaiah 65:17, Revelation 21–22).

I can't wait until we are an integral part of what the Creator of the universe is going to do in that day. We will serve as his brand-new ambassadors to the ages yet to come—newborn dimensions and worlds, bursting into life at the divine command of Yeshua Himself.[416]

Like Eddie Red's transformation out of the fish tank and into another dimension of glorified life, we too will have the ability to go through dimension after dimension of God's glorious and endless domain.[417] As we serve him, we will be accompanied by the heavenly host of the divine council of Yahweh, who have been patiently waiting for us to join them all along (Ephesians 1:3–14, 3:14–21).

I yearn for the day when God's paradise is finally unveiled before our longing eyes and we hear those cherished and blood-bought words—*"Welcome home! Well done my children!"*

Until then, my dear fellow ambassadors...*press on!*

There is still so much kingdom work yet to be finished. As surely as Jesus chose John the Baptizer, John the Revelator, and all the other faithful ones to walk by his side during the amazingly prophetic days of their time, He has chosen us to do the same thing, within the unveiling of our own prophetic days.

And never forget, because of our victory in Jesus, one day very soon Satan will finally become the *prince of nothing*. We will see him no more—*forever*.

And on that glorious day...the Final Kingdom will be ours.

Like it was meant to be—*from the beginning*.

Not that I have already obtained all this, or have already arrived at my goal, but I press on to take hold of that for which Christ Jesus took hold of me. Brothers and sisters, I do not consider myself yet to have taken hold of it. But one thing I do: Forgetting what is behind and straining toward what is ahead, I press on toward the goal to win the prize for which God has called me heavenward in Christ Jesus.

— PHILIPPIANS 3:12–14

ABOUT THE AUTHOR

Carl Gallups has been the senior pastor of Hickory Hammock Baptist Church in Milton, Florida, since 1987. He is a graduate of the Florida Law Enforcement Training Academy, Florida State University (BSc., Criminology) and New Orleans Baptist Theological Seminary (MDiv), and serves on the Board of Regents at the University of Mobile in Mobile, Alabama.

Carl is a former decorated Florida law enforcement officer, having served under three sheriffs with two different sheriff's offices, as well as having served in an administrative capacity in the Central Office of the Florida Department of Corrections. He was also appointed as a special deputy, in January 2016, under former Sheriff Joe Arpaio, Maricopa County, Arizona.

Pastor Gallups is a critically acclaimed, Amazon Top 60 bestselling author of multiple books, a talk-radio host since 2002, and a regular guest pundit on numerous television and radio programs as well as in various print media sources. He is also a frequent guest preacher at national prophecy and Bible conferences. He has preached the gospel of Jesus Christ on three continents, and in four nations—including Israel—and all over the United States, including Hawaii and Alaska. He has also preached in the Canadian provinces of British Columbia, Alberta, and Ontario.

Carl was featured on Fox News Business Report in 2016 as an "influential evangelical leader," publicly endorsing candidate Donald Trump for the office of president. Carl was asked by the Trump campaign to open the internationally broadcast Trump for President Rally in Pensacola, Florida, in January 2016. More than twelve thousand people attended that rally.

Carl lives in Milton, Florida, with his wife, Pam. You can find more information about him at www.carlgallups.com.

NOTES

1. 1 John 3:8, "Pulpit Commentary," Biblehub.com, https://biblehub.com/commentaries/1_john/3-8.htm.

2. If an angelic encounter is given to us, it is not so that we can convince others of how "spiritual" we are. Apparently there were false teachers in the early church who engaged in this type of practice. Attempting to "conjure" this kind of experience could easily result in demonic infiltration into the event, or, at the very least, a dangerous psychological delusion that plays upon our fallen sin nature. The rule is: Follow only the Lord Jesus Christ, by faith. If He determines to assist us by sending an angelic messenger, not only will we not be required to ask him for it—but ample evidence of the genuineness of the visitation will be given to us as well.

   > Do not let anyone who delights in false humility and the wor-
   > ship of angels disqualify you. Such a person also goes into great
   > detail about what they have seen; they are puffed up with idle
   > notions by their unspiritual mind. (Colossians 2:18)

   Expositor's Greek Testament
   > [In reference to these false teachers] "The Worship of
   > Angels"—This should probably be explained with reference to
   > the invisible world, with which they professed to hold commu-
   > nion, but which really was closed to them.

Jamieson-Fausset-Brown Bible Commentary

> Plainly the [manifestations] were actually seen…***whether of demoniacal origination (1 Sa 28:11–20), or phenomena resulting from natural causation, mistaken…as if [it were] supernatural.*** Paul, not stopping to discuss the nature of the things so seen, fixes on the radical error. https://biblehub.com/commentaries/colossians/2-18.htm.

3. See Matthew 18:15–17, 1 Corinthians 5:1–13.
4. The moment I heard the man say, "I am a fellow minister with you," the following passage came to mind. However, the truth of it did not fully register with me, until several days later:

    > [The angel said to John: "Do not worship me!] I am a fellow servant with you and with your fellow prophets and with all who keep the words of this scroll. Worship God!" (Revelation 22:9, brackets added for context).

5. **Sons of God** (i.e., Job 1:6). A Hebrew expression used in the Old Testament for angels—the members of God's divine court and thus members of the obedient realm of God's creation.

    Pulpit Commentary

    > By "the sons of God" it is generally admitted that, in this place [Job 1:6], the angels are meant (so again in Job 38:7). https://biblehub.com/commentaries/job/1-6.htm.

6. Hebrews 13:2, Genesis 18:1–2, 19:1–2.

    Regarding the account of "three men" in Genesis 18, who were only later to be revealed as angels, observe the following:

    Cambridge Bible for Schools and Colleges

    > The sudden appearance of the three men before the tent is especially recorded. Their approach had not been observed. As in the case of Genesis 32:24, Joshua 5:13, Judges 13:10-11, the angelic visitants are not distinguishable from ordinary men. https://biblehub.com/commentaries/genesis/18-2.htm.

7. Genesis 3:24.
8. Galatians 3:16–29.
9. **The stars will fall from the heavens**. I deal with this biblical declaration in great detail in later chapters.

10. **Part Two** through **Part Four** of this book comprise chapters that are a fictional narrative-style recounting of the scriptural records as they are presented in Genesis 3, Genesis 6, Matthew 3, Luke 3, Mark 1, and John 1. Though these chapters are presented in this narrative manner, the main theological details are factually confirmed through the contextual interpretation of the Scriptures, and through respected scholarly affirmation, all of which are explained in the chapters that follow.

11. Ezekiel 28:12–14.

12. **Elohim**—*Elohim* is the second most prolific name by which the Creator is known in the Bible—the most-often used name for God is *Yahweh*. However, Elohim is the first name of God to which we are introduced in the Scriptures. Genesis 1:1, "In the beginning, Elohim created the heavens and the earth."

    Elohim is often translated as "God" in the English translations. However, it can also be translated as "gods," "angels," or "divine beings." This is a complex Hebrew word, as the same word can be either singular or plural, depending upon the qualifying words that surround it. In that way, the word is similar in nature to our words: deer, or buffalo. However, when the word is used in the plural, its proper interpretation is: divine beings, angels, rulers, the demonic realm, or as *gods*—as in "Thou shalt have no other *gods* before me."

    Please see my book, *Gods and Thrones* (Defender Publishing, October 2017) for a detailed scholarly examination of this important Hebrew word and the importance of its proper contextual understanding.

13. Ezekiel 28:13–19.

14. **The divine council**: The biblical understanding of the heavenly "court" of angels that serve as God's witnesses, and assistants in the administration of God's decrees throughout his creation.

    God has taken his place **in the divine council**; in the **midst of the gods** he holds judgment. (Psalm 82:1)

    In the **council of the holy ones** God is greatly feared; he is more awesome than all who surround him. (Psalm 89:7)

15. See my book *Gods and Thrones* (Defender Publishing, October 2017) for a detailed examination of the matter of the divine council.

Cherubim "great, mighty" **See**: OT:3742, *Kerub*. "Brown-Driver-Briggs"
(Noun: masculine), https://biblehub.com/hebrew/3742.htm.

Also see: Abarim Publications. "Cherubim Meaning," (See especially the
bottom of the page, Subsection: Cherubim Meaning), Accessed on November 12, 2018, http://www.abarim-publications.com/Meaning/Cherubim.
html#.W8Jz0WhKhdg.

16. Even though the passage does not reveal that God specifically told Eve about
"not touching" the fruit—a number of scholars understand that Eve was
merely repeating what God had in fact told her at an early time. Otherwise,
Eve would have flatly lied and, at the same time, falsely accused God, when
she made this statement to Satan. If that were the case, then these words
would have been Eve's first "sin" and not the "eating" of the fruit.

17. Adam and Eve were together during the temptation event. Eve was not
alone in the affair—as some mistakenly interpret the account.
Genesis 3:6, "She also gave some to her husband, *who was with her*, and he
ate it." (NIV)
Keil and Delitzsch Biblical Commentary on the Old Testament
    She took of its fruit and ate, and gave to her husband by her
    (who was present), and he did eat. (Parenthesis in the original).
    https://biblehub.com/commentaries/genesis/3-6.htm.
Gill's Exposition of the Entire Bible
    The Jews infer from hence, that Adam was with her all the
    while, and heard the discourse between the serpent and her, yet
    did not interpose nor dissuade his wife from eating the fruit.
    https://biblehub.com/commentaries/genesis/3-6.htm.
Ellicott's Commentary for English Readers
    The demeanor of Adam throughout is extraordinary. It is the
    woman who is tempted—not as though Adam was not present...for she has not to seek him—but he shares with her at
    once the gathered fruit. https://biblehub.com/commentaries/
    genesis/3-6.htm.
See my book *Gods of Ground Zero* (Defender Publishing) for an in-depth
examination of the Garden temptation and sin.

18. *Whedon's Commentary on the Bible*
    That these "sons of God" **should be called upon at stated times**
    [summoned] **to give account of their deeds** is not an unreasonable thought for us—a race upon whom the sense of responsi-

bility is stamped; and **who will be summoned to undergo our ordeal** at the close of life. (Brackets and emphasis added)

Job 1:6–7. "Whedon's Commentary on the Bible," Studylight.org, https://www.studylight.org/commentaries/whe/job-1.html.

Matthew Poole's Commentary

Satan came also among them; **being forced to come**, and give up his account. (Emphasis added)https://biblehub.com/commentaries/job/1-6.htm.

Nachash—OT: 5172 and 5175 "Nachash." (A serpent—literal. Or figurative—one who hisses magically or seductively. A seducer. One who whispers magically and manipulates. i.e.—"He's a snake in the grass. Be careful of him! you can't trust that one!").

19. See Proverbs 6:16–19.

20. Dr. John McArthur says, regarding the third chapter of Genesis:

    Here's what Satan is thinking: "I failed to a degree in heaven and yet I succeeded. I was thrown out of heaven but I took a third of the angels with me so I have my kingdom." He's trying to be a sovereign in his own right. And he is successful in capturing Adam and Eve. He's successful. And at this point Satan may well have felt that he had made a massive dent in the divine purpose, that God had gone to all of this wondrous effort to create a universe and place man and woman in His universe on the earth and it was so magnificent and it was a paradise like the original paradise of heaven before the angels were thrown out and Satan succeeded in wrecking paradise. He succeeded in gaining the devotion of Adam and Eve. And that is really essentially what happened. https://www.gty.org/library/sermons-library/90-241/the-curse-on-the-serpent-part-1.

21. In Ezekiel 28:13,16; Yahweh declares that He cast Satan out of the Garden and off the divine council because of his "profanity" in the Garden:

    You were in Eden, the garden of God…. Thou hast sinned: therefore I will **cast thee** *as profane* **out of the mountain of God**: and I will destroy thee, O covering cherub, from the midst of the stones of fire. (KJV)

The Hebrew word for profane is *chalal*. It is OT:2490. The word is particularly hideous and according to *Brown-Driver-Briggs* Hebrew lexicon and dictionary it can sometimes be used to speak of : "defile, pollute: sexually, Genesis 49:4 (poem) = 1 Chronicles 5:1 (the father's bed); a woman = זנה Leviticus 19:29; Leviticus 21:7, 9 (H); זֶרְעוֹ Leviticus 21:15 (H). See: OT:2490. "Brown-Driver-Briggs," (Verb form: Pollute, Defile, Profane), Biblehub.com, https://biblehub.com/hebrew/2490.htm.

Also see my book *Gods of Ground Zero* for an in-depth development of the full meaning of this word, and its connections to the Garden of Eden.

22. See Hebrews 8:5.
23. See Isaiah 14:12–14.
24. Genesis 3:15.
25. See Genesis 6.
26. See two of my previous books, *Gods and Thrones* and *Gods of Ground Zero*, (Defender Publishing) for thorough studies of each of these biblical truths.
27. Romans 8:21, Ephesians 1:4, 1 Peter 1:20, Revelation 13:8.
28. Ibid.
29. Luke 17:26–30.
30. Ezekiel 5:5: "This is what the Sovereign LORD says: This is Jerusalem, which I have set in the center of the nations, with countries all around her.
31. **The Divine Son of God**—*Divi Augusti filius.* His official title was: Tiberius Caesar Augustus Divi Augusti filius. Tiberius was Roman emperor from AD 14 to AD 37, succeeding the first emperor, Augustus.
32. The prince of this world; see John 12:31 and 14:30.
33. Luke 3:10–14.
34. Jesus would also call these religious leaders a "brood of vipers." Each time He does it, the context of His charge is the accusation of their direct alliance with Satan (Matthew 12:34, 23:33; John 8:44, Matthew 23:13).
35. *Gill's Exposition of the Entire Bible*

    Expresses their craft and subtlety, their inward poison, and venomous nature; their fair outside, and specious pretenses; their hypocrisy, malice, and wickedness; **in which they were like to the old serpent, their father the devil.** (Bold emphasis added) https://biblehub.com/commentaries/matthew/23-33.htm.

    Pulpit Commentary

    They were of devilish nature, inherited from their very birth the disposition and character of Satan. So Christ said on another occasion, "Ye are of your father the devil, and the lusts of your father it is your will to do. He was a murderer from the beginning, and stood not in the truth." https://biblehub.com/commentaries/matthew/23-33.htm.

36. Isaiah 40:3.

37. **Yeshua.** Hebrew for Jesus. In Hebrew, His name means "Salvation."

38. Isaiah 53:2–3.

39. See my book, *The Rabbi, the Secret Note, and the Identity of Messiah* (Defender Publishing, February 2019) for an in-depth look at this orthodox Jewish belief.

40. See John 1:35–36. The two men Jesus referenced were Andrew and John, the son of Zebedee. John would go down in history as "the disciple whom Jesus loved." He would later give the world five New Testament books: the Gospel of John, 1–3 John, and the Book of Revelation.

    Meyer's New Testament Commentary

    One was Andrew, John 1:41. The other? Certainly John himself,[120] partly on account of that peculiarity of his which leads him to refrain from naming himself, and partly on account of the special vividness of the details in the following account, which had remained indelibly impressed upon his memory ever since this first and decisive meeting with his Lord. https://biblehub.com/commentaries/john/1-35.htm.

41. The potentialities of the narration of this section are attested to, at least in foundation, by numerous and reputable scholarly sources. Observe the following examples:

    Expositor's Greek Testament

    [This event] **does not necessarily involve that an actual dove was visible. It was not the dove which was to be the sign;** what he saw **was the Spirit** descending....It was the possession of this spirit by Jesus that convinced John that He could baptize with the Holy Spirit. That this conviction came to him at the baptism of Christ with a clearness and firmness which authenticated it as divine is guaranteed by the words of this verse. It was as plain to him that Jesus was **possessed by the Spirit** as if **he had seen the Spirit in a visible shape alighting upon him.** (Emphasis added). https://biblehub.com/commentaries/john/1-32.htm.

Ellicott's Commentary for English Readers
> The narrative implies (1) that our Lord and the Baptist were either alone, or that **they alone saw what is recorded.** "The **heavens were opened** to *him*" **as they were to Stephen** (Acts 7:56). The Baptist bears record that he too beheld the Spirit descending (John 1:33–34), but there is **not the slightest ground for supposing that there was any manifestation to others.** The [overshadowing of the Holy Spirit upon Jesus "in bodily form" is here pictured in the] perfection of the tenderness, the purity, the gentleness of which **the dove was the acknowledged** *symbol.* (Brackets and emphasis added) ttps:// biblehub.com/commentaries/matthew/3-16.htm.

42. In John 1:30–34, we hear John the Baptizer explain this truth, in detail: This is the one I meant when I said, "A man who comes after me has surpassed me because he was before me." **I myself did not know him,** but the reason I came baptizing with water was that he might be revealed to Israel. Then John gave this testimony:
> I saw the Spirit come down from heaven as a dove and remain on him. **And I myself did not know him, but the one who sent me** *[God himself. Ref. John 1:6]* **to baptize with water told me,** "The man on whom you see the Spirit come down and remain is the one who will baptize with the Holy Spirit." **I have seen and I testify** that this is God's Chosen One."
> (Emphasis and brackets added)

Jamieson-Fausset-Brown Bible Commentary gives further clarification to John the Baptist's claim:
> **Knew him not**—Living mostly apart, the one at Nazareth, the other in the Judean desert—to prevent all appearance of collusion, John only knew that at a definite time after his own call, his Master would show himself.... **But the sign which he was told to expect was the visible descent of the Spirit** upon him as He emerged out of the baptismal water. Then, catching up the voice from heaven, "he saw and bare record that this is the Son of God." (Emphasis added) https://biblehub.com/commentaries/john/1-31.htm.

43. The Gospel of John (1:29) records: "The **next day** John saw Jesus coming

toward him and said, "Behold, the Lamb of God, who takes away the sin of the world!" (Emphasis added).

There is some disparity among highly renowned scholars as to exactly *when* this "next day" was. At first glance, one would assume that it was the *very next day - the* one after John had confronted the Sanhedrin representatives at the Jordan River. This is the position that most commentators take. However, the uncertainty comes into play because of the fact that John, the writer of the Gospel, has Jesus returning to the river, on the "next day" yet again—for two "next days" in a row. On this particular second "next day" the declaration of the "Lamb of God" is again declared to the crowds. Furthermore, it is on this second "next day" event that we are told some in the crowd began to follow Jesus as His disciples. We are also told it was at this specific point that Jesus immediately began His earthly ministry. Oddly, John never mentions the wilderness temptation. John's account was the last one to be written, of the four Gospel accounts. However, Matthew, Mark, and Luke all record the fact of Jesus' temptation experience, and the selection of His disciples *after* that temptation.

See an example of thirteen scholarly commentary speculations on this matter at https://biblehub.com/commentaries/john/1-29.htm.

Of the thirteen, five conclude that John's declaration of Jesus being the Lamb of God was made *after* the wilderness temptation. Eight agree it was made *at the baptism* event, and *before* the temptation in the wilderness – as I have represented in my narrative.

44. *Cambridge Bible for Schools and Colleges*

    The desert unpeopled by men was thought to be the abode of demons. So Jesus meets the evil spirit in his own domains, the Stronger One coming upon the strong man who keepeth his palace (Luke 11:21-22). https://biblehub.com/commentaries/matthew/4-1.htm.

45. Matthew 12:29.

46. Mark's mention (1:13) of the wild animals in the wilderness temptation event is yet another connection to the Garden of Eden. This fact has not escaped the attention of numerous scholars.

    Cambridge Bible for Schools and Colleges

    The Saviour was "with the wild beasts," unhurt by them, as Adam was in Paradise.

Bengel's Gnomen

He even now, in the very height of His humiliation (self-emptying), exercised over the beasts the dominion which Adam had so soon suffered himself to lose.

Pulpit Commentary

He dwelt amongst them as Adam lived with them in his state of innocence in Paradise.

Gill's Exposition of the Entire Bible

[Jesus] was with the wild beasts…as Adam in Eden's garden.

47. *Cambridge Bible for Schools and Colleges*

The desert unpeopled by men was thought to be the abode of demons. So Jesus meets the evil spirit in his own domains, the Stronger One coming upon the strong man who keepeth his palace (Luke 11:21-22). https://biblehub.com/commentaries/matthew/4-1.htm.

48. See my book, *Gods of Ground Zero*, for a thorough study of this biblical truth. (Defender Publishing, August 2018)

In Ezekiel 28:16, Yahweh calls what Satan did in the Garden a "profane" thing:

"Therefore I will cast thee as profane (Heb. *chalal*) out of the mountain of God: and I will destroy thee." (KJV)

The Hebrew word for profane is *chalal*. It is OT: 2490. The word is particularly hideous in nature, and according to Brown-Driver-Briggs Hebrew lexicon and dictionary it can sometimes be used to express : "to defile or *pollute sexually*, Genesis 49:4 (poem) = 1 Chronicles 5:1 (the father's bed); a woman Leviticus 19:29; Leviticus 21:7, 9 (H); Leviticus 21:15.

OT: 2490. "Brown-Driver-Briggs," (Verb form: Pollute, Defile, Profane), Biblehub.com, https://biblehub.com/hebrew/2490.htm.

49. 1 Corinthians 15:22–45 (Jesus as the Second Adam).

John Lightfoot's Commentary on the Gospels

Jesus was led up by the Spirit into the wilderness to be tempted. The war, proclaimed of old in Eden between the serpent, and the seed of the serpent, and the seed of the woman, Genesis 3:15, now takes place; when that promised seed of the woman comes forth into the field (being initiated by baptism, and anointed by the Holy Ghost, unto the public office of his ministry) to fight with that old serpent, and at last to bruise his head.

Matthew 4. "John Lightfoot's Commentary on the Gospels," Studylight.org, https://www.studylight.org/commentaries/jlc/matthew-4.html#1.

50. *Barnes' Notes on the Bible*

> **When the first Adam** was created he was subjected to the temptation of the devil, and he fell and involved the race in ruin: it was not improper that **the second Adam** - the Redeemer of the race - should be subjected to temptation, in order that it might be seen that there was no power that could alienate him from God; that there was a kind and a degree of holiness which no art or power could estrange from allegiance. https://biblehub.com/commentaries/matthew/4-1.htm.

51. **Nehushtan—the brazen one:**

Nehushtan is the disparaging name tagged to the bronze serpent on a pole. It was first described in the Book of Numbers. (Numbers 21:4–9)

In the book of 2 Kings, King Hezekiah institutes a reform of an existing heresy among the Israelites. Hezekiah insisted upon the destruction of "the brazen serpent that Moses had made; for unto those days the children of Israel did burn incense to it; and it was called *Nehushtan.*" The term means "a brazen thing" (2 Kings 18:4).

Nehushtan comes from OT: 5174, 5178, and 5180. See*: New Exhaustive Strong's Numbers and Concordance with Expanded Greek-Hebrew Dictionary.*

52 *Matthew Henry's Concise Commentary*

> Mark notices his being in the wilderness and that he was with the wild beasts…The serpent tempted the first Adam in the garden, the Second Adam in the wilderness; with different success indeed.

Reference for all of the above commentaries: https://biblehub.com/commentaries/mark/1-13.htm.

Matthew 4:2 clarifies this point: "**After** fasting forty days and forty nights, he was hungry. The tempter **came to him** and said." (Emphasis added).

Pulpit Commentary

> **It was only after** his six weeks meditation that he felt the need of food… It was the moment the tempter had waited for to make his decisive assault. (Emphasis added). https://biblehub.com/commentaries/matthew/4-2.htm.

Barnes' Notes on the Bible
> The temptations, however, which are recorded by Matthew and Luke **did not take place until the forty days were finished.** https://biblehub.com/commentaries/luke/4-5.htm.

53. 2 Corinthians 4:4.
54. I deal with the supernatural mechanics that were in play in this scene, and the scholarly attestations of it, in a later section of this book.
55. Ephesians 2:2.
56. See Job 1:6–7 (and the following commentary entries for this passage).
Jamieson-Fausset-Brown Bible Commentary
> Sons of God—angels (Job 38:7; 1Ki 22:19). They **present themselves to render account** of their "ministry" in other parts of the universe (Heb. 1:14). [In other words, they had been "summoned" by Yahweh—they didn't merely enter into His presence at will].... Satan had been the agent in Adam's temptation. Hence his name is given without comment. The feeling with which he looks on Job is similar to that with which he looked on Adam in Paradise. (Emphasis added, brackets added as my commentary) https://biblehub.com/commentaries/job/1-6.htm.

The *Pulpit Commentary* also agrees with my assessment:
> We may gather, perhaps, from this place and Job 2:1 that **there are fixed times** at which the angelic host, often sent out by the Almighty on distant errands, *has to gather* **together**, [they are summoned] one and all, before the great white throne, to pay homage to their Lord, and probably **to give an account** of their doings. (Emphasis and brackets added). https://biblehub.com/commentaries/job/1-6.htm.

57. Revelation 12:9, 20:2.
58. The corresponding Greek word, used in the New Testament, is NT: 3789 "Ophis." Literally—a snake, or figuratively (as a type of sly cunning) an artful malicious person, especially Satan.
The Masquerade—The majority of scholars agree that, at this point, Satan's manifestation was in the realm of the physical and had moved far beyond any "mental" and "emotional" temptations that Jesus had thus far encountered. I quote, and analyze, a number of scholarly attestations to this fact in a later chapter.

59. Lucifer—"the shining one." Another name for Satan. See Isaiah 14:12 (KJV).

60. Dr. Stewart, Don. "What Do We Know about Jesus' Earthly Parents: Joseph and Mary?" Blue Letter Bible, https://www.blueletterbible.org/faq/don_stewart/don_stewart_198.cfm.

61. "The village seems to have been held in some contempt in 1st century Palestine. It was a nondescript dot on the map with not much to offer, overshadowed by nearby Sepphoris, the luxurious Greek-style capital of Herod Antipas."
Fletcher, Elizabeth. "Basic Facts about Nazareth," accessed October 22, 2018, http://www.jesus-story.net/nazareth_about.htm.
John 1:46, "And Nathanael said to him, can there any good thing come out of Nazareth? Philip said to him, Come and see."
Barnes' Notes on the Bible
> The character of Nazareth was proverbially bad. To be a Galilean or a Nazarene was an expression of decided contempt. https://biblehub.com/commentaries/john/1-46.htm.

For an in-depth Hebrew study of the word "Nazareth," see: http://www.abarim-publications.com/Meaning/Nazareth.html#.XGhu1uhKjIU.

62. See Genesis 3:15, Genesis 22:18, and Galatians 3:19.
A Commentary on the New Testament from the Talmud and Hebraica by John Lightfoot
> The war, proclaimed of old in Eden between the serpent, and the seed of the serpent, and the seed of the woman, Genesis 3:15, now takes place; when that promised seed of the woman comes forth into the field (being initiated by baptism, and anointed by the Holy Ghost, unto the public office of his ministry) to fight with that old serpent, and at last to bruise his head.See: https://www.biblestudytools.com/commentaries/lightfoot-new-testament/matthew/4.html.

63. **How did Satan get Jesus to the Temple in Jerusalem?** I deal with this topic in great detail, quoting a number of renowned scholars, in a later chapter.

64. See Psalm 91.

65. **How did Satan get Jesus to a place where He could observe all the nations of the world in an instant?** I deal with this topic in great detail, quoting a number of renowned scholars, in a later chapter.

66. Some translations of this verse render "Away from me Satan!" with an

exclamation point at the end. Others do not. It is a matter of choice on the part of the translators.

In the New Testament era, when Koine Greek was used as the everyday common language, Greek was most often written with no punctuation. The words ran together, with no spacing or markup. With very few exceptions—accents, breathing marks, spaces, and other punctuation were not added until a much later time.

I prefer to think that Yeshua had no need to raise His voice to Satan at this point. Yeshua's words alone were enough to silence and tame the evil one. Also note the most important point: Satan *obeyed* Jesus—and it wasn't because Jesus had raised His voice.

67. Isaiah 14:13–14.
68. Matthew 4:3. "Clarke's Commentary on the Whole Bible," Bible Study Tools, https://www.bibletools.org/index.cfm/fuseaction/Bible.show/sVerseID/23213/eVerseID/23213/RTD/clarke/version/nasb.
69. Ibid.
70. Matthew 4:3. "People's Bible Commentary," Bible Study Tools, https://www.bibletools.org/index.cfm/fuseaction/Bible.show/sVerseID/23213/eVerseID/23213/RTD/pcnt/version/nasb.
71. Matthew 4:3. "Jamieson-Fausset-Brown: Commentary Critical and Explanatory on the Whole Bible," Bible Study Tools, https://www.biblestudytools.com/commentaries/jamieson-fausset-brown/matthew/matthew-4.html.
72. Luke 4:3, "Cambridge Bible for Schools and Colleges," Biblehub.com, https://biblehub.com/commentaries/luke/4-3.htm.
73. Luke 4:3, "Gill's Exposition of the Entire Scripture," Biblehub.com, https://biblehub.com/commentaries/luke/4-3.htm.
74. Matthew 4, "Biblical Illustrator," (What Satan Knew of Christ), Biblehub.com, https://biblehub.com/commentaries/illustrator/matthew/4.htm.
75. 1 Peter 1:12. "Ellicott's Commentary," Biblehub.com, https://biblehub.com/commentaries/1_peter/1-12.htm.
76. 1 Peter 1:12. "Barnes' Notes on the Bible," Biblehub.com, https://biblehub.com/commentaries/1_peter/1-12.htm.
77. 1 Peter 1:12. "Pulpit Commentary," Biblehub.com, https://biblehub.com/commentaries/1_peter/1-12.htm.
78. This attitude of Satan is said to be explicitly expressed in Isaiah 14:13–14: You said in your heart, "I will ascend to the heavens; I will raise my throne

above the stars of God; I will sit enthroned on the mount of assembly, on the utmost heights of Mount Zaphon. I will ascend above the tops of the clouds; I will make myself like the Most High."

The *David Guzik Commentary* for the *Blue Letter Bible* online Bible study resource says of this passage:

> As this prophecy continues from the context of Isaiah 13, it is important to remember that Isaiah has two aspects of prophetic fulfillment in mind. First, there is the immediate and partial fulfillment regarding the empire of Babylon and its king. Second, there is the distant and **ultimate fulfillment regarding the spiritual empire of Babylon - the world system - and its king, Satan.** (Emphasis added) https://www.blueletterbible.org/Comm/guzik_david/StudyGuide2017-Isa/Isa-14.cfm.

79. Matthew 4:3. "Pulpit Commentary," Biblehub.com, https://biblehub.com/commentaries/matthew/4-3.htm.
80. Matthew 4:3. "Meyer's New Testament Commentary," Biblehub.com, https://biblehub.com/commentaries/matthew/4-3.htm.
81. **Theophany**
    Manifestation of God that is tangible to the human senses. In its most restrictive sense, it is a visible appearance of God in the Old Testament period often, but not always, in human form. Some would also include in this term Christophanies (preincarnate appearances of Christ) and angelophanies (appearances of angels).
    See: Theophany. "Baker's Evangelical Dictionary of Biblical Theology," Biblestudytools.com, https://www.biblestudytools.com/dictionary/theophany.
82. A study of the *Only Begotten* is set forth in my book, *Gods and Thrones* (Defender Publishing, Oct. 2017).
83. OT: 3439. *Monogenes.* "Helps Word-studies," Biblehub.com, https://biblehub.com/greek/3439.htm.
84. For ages, various writers have endeavored to unwrap this mystery. And, some of the most unusual suggestions have been made in this attempt. First, there was the idea that Mary was somehow "sinless" as a special "gift" of God. Therefore, her child, through the Holy Spirit—and not Joseph, could be sinless as well. This notion is often referred to as the Immaculate

Conception. The problem with this interpretation is that nowhere in scripture is this possibility even intimated. In fact, the whole idea goes against the contextual grain of biblical truth—from Genesis to Revelation, especially regarding the thoroughly fallen condition of the entire human race, of which Mary was undoubtedly a part. (SEE: Staples, Tim. "Hail Mary, Conceived without Sin," Catholic Answers, 9-1-07, https://www.catholic.com/magazine/print-edition/hail-mary-conceived-without-sin.) Others have attempted to explain the matter by insisting that the "sin nature" is passed to the child through the father only, and not the mother. Therefore since the "father," in Jesus' case, was the "power of the Holy Spirit," then Mary could be the mother of a child without that child possessing a sin nature. This idea is sometimes referred to as the Father's Line model. SEE: Slick, Matt. "Why wasn't Jesus born with original sin?" CARM (Christian Research and Apologetics Ministry), accessed Jan. 2, 2019, https://carm.org/why-wasnt-jesus-born-original-sin. Suffice it to say, the Father's Line idea simply does not hold up to thorough biblical scrutiny. (SEE: Hodge, Bodie, "Is Original Sin (Sin Nature) Passed through the Father's Genetic Line?" Answers in Genesis, 2-23-10, https://answersingenesis.org/sin/original-sin/sin-nature-passed-through-fathers-genetic-line.)

85. Some have wondered how it could be that Satan was not privy to the plan of the incarnation. How did he not know of Gabriel's visit to Mary, and the plans that had been revealed there? The answer should be clear by now. Satan is not omnipresent, nor is he omniscient. Elohim had obviously arranged for Gabriel's visit to be completely unnoticed by the demonic realm. Satan never fully understood what happened to him, until the morning of the resurrection. Notice that, in the scriptural accounts, we never again hear of Satan personally appearing to or harassing Jesus—after the resurrection. For the entire forty days before the ascension, Satan's name or presence is never mentioned again. It was at the resurrection that *he finally knew*.

86. Wesley, Charles. "Hark! The Herald Angels Sing," http://www.hymntime.com/tch/htm/h/h/a/hhangels.htm.

87. Hagios. NT #40. "Helps Word-studies," Biblehub.com, https://biblehub.com/greek/40.htm.

88. Shead, Sam. "Can Two People Have the Same DNA?" *Science Focus*, accessed Jan. 2, 2019, https://www.sciencefocus.com/the-human-body/can-two-people-have-the-same-dna.

89. See these articles:
    a. Hall, Harriet. "Baby's DNA in Mom's Blood: Noninvasive Prenatal Testing," *Science Base Medicine*, 9-17-13, https://sciencebasedmedicine.org/babys-dna-in-moms-blood-noninvasive-prenatal-testing.
    b. McAdam, Cormac. "The Placenta: The Fetal Life Support System," Health Research Board—Ireland, 4-7-17, http://www.hrb-mbctni.ie/2017/04/placenta-fetal-life-support-system.
90. Bible.org. "Is Mary's Lineage in One of the Gospels?" Accessed Jan. 2, 2019, https://bible.org/question/mary%E2%80%99s-lineage-one-gospels.
91. Luke 1:35, "Barnes' Notes on the Bible," Biblehub.com, https://biblehub.com/commentaries/luke/1-35.htm.
92. Matthew 1:18, "Ellicott's Commentary for English Readers," Biblehub.com, https://biblehub.com/commentaries/matthew/1-18.htm.
93. Luke 1:35, "Pulpit Commentary," Biblehub.com, https://biblehub.com/commentaries/luke/1-35.htm.
94. Luke 1:35, "Gill's Exposition of the Entire Bible," Biblehub.com, https://biblehub.com/commentaries/luke/1-35.htm.
95. Luke 1:35, "Expositor's Greek Testament," Biblehub.com, https://biblehub.com/commentaries/luke/1-35.htm.
96. Matthew 1:20 "Matthew Poole's Commentary," Biblehub.com, https://biblehub.com/commentaries/matthew/1-20.htm.
97. Luke 1:35, "Matthew Poole's Commentary," Biblehub.com, https://biblehub.com/commentaries/luke/1-35.htm.
98. Matthew 1:20 "Benson's Commentary," Biblehub.com, https://biblehub.com/commentaries/matthew/1-20.htm.
99. Luke 1:35, "Expository Notes of Dr. Thomas Constable," Studylight.org, https://www.studylight.org/commentaries/dcc/luke-1.html.
100. Luke 1:35, "Lange's Commentary on the Holy Scriptures: Critical, Doctrinal, and Homiletical," Studylight.org, https://www.studylight.org/commentaries/lcc/luke-1.html.
101. Matthew 4:6, "Matthew Henry's Commentary on the Bible," Biblehub.com, https://biblehub.com/commentaries/matthew/4-6.htm.
102. Matthew 4:1. "Barnes' Notes on the Bible," Biblehub.com, https://biblehub.com/commentaries/matthew/4-1.htm.
103. 1 Corinthians 15:45. "Meyer's New Testament Commentary," Biblehub.com, https://biblehub.com/commentaries/1_corinthians/15-45.htm.

104. Hebrews 4:15. "Dr. John W. Ritenbaugh—Forerunner Commentary," BibleTools.org, https://www.bibletools.org/index.cfm/fuseaction/Bible.show/sVerseID/30030/eVerseID/30030/version/nasb.

105. Hebrews 4:15, "*Pulpit Commentary*," Biblehub.com, https://biblehub.com/commentaries/hebrews/4-15.htm.

106. Hebrews 4:15, "*Gill's Exposition of the Entire Bible*," Biblehub.com, https://biblehub.com/commentaries/hebrews/4-15.htm.

107. Hebrews 4:15, "*Matthew Poole's Commentary*," Biblehub.com, https://biblehub.com/commentaries/hebrews/4-15.htm.

108. Hebrews 4:15. "Commentary - Hebrews 4:15," https://www.biblestudy-tools.com/commentaries/robertsons-word-pictures/hebrews/hebrews-4-15.html.

109. Hebrews 4:15. "Expository Notes of Dr. Thomas Constable," Studylight.org, "https://www.studylight.org/commentaries/dcc/hebrews-4.html.

110. Mark 1:24, "Pulpit Commentary," Biblehub.com, https://biblehub.com/commentaries/mark/1-24.htm.

111. Luke 4:34, "The IVP New Testament Commentary," The Bible Gateway, https://www.biblegateway.com/resources/ivp-nt/Examples-Jesus-Ministry.

112. John 19:38–42, "Joseph and Nicodemus Bury Jesus' Body," (The IVP New Testament Commentary Series), accessed October 22, 2018, https://www.biblegateway.com/resources/ivp-nt/Joseph-Nicodemus-Bury-Jesus-Body.

113. John 8:44. "Expositor's Greek Testament," Biblehub.com, https://biblehub.com/commentaries/john/8-44.htm.

114. John 8:44. "Jamieson-Fausset-Brown Bible Commentary," Biblehub.com, https://biblehub.com/commentaries/john/8-44.htm.

115. John 8:44. "Barnes' Notes on the Bible," Biblehub.com, https://biblehub.com/commentaries/john/8-44.htm.

116. OT: 1537. *Ek.* "Helps Word-studies," Biblehub.com, https://biblehub.com/greek/1537.htm.

117. OT: 1537. *Ek.* "Strong's Exhaustive Concordance,"Biblehub.com, https://biblehub.com/greek/1537.htm.

118. OT: 1537. *Ek.* "Thayer's Greek Lexicon," Biblehub.com, https://biblehub.com/greek/1537.htm.

119. Matthew 21:38. "Ellicott's Commentary on the Bible," Biblehub.com, https://biblehub.com/commentaries/matthew/21-38.htm.

120. Matthew 21:38. "Pulpit Commentary," Biblehub.com, https://biblehub.com/commentaries/matthew/21-38.htm.

121. Matthew 21:38. "Jamieson-Fausset-Brown Bible Commentary," Biblehub.com, https://biblehub.com/commentaries/matthew/21-38.htm.

122. John 12:10. "Ellicott's Commentary on the Bible," Biblehub.com, https://biblehub.com/commentaries/john/12-10.htm.

123. John 12:10. "Bengel's Gnomen," Biblehub.com, https://biblehub.com/commentaries/john/12-10.htm.

124. John 12:10. "Pulpit Commentary," Biblehub.com, https://biblehub.com/commentaries/john/12-10.htm.

125. John 12:10. "Jamieson-Fausset-Brown Bible Commentary," Biblehub.com, https://biblehub.com/commentaries/john/12-10.htm.

126. Revelation 12. "Cambridge Bible for Schools and Colleges," Biblehub.com, https://biblehub.com/commentaries/cambridge/revelation/12.htm.

127. John 6:64. "Bengel's Gnomen," Biblehub.com, https://biblehub.com/commentaries/john/6-64.htm.

128. Matthew 27:3–27:8

> Then Judas, who betrayed him, seeing that he was condemned, repenting himself, brought back **the thirty pieces of silver** to the chief priests and ancients, saying: "I have sinned in betraying innocent blood." But they said: "What is that to us? Look thou to it." **And casting down the pieces of silver in the temple**, he departed, and went and hanged himself with a halter. But the chief priests, having taken the pieces of silver, said: "It is not lawful to put them into the corbona, because it is the price of blood." And after they had consulted together, **they bought with them the potter's field**, to be a burying place for strangers. For this the field was called Haceldama, that is, the field of blood, even to this day. (Douay-Rheims Bible Translation)

129. Matthew 27. "Aramaic Bible in Plain English," Biblehub.com, https://biblehub.com/aramaic-plain-english/matthew/27.htm.

130. Matthew 27:9 (in most English translations) ascribes this prophecy to Jeremiah, rather than its correct location, which is clearly from the prophet Zechariah.

The *Benson's Commentary* (as do many others) explains the discrepancy in this manner:

> The words here quoted are not in any copy of Jeremiah extant. But they bear a strong resemblance to the words of Zechariah 11:12-13. One MS., not of great account, has Ζεχαριου, of Zechariah. Another adds no name to the word prophet, and there is none added in the Syriac version, the words being only, which was spoken by the prophet. And it seems, from a remark of Augustine, that some copies in his time named no prophet. Indeed it is not improbable that the name Jeremiah was inserted by some officious transcriber. Or we may suppose, with Bishop Hall, that in copying the words, Jeremiah was put down for Zechariah, a blunder which transcribers might easily commit, especially if the names were written by abbreviation, Ιριου for Ζριου. See Matthew 27:9. "Benson's Commentary," Biblehub.com, https://biblehub.com/commentaries/matthew/27-9.htm.

The *Aramaic Bible in Plain English* accounts for this apparent scribal error with the following translation:

> Then was fulfilled what was spoken by the Prophet who said, "I took thirty silver coins, the price of The Precious One on which they of the children of Israel had agreed.

See Matthew 27:9. "Aramaic bible in Plain English," Biblehub.com, https://biblehub.com/matthew/27-9.htm.

131. Revelation 11:19 "Bible Exposition Commentary—New Testament." (David C. Cook; New edition, November 1, 2007): p.1065.

132. See my book, *Gods of Ground Zero* (Defender Publishing, August 2018) for an in-depth scholarly analysis of this contextual biblical truth.

133. John 2:23–25 proves this biblical truth:

> Now while [Jesus] was in Jerusalem at the Passover Festival, many people saw the signs he was performing and believed in his name. But Jesus would not entrust himself to them, for he knew all people. He did not need any testimony about mankind, for he knew what was in each person.

134. John 2:24–25. "Barnes' Notes on the Bible," Biblehub.com, https://biblehub.com/commentaries/john/2-25.htm.

135. John 2:23–25. (PC Study Bible V5. From the Bible Exposition Commen-

tary—New Testament. Copyright © 1989 by Chariot Victor Publishing, and imprint of Cook Communication Ministries. All rights reserved. Used by permission.)

136. John 6:70. "Pulpit Commentary," Biblehub.com, https://biblehub.com/commentaries/john/6-70.htm.

137. John 6:70. "Meyer's New Testament Commentary," Biblehub.com, https://biblehub.com/commentaries/john/6-70.htm.

138. John 6:70. "Gill's Exposition of the Entire Bible," Biblehub.com, https://biblehub.com/commentaries/john/6-70.htm.

139. John 6:70. "Vincent's Word Studies," Biblehub.com, https://biblehub.com/commentaries/john/6-70.htm.

140. Luke 22:3. "Meyer's New Testament Commentary," Biblehub.com, https://biblehub.com/commentaries/luke/6-3.htm.

141. John 14:30. "Ellicott's Commentary for English Readers," Biblehub.com, https://biblehub.com/commentaries/john/14-30.htm.

142. John 14:30. "Expositor's Greek Testament," Biblehub.com, https://biblehub.com/commentaries/john/14-30.htm.

143. John 14:30. "Cambridge Bible for Schools and Colleges," Biblehub.com, https://biblehub.com/commentaries/john/14-30.htm.

144. John 14:30. "Pulpit Commentary," Biblehub.com, https://biblehub.com/commentaries/john/14-30.htm.

145. John 14:30. "Matthew Poole's Commentary," Biblehub.com, https://biblehub.com/commentaries/john/14-30.htm.

146. John 13:27. "Meyer's New Testament Commentary," Biblehub.com, https://biblehub.com/commentaries/john/13-27.htm.

147. John 13:27. "Cambridge Bible for Schools and Colleges," Biblehub.com, https://biblehub.com/commentaries/john/13-27.htm.

148. John 13:27. "Pulpit Commentary," Biblehub.com, https://biblehub.com/commentaries/john/13-27.htm.

149. Licona, Michael (2010). *The Resurrection of Jesus: A New Historiographical Approach*. InterVarsity Press. p. 304.

150. Luke 23:34. "Barnes Notes," Biblehub.com, https://biblehub.com/commentaries/luke/23-34.htm.

151. Of course, John the Baptist would be put to death before the crucifixion and resurrection. His "proof" that Jesus was the genuine Messiah was the fact that he literally saw the throne of Heaven and heard God's voice.

152. Revelation 20:3, "Jamieson-Fausset-Brown Bible Commentary," Biblehub. com, https://biblehub.com/commentaries/revelation/20-3.htm.

153. NT: 758. Archón (rulers). "Thayer's Greek Lexicon," Biblehub.com, https://biblehub.com/greek/758.htm.

154. Also see my previous books *Gods and Thrones* and *Gods of Ground Zero* (Defender Publishers, Crane, MO) for a thorough biblical study of this prevalent biblical truth.

155. Rochford, James M. "Why Did Satan Crucify Jesus?" Evidenceunseen. com, accessed 10-31-18, http://www.evidenceunseen.com/theology/ satanology/why-did-satan-crucify-jesus/#_ftn5.
I want to give credit for creative inspiration to James M. Rochford for the brilliant and original fleshing out of the material I eventually put into my own words in this chapter, under my section titled "Why Did God Go to All That Trouble?"
James Rochford is the author of *Evidence Unseen: Exposing the Myth of Blind Faith*, (2013), *Endless Hope or Hopeless End: The Bible and the End of Human History* (2016), and *Too Good to Be True? How we get to Heaven, What it will be like, and Why we can't live without it* (2016).

156. 2 Peter 1:3–4.

157. Forster, Roger T., and V. Paul Marston. God's Strategy in Human History. (Minneapolis, Minnesota: Bethany House Publishers, 1974): 8.

158. Ibid. Rochford, James M. "Why Did Satan Crucify Jesus?"

159. Colossians 2:15, "Barnes' Notes on the Bible," Biblehub.com, https:// biblehub.com/commentaries/colossians/2-15.htm.

160. Colossians 2:15, "Jamieson-Fausset-Brown Bible Commentary," Biblehub. com, https://biblehub.com/commentaries/colossians/2-15.htm.

161. Colossians 2:15, "Matthew Poole's Commentary," Biblehub.com, https:// biblehub.com/commentaries/colossians/2-15.htm.

162. Warmflash, David. "Three Totally Mind-bending Implications of a Multidimensional Universe," Discover Magazine, 12-04-14, http://blogs. discovermagazine.com/crux/2014/12/04/multidimensional-universe/#. W9uSRJNKhdg.

163. String theory, by using the known scientific information of quantum mechanics, predicts that there truly are multiple universes and dimensions beyond the ones we know. https://www.aps.org/careers/physicists/profiles/ kaku.cfm.

164. Freudenrich, Craig, PhDD "What are the Four Fundamental Forces of Nature?" Science, accessed 11-3-18, https://science.howstuffworks.com/environmental/earth/geophysics/fundamental-forces-of-nature.htm.

165. Kaku, Micho. "Nobel Prize Awarded to Two Quantum Physicists," *Big Think*, 10-10-12, https://bigthink.com/dr-kakus-universe/nobel-prize-awarded-to-two-quantum-physicists.

166. Ball, Philip. "How Big Can Schrödinger's Kittens Get?" Nautilus, 10-8-15, http://nautil.us/issue/29/scaling/how-big-can-schr246dingers-kittens-get.

167. Williams, Matt. "A Universe of 10 Dimensions," 12-11-14, *PHYS.org*, https://phys.org/news/2014-12-universe-dimensions.html.
Also see: Glanz, J. 1997. *Strings Unknot Problems in Particle Theory, Black Holes. Science* 276:1969-1970.
Also see: Kestenbaum, D. 1998. Practical Tests for an "Untestable" Theory of Everything? *Science* 281:758–759.

168. Tate, Karl. "How Quantum Entanglement Works (Infographic)" Live Science, 4-8-13, https://www.livescience.com/28550-how-quantum-entanglement-works-infographic.html.

169. Universitat Autonoma de Barcelona. "Record Quantum Entanglement of Multiple Dimensions," PHYS.org, 3-27-14, https://phys.org/news/2014-03-quantum-entanglement-multiple-dimensions.html.

170. Kaku, Micho. "4 Things That Currently Break the Speed of Light Barrier," *Big Think*, 11-9-10, https://bigthink.com/dr-kakus-universe/what-travels-faster-than-the-speed-of-light.

171. CERN. "The Large Hadron Collider," CERN.com, accessed 11-10-18, https://home.cern/science/accelerators/large-hadron-collider.

172. CERN is the European Organization for Nuclear Research. The name CERN is derived from the acronym for the French Conseil Européen pour la Recherche Nucléaire, a provisional body founded in 1952 with the mandate of establishing a world-class fundamental physics research organization in Europe. (https://en.wikipedia.org/wiki/CERN.)

173. Ibid. Cern. "The Large Hadron Collider."

174. Milton-Barker, Adam. "How CERN plan to use the Large Hadron Collider to open portals to other dimensions, and possibly already have." *Techbubble.info*, 5-4-15, https://www.techbubble.info/blog/quantum-physics/entry/how-cern-plan-to-use-the-large-hydrogen-collider-to-open-portals-to-other-dimensions.

175. Page, Lewis. "'Something May Come through' Dimensional 'Doors' at LHC," *The Register*, 10-6-09, https://www.theregister.co.uk/2009/11/06/lhc_dimensional_portals.
This Bertolucci quote was reported all over the Internet, including through *Charisma Magazine* and *Breaking Israel News*. I am not aware of any reputable source that claims Bertolucci or CERN denies the veracity of the quote.
176. Ibid. Tate, Karl. "How Quantum Entanglement Works (Infographic)."
177. Thompson, Avery. "China Plans to Build a Particle Collider Five Times More Powerful than the LHC," Popular Mechanics, 11-14-18, https://www.popularmechanics.com/science/a25101820/china-lhc-particle-collider-cepc.
178. Orzel, Chad. "What Has Quantum Mechanics Ever Done For Us?" 8-13-15, Forbes.com, https://www.forbes.com/sites/chadorzel/2015/08/13/what-has-quantum-mechanics-ever-done-for-us/#173c98664046.
179. I first heard this illustration, many years ago, from a lecture given by Dr. Kent Hovind. I give him the credit for my use, and the expanding, of that illustration here.
180. Moskowitz, Clara. "5 Reasons We May Live in a Multiverse," Space.com, 12-7-12, https://www.space.com/18811-multiple-universes-5-theories.html.
181. Hawking, Stephen. "The Beginning of Time," (Lecture), accessed 11-3-18, http://www.hawking.org.uk/the-beginning-of-time.html.
182. Cho, Adrian. "Stephen Hawking's (almost) last paper: putting an end to the beginning of the universe," Sciencemag.org, 5-2-18, https://www.sciencemag.org/news/2018/05/stephen-hawking-s-almost-last-paper-putting-end-beginning-universe.
183. Cosmology. "The branch of philosophy dealing with the origin and general structure of the universe, with its parts, elements, and laws, and especially with such of its characteristics as space, time, causality, and freedom." https://www.dictionary.com/browse/cosmology.
184. Johnson, George, "Beyond Energy, Matter, Time and Space," New York Times, 7-21-14, https://www.nytimes.com/2014/07/22/science/beyond-energy-matter-time-and-space.html.
185. Redd, Nola Taylor. Space.com Contributor. "What Is Cosmology? Definition & History," Space.com, 9-25-17, https://www.space.com/16042-cosmology.html.
186. Kitching, Thomas. "What is time—and why does it move forward?"

PHYS.org, 2-23-16, https://phys.org/news/2016-02-what-is-time-and-why.html.

187. Psalm 90:4, "Cambridge Bible for Schools and Colleges," Biblehub.com, https://biblehub.com/commentaries/psalms/90-4.htm.

188. Psalm 90:4, "Pulpit Commentary," Biblehub.com, https://biblehub.com/commentaries/psalms/90-4.htm.

189. 2 Peter 3:8, "Ellicott's Commentary for English Readers," Biblehub.com, https://biblehub.com/commentaries/2_peter/3-8.htm.

190. 2 Peter 3:8, "Expositor's Greek New Testament," Biblehub.com, https://biblehub.com/commentaries/2_peter/3-8.htm.

191. 2 Peter 3:8, "Jamieson-Fausset-Brown Bible Commentary," Biblehub.com, https://biblehub.com/commentaries/2_peter/3-8.htm.

192. Dr. Schaefer, Henry F. III. "Stephen Hawking, the Big Bang, and God," Accessed 11-3-18, http://www.leaderu.com/offices/schaefer/docs/bigbang.html.

193. Hebrews 11:3, "Benson's Commentary," Biblehub.com, https://biblehub.com/commentaries/hebrews/11-3.htm.

194. Dr. Jason Lisle. "God & Natural Law," Answers in Genesis, 8-28-06, https://answersingenesis.org/is-god-real/god-natural-law.

195. Siegel, Ethan. "The Biggest Myth in Quantum Physics," Forbes, 2-7-18, https://www.forbes.com/sites/startswithabang/2018/02/07/the-biggest-myth-in-quantum-physics/#262313e353fa.

196. Robertson, Bill. "How Do We Know Protons, Electrons, and Quarks Really Exist?" *NSTA WebNews Digest*, 9-27-05, https://www.nsta.org/publications/news/story.aspx?id=51054.
Also see: *PHYS.org*. "Electron Filmed for First Time Ever," 2-22-08, https://phys.org/news/2008-02-electron.html. This article says that the "motion of an election" has been filmed. However, the actual element of the electron apparently has yet to be "seen." This is similar to saying that we have never "seen" the wind—only the effects and motions of it. Yet, we know the wind is there because of those motions and effects.

197. Job 1:7, "Benson's Commentary," Biblehub.com, https://biblehub.com/commentaries/job/1-7.htm.

198. Job 1:7, "Barnes' Notes on the Bible," Biblehub.com, https://biblehub.com/commentaries/job/1-7.htm.

199. Job 1:7, "Gill's Exposition of the Bible," Biblehub.com, https://biblehub.com/commentaries/job/1-7.htm.

200. Matthew 24:29, "Meyer's New Testament Commentary," Biblehub.com, https://biblehub.com/commentaries/matthew/24-29.htm.

201. Rabbi Dov Ber Weisman. "Revealing the Hidden," TFDixie, accessed 3-18-19, http://www.tfdixie.com/parshat/tetzaveh/004.htm.

202. Isaiah 34:4. "Benson's Commentary," Biblehub.com, https://biblehub.com/commentaries/isaiah/34-4.htm.

203. Isaiah 34:4. "Barnes' Notes on the Bible," Biblehub.com, https://biblehub.com/commentaries/isaiah/34-4.htm.

204. Isaiah 34:4. "Jamieson-Fausset-Brown Bible Commentary," Biblehub.com, https://biblehub.com/commentaries/isaiah/34-4.htm.

205. Isaiah 34:4. "Matthew Poole's Commentary," Biblehub.com, https://biblehub.com/commentaries/isaiah/34-4.htm.

206. Isaiah 34:4. "Pulpit Commentary," Biblehub.com, https://biblehub.com/commentaries/isaiah/34-4.htm.

207. Revelation 6:12, "Forerunner Commentary," Bibletools.org, https://www.bibletools.org/index.cfm/fuseaction/Bible.show/sVerseID/30806/eVerseID/30811/version/nasb.

208. 2 Peter 3:10. "Jamieson-Fausset-Brown Bible Commentary," Biblehub.com, "https://biblehub.com/commentaries/2_peter/3-10.htm.

209. 2 Peter 3:10. "Vincent's Word Studies," Biblehub.com, "https://biblehub.com/commentaries/2_peter/3-10.htm.

210. 2 Peter 3:10. "Pulpit Commentary," Biblehub.com, "https://biblehub.com/commentaries/2_peter/3-10.htm.

211. 2 Peter 3:10, "Ellicott's Commentary for English Readers," Biblehub.com, https://biblehub.com/commentaries/2_peter/3-10.htm.

212. 2 Peter 3:10, "Meyer's New Testament Commentary," Biblehub.com, https://biblehub.com/commentaries/2_peter/3-10.htm.

213. 2 Peter 3:10, "Expositor's Greek Commentary," Biblehub.com, https://biblehub.com/commentaries/2_peter/3-10.htm.

214. Revelation 21:5, "McLaren's Expositions," Biblehub.com, https://biblehub.com/commentaries/revelation/21-5.htm.

215. Revelation 21:1, "Ellicott's Commentary for English Readers," Biblehub.com, https://biblehub.com/commentaries/revelation/21-1.htm.

216. Isaiah 65:17, "Cambridge Bible for Schools and Colleges," Biblehub.com, https://biblehub.com/commentaries/isaiah/65-17.htm.

217. Isaiah 65:17, "Barnes' Notes on the Bible," Biblehub.com, https://biblehub.com/commentaries/isaiah/65-17.htm.

218. Isaiah 65:17, "Jamieson-Fausset-Brown Bible Commentary," Biblehub. com, https://biblehub.com/commentaries/isaiah/65-17.htm.

219. Acts 8:39, "Meyer's N.T. Commentary," Biblehub.com, https://biblehub. com/commentaries/acts/8-39.htm.

220. Acts 8:39, "Expositor's Greek Testament," Biblehub.com, https://biblehub. com/commentaries/acts/8-39.htm.

221. Acts 8:39, "Jamieson-Fausset-Brown Bible Commentary," Biblehub.com, https://biblehub.com/commentaries/acts/8-39.htm.

222. Matthew 4:5, "The Pulpit Commentary," Biblehub.com, https://biblehub. com/commentaries/matthew/4-5.htm.

223. Matthew 4:5, "Gill's Exposition of the Entire Bible," Biblehub.com, https://biblehub.com/commentaries/matthew/4-5.htm.

224. Davis, John. "Strange behavior of quantum particles may indicate the existence of other parallel universes," *PHYS.org*, 6-3-15, https://phys.org/ news/2015-06-strange-behavior-quantum-particles-parallel.html.

225. Matthew 4:5, "Meyer's New Testament Commentary," Biblehub.com, https://biblehub.com/commentaries/matthew/4-5.htm.

226. Matthew 4:5, "Bengel's Gnomen," Biblehub.com, https://biblehub.com/ commentaries/matthew/4-5.htm.

227. Matthew 4:5, "Vincent's Word Studies," Biblehub.com, https://biblehub. com/commentaries/matthew/4-5.htm.

228. Matthew 4:5, "Ellicott's Commentary for English Readers," Biblehub. com, https://biblehub.com/commentaries/matthew/4-5.htm.

229. Revelation 21:10, "Ellicott's Commentary for English Readers," Biblehub. com, https://biblehub.com/commentaries/revelation/21-10.htm.

230. Revelation 21:10, "Gill's Exposition of the Entire Bible," Biblehub.com, https://biblehub.com/commentaries/revelation/21-10.htm.

231. Matthew 4:8, "Jamieson-Fausset-Brown Bible Commentary," https:// biblehub.com/commentaries/matthew/4-8.htm.

232. Matthew 4:8, "Gill's Exposition of the Entire Bible," https://biblehub. com/commentaries/matthew/4-8.htm.

233. Luke 4:1, "Pulpit Commentary," Biblehub.com, http://biblehub.com/ commentaries/Luke/4-1.htm.

234. Job 1:6. "Ellicott's Commentary for English Readers," Biblehub.com, https://biblehub.com/commentaries/job/1-6.htm.

235. 2 Corinthians 12:2, "Ellicott's Commentary for English Readers," Bible-hub.com, https://biblehub.com/commentaries/2_corinthians/12-2.htm.

236. 2 Corinthians 12:2, "Benson's Commentary," Biblehub.com, https://bible-hub.com/commentaries/2_corinthians/12-2.htm.

237. Bown, Willian. "Science: How a Photon Can Be in Two Places at Once," New Scientist, 3-30-1991, https://www.newscientist.com/article/mg12917624-000-science-how-a-photon-can-be-in-two-places-at-once.

238. "Atoms Can Be in Two Places at the Same Time," *PHYS.org*, January 20, 2015, https://phys.org/news/2015-01-atoms.html.

239. Matthew 4:3, "Whedon's Commentary on the Bible," Studylight.org, https://www.studylight.org/commentaries/whe/matthew-4.html.

240. Matthew 4:3. "Expository Notes of Dr. Thomas Constable," Studylight. org, https://www.studylight.org/commentaries/dcc/matthew-4.html.

241. Genesis 28:12. "Ellicott's Commentary for English Readers," Biblehub. com, https://biblehub.com/commentaries/genesis/28-12.htm.

242. *Benson's Commentary*

The veil, separating the most holy place from the holy, or the outermost part of the temple, is supposed to be taken away, for the prophet, to whom the whole is exhibited. https://biblehub.com/commentaries/isaiah/6-1.htm.

Pulpit Commentary

To see [the Temple's] veils drawn aside, and instead of the Shechinah enthroned on the cherubim, to behold the King of glory, enthroned on high...It is the heavenly palace of the King of kings into which the prophet's gaze is allowed to penetrate. https://biblehub.com/commentaries/isaiah/6-1.htm.

Ellicott's Commentary for English Readers

Suddenly [Isaiah] passes, as St. Paul afterwards passed, under the influence of like surroundings (Acts 22:17), into a state of ecstatic trance, and as though the veil of the Temple was withdrawn, he saw the vision of the glory of the Lord, as Moses (Exodus 24:10). https://biblehub.com/commentaries/isaiah/6-1.htm.

243. Genesis 3:15, "Benson's Commentary," Biblehub.com, http://biblehub.com/commentaries/genesis/3-15.htm.

244. Genesis 3:15, "Pulpit Commentary," Biblehub.com, http://biblehub.com/commentaries/genesis/3-15.htm.

245. Strauss, Dr. Lehman. "Bible Prophecy (The First Prophecy)," Bible.org, accessed November 4, 2017, https://bible.org/article/bible-prophecy.

246. Dr. Deffinbaugh, Bob. "The Anticipation of Israel's Messiah," Bible.org, June 22, 2004, https://bible.org/article/anticipation-israels-messiah#P24_5301.

247. Dr. Stewart, Don. "What Does Genesis 3:15 Mean?" Blue Letter Bible—Commentary, accessed November 29, 2017, https://www.blueletterbible.org/faq/don_stewart/don_stewart_756.cfm.

248. Revelation 12:2, "Cambridge Bible for Schools and Colleges," Biblehub.com, https://biblehub.com/commentaries/revelation/12-2.htm. See also: Revelation 12:3, "Cambridge Bible for Schools and Colleges," Biblehub.com, https://biblehub.com/commentaries/revelation/12-2.htm.

249. Revelation 12:3, "Ellicott's Commentary for English Readers," Biblehub.com, https://biblehub.com/commentaries/revelation/12-3.htm.

250. Revelation 12:3, "Meyer's New Testament Commentary," Biblehub.com, https://biblehub.com/commentaries/revelation/12-3.htm.

251. **The prince of the power of the air** (Ephesians 2:2)—This phrased, used by the Apostle Paul, also speaks of an interdimensional realm in which Satan operates—thus exercising his diabolical control over earthly matters. Following are several classical commentary attestations of this truth:
Expositor's Greek Commentary
Describes these demonic powers as between earth and heaven, in that "supra-terrestrial but subcelestial region which seems to be, if not the abode, yet the haunt of evil spirits". Thus the prince of evil is described as the Lord-Paramount over all the demonic powers; and these demonic powers, as having their seat in the air, are distinguished from the angels whose abode is in heaven.
Barnes' Notes on the Bible
The Bible teaches tha …they must have "some" locality—some part of the universe where they dwell. Who can tell what may be in the invisible world, and what spirits may be permitted to fill up the vast space that now composes the universe? https://biblehub.com/commentaries/ephesians/2-2.htm.

252. See Dr. Walker's Bio here (Who Is Eric Walker?), Igniting a Nation Ministries and TV, accessed 11-6-18, https://ianbn.com.

253. Rabbi Eric Walker has read and approved the following words attributed to him.

254. See Revelation 12 for the biblical attestation of this eternal truth. "The

called out ones" is the English translation of the Greek word *ekklesia*. It is found in the New Testament 114 times. The use of this Greek word in the New Testament is translated as "the church."

For further study on this subject, see this article: https://www.christiancourier.com/articles/1500-what-is-the-meaning-of-ekklesia.

255. *Matthew Poole's Commentary* on Genesis 22:14: This was but an earnest of further and greater blessings to be expected in this place, where the temple was built, and the Lord Christ was manifested in the flesh.

Gill's Exposition of the Entire Bible on Genesis 22:14:

This may also refer to the presence of God in this mount, when the temple should be built on it, as it was, 2 Chronicles 3:1; and to the appearance of Christ in it, who was often seen here: some choose to render the words, "in the mount the Lord shall be seen" (n); "God manifest in the flesh", 1 Timothy 3:16, the "Immanuel", "God with us", Matthew 1:23, who was frequently in the temple built on this mount, and often seen there in his state of humiliation on earth. https://biblehub.com/commentaries/genesis/22-14.htm.

256. Genesis 22:17, "Barnes' Notes on the Bible," Biblehub.com, https://biblehub.com/commentaries/genesis/22-17.htm.

257. Genesis 22, "Gill's Exposition of the Entire Bible," Biblehub.com, https://biblehub.com/commentaries/gill/genesis/22.htm.

258. Exodus 1:16, "Matthew Henry's Concise Commentary," Biblehub.com, https://biblehub.com/commentaries/exodus/1-16.htm.

259. Revelation 12:4, "Pulpit Commentary," Biblehub.com, https://biblehub.com/commentaries/revelation/12-4.htm.

260. Revelation 12:4, "Ellicott's Commentary for English Readers," Biblehub.com, https://biblehub.com/commentaries/revelation/12-4.htm.

261. Revelation 12:4, "Jamieson-Fausset-Brown Bible Commentary," Biblehub.com, https://biblehub.com/commentaries/revelation/12-4.htm.

262. Revelation 12:4, "Vincent's Word Studies," Biblehub.com, https://biblehub.com/commentaries/revelation/12-4.htm.

263. Although I will, in this chapter, present plenty of scholarly evidence that supports this biblical claim, I would also refer the reader to my book, *Gods of Ground Zero*, wherein a lengthy scholarly case is solidly made to support this assertion.

264. **Paradise.** Thayer' Greek Lexicon says this word (NT: 3857 paradeisos) means: "Universally, a garden, pleasure-ground; grove, park…that delightful region, '**the garden of Eden,' in which our first parents dwelt before the fall.**"
     See: The Hebrew Bible. "Gan Eden," accessed November 12, 2018, https://theisraelbible.com/glossary/gan-eden.
     "The Garden of Eden (Hebrew *Gan Eden*) or often paradise, is the biblical "garden of God", described most notably in the Book of Genesis chapters 2 and 3, and also in the Book of Ezekiel."
     See: Eden, "Strong's Concordance," Biblehub.com, http://biblehub.com/strongs/hebrew/5730.htm.
     See: Thayer's Greek Lexicon, http://biblehub.com/greek/3857.htm.
     See: Gill's Exposition of the Entire Bible, http://biblehub.com/commentaries/2_corinthians/12-4.htm.
265. 2 Corinthians 2:4, "Geneva Study Bible," Biblehumb.com, https://biblehub.com/commentaries/2_corinthians/12-4.htm.
266. Revelation 12:2, "Cambridge Bible for Schools and Colleges," Biblehub.com, https://biblehub.com/commentaries/revelation/21-2.htm.
267. Revelation 12:2, "Barnes' Notes on the Bible," Biblehub.com, https://biblehub.com/commentaries/revelation/21-2.htm.
268. Revelation 21:2, "Commentary Critical and Explanatory on the Whole Bible," Bible Study Tools, https://www.biblestudytools.com/commentaries/jamieson-fausset-brown/revelation/revelation-21.html.
269. Dr. Krell, Keith. "Party in Paradise" (Genesis 2:4-25)," Bible.org, accessed December 7, 2017, https://bible.org/seriespage/5-party-paradise-genesis-24-25#P36_11331.
270. Berkowitz, Adam Eliyahu. "Has the Location of the Garden of Eden Been Found?" Breaking Israel News, September 21, 2016, https://www.breakingisraelnews.com/76029/prophetic-rebirth-dead-sea-reveal-garden-eden/#63wcA3e9kqg0prA3.99.
271. Genesis 2:8, "Benson's Commentary," Biblehub.com, http://biblehub.com/commentaries/genesis/2-8.htm.
272. Hosea 6:7, "Pulpit Commentary," Biblehub.com, http://biblehub.com/commentaries/hosea/6-7.htm.
273. The Israel Bible, "Gan Eden," accessed December 8, 2018, https://theisraelbible.com/glossary/gan-eden/#7QIdZLlMJxLCuFrf.99.

274. CMJ—USA, "Sibley," accessed Dec. 23, 2017, http://www.cmj-usa.org/content/sibley.

275. Wellman, Jared. "WELLMAN: Where on Earth was the Garden of Eden?" OA Online, 1-3-15, http://www.oaoa.com/people/religion/article_7d948064-935d-11e4-90c2-4b09cc36f260.html.

276. Baker, Eric W. "The Eschatological Role of the Jerusalem Temple: An Examination of Jewish Writings Dating from 586 BCE to 70 CE," (Andrews University -Digital Commons, 2014): 33-36, https://digitalcommons.andrews.edu/cgi/viewcontent.cgi?article=1012&context=dissertations.

277. Barker, Margaret. "The Gate of Heaven: The History and Symbolism of the Temple in Jerusalem," (London: SPCK, 1991): 57, 63–64.

278. Singer, Bethany. "Holy Ground: The Importance of Jerusalem for Jews," IMB.org, 8-3-18, https://www.imb.org/2018/08/03/holy-ground-the-importance-of-jerusalem-for-jews.

279. Keidar, Doron. "Jewish history on the Temple Mount: Did the Jews Abandon it?" Cry for Zion, 3-30-2015, http://cryforzion.com/jewish-history-on-the-temple-mount-did-jews-abandon-it/#_ftn7.

280. Israeli, Raphael. "War, Peace and Terror in the Middle East." (Psychology Press. 2003): 21. Accessed Nov. 21, 2018. "During the process of the Islamization of Jerusalem, a mosque was built on the site…. The Islamicized Mount became the destination of Muhammad's isra'…", https://books.google.com/books?id=I4B11CFdP-oC&pg=PA21#v=onepage&q&f=false.

281. Vilnay, Zev. "The Legends of Jerusalem," Philadelphia Copyright © 1973 by The Jewish Publication Society of America, accessed April 12, 2019, https://archive.org/stream/VILNAYLegendsOfJerusalem/VILNAY_Legends-Of-Jerusalem_djvu.txt.
See also: Dolphin, Lambert. "Early history of the Temple Mount," accessed December 12, 2017, http://www.templemount.org/earlytm.html

282. Strong's 3857, "paradise" (Outline of Biblical Usage), https://www.blueletterbible.org/lang/lexicon/lexicon.cfm?t=kjv&strongs=g3857.

283. Dywer, Colin. "U.N. Votes Overwhelmingly to Condemn U.S. Decision on Jerusalem," NPR, 12-21-17, https://www.npr.org/sections/thetwo-way/2017/12/21/572565091/u-n-votes-overwhelmingly-to-condemn-trumps-jerusalem-decision.

284. Mateus Kadesh. "Fox News Host Under Fire after Controversial

Segment," IPatriot.com, March 13, 2019, https://ipatriot.com/fox-news-host-under-fire-after-controversial-segment-watch-it-here.

285. Bible History Online. "Herod's Cruelty," Accessed Nov. 2, 2018, https://www.bible-history.com/herod_the_great/HERODhis_Cruelty.htm.

286. Matthew 2:16, "Expositor's Greek Testament," Biblehub.com, https://biblehub.com/commentaries/matthew/2-16.htm.

287. Revelation 12:4. "Ellicott's Commentary for English Readers," Biblehub.com, https://biblehub.com/commentaries/revelation/12-4.htm.

288. Revelation 12:4. "Cambridge Bible for Schools and Colleges," Biblehub.com, https://biblehub.com/commentaries/revelation/12-4.htm.

289. Revelation 12:4. "Gill's Commentary on the Entire Bible," Biblehub.com, https://biblehub.com/commentaries/revelation/12-4.htm.

290. Revelation 12:4. "Barnes' Notes on the Bible," Biblehub.com, https://biblehub.com/commentaries/revelation/12-4.htm.

291. Vermaat, Robert. "The Draco, The Late Roman Military Standard," Fectio.org, accessed November 2, 2018, http://www.fectio.org.uk/articles/draco.htm.
Also see: Yust, Walter (1953). Encyclopædia Britannica: A New Survey of Universal Knowledge: Encyclopædia Britannica. P. 570.

292. Roman Military Standards. "The Draco," Accessed November 2, 2018, https://romanlegionmilitarystandards.weebly.com/the-draco.html.

293. The Ghost Dance of 1890 was a religious movement incorporated into numerous Native American belief systems. According to the teachings of the Northern Paiute spiritual leader Wovoka (renamed Jack Wilson), proper practice of the dance would reunite the living with spirits of the dead, bring the spirits to fight on their behalf, make the white colonists leave, and bring peace, prosperity, and unity to Native American peoples throughout the region—as well as the belief that there would eventually be a fundamental movement in society, after which all things will be changed. See: Wikipedia, "Ghost Dance," (reference by reliable historical sources) accessed February 2, 2019, https://en.wikipedia.org/wiki/Ghost_Dance.

294. Revelation 12, "Jamieson-Fausset-Brown Bible Commentary," Biblehub.com, https://biblehub.com/commentaries/jfb/revelation/12.htm.

295. Kumar, Anugrah, "Christian Persecution Hits All-Time High Worldwide: Report," Christian Post, 10-14-17, https://www.christianpost.com/news/christian-persecution-all-time-high-worldwide-report.html.

296. "Christian Persecution at an All Time High," Orthodox Christian Network, 2-14-18, http://myocn.net/christian-persecution-at-an-all-time-high.

297. Mora, Edwin. "Report: Half a Billion Christians Facing Global Persecution," Breitbart, 11-24-18, https://www.breitbart.com/national-security/2018/11/24/report-half-billion-christians-facing-global-persecution.

298. Lindy Lowry. "11 Christians Killed Every Day for Their Decision to Follow Jesus," Open Doors USA, March 13, 2019, https://www.open-doorsusa.org/christian-persecution/stories/11-christians-killed-every-day-for-their-decision-to-follow-jesus/?fbclid=IwAR1IJi2IdDNeWbWM77HpM9Ye1Cl5BGDaPP2AkF48ikQ9y-0MF7wuROFtLqM.

299. Mora, Edwin. "Report: 245 Million Christians Facing 'Extreme' Persecution Worldwide," Breitbart, 1-16-19, https://www.breitbart.com/national-security/2019/01/16/report-245-million-christians-facing-extreme-persecution-worldwide.

300. Williams, Thomas D. Ph.D. "Abortion Leading Cause of Death in 2018 with 41 Million Killed," Breitbart.com, Dec. 31, 2018, https://www.breitbart.com/health/2018/12/31/abortion-leading-cause-of-death-in-2018-with-41-million-killed.

301. For confirmation of the huge number of globally unreported abortions, **See:**
1. Astbury-Ward E, Parry O and Carnwell R, Stigma, abortion, and disclosure—findings from a qualitative study, Journal of Sexual Medicine, 2012, 9(12):3137–3147, http://dx.doi.org/10.1111/j.1743-6109.2011.02604.x.
2. Jones RK and Kost K, Underreporting of induced and spontaneous abortion in the United States: an analysis of the 2002 National Survey of Family Growth, Studies in Family Planning, 2007, 38(3):187–197.
3. Susheela Singh,Lisa Remez,Gilda Sedgh,Lorraine KwokandTsuyoshi Onda. "Abortion Worldwide 2017: Uneven Progress and Unequal Access," Guttmacher Institute, March 2018 Report, https://www.guttmacher.org/report/abortion-worldwide-2017.

302. See the following articles of attestation:
1. Stevelos, JoAnn. "Child Sexual Abuse Declared an Epidemic: World Health Organization publishes CSA guidelines," Psychology Today, 11-29-17, https://www.psychologytoday.com/us/blog/children-the-table/201711/child-sexual-abuse-declared-epidemic.
2. John, Tara, "FBI: Child Abuse 'Almost at an Epidemic Level' in U.S."

Time, 7-20-15, http://time.com/3978236/american-children-sold-sex.
3. Siddharth Chatterjee. "The Global Epidemic of Violence Against Children," Huffington Post, 4-16-17, https://www.huffpost.com/entry/the-global-epidemic-of-violence-against-children_b_58e7ca87e4b06f8c18beeb55.

303. I address this specific truth in several chapters that follow.

304. Acosta, Judith. "Death Fear: Why Do We Dread Being Dead?" Huffington Post, 02/23/2011 | Updated January 14, 2012, https://www.huffpost.com/entry/death-fear_b_825726.

305. Acosta, Judith. "Judith Acosta, LISW, CCH," Huffington Post, accessed January 12, 2019, https://www.huffingtonpost.com/author/verbal-firstaid-348. Also see: https://www.classicalhomeopathynewmexico.com.

306. Ibid. Acosta, Judith. "Death Fear: Why Do We Dread Being Dead?"

307. Acosta, Judith. "Why Is Death So Shocking?" The Huffington Post, 06/01/2012 | Updated August 1, 2012, https://www.huffpost.com/entry/pet-death_b_1559033?ec_carp=1008136760964720286.

308. Specktor, Brandon. "What Happens in Hours before Death? Many Don't Know," Fox News, 5-9-19, https://www.foxnews.com/health/what-happens-before-death.

309. "**Annihilationism** (also known as extinctionism or destructionism) is a belief that after the final judgment some human beings and all fallen angels (all of the damned) will be totally destroyed so as to not exist, or that their consciousness will be extinguished, rather than suffer everlasting torment in hell (often synonymized with the lake of fire)." https://en.wikipedia.org/wiki/Annihilationism.
See: James Packer on "Why Annihilationism is Wrong." https://www.thegospelcoalition.org/article/j.i.-packer-on-why-annihilationism-is-wrong.

310. **This is a view commonly referred to as "soul sleep."** There are several denominations that teach the view that the departed soul "sleeps" in the grave until a future date when the "resurrection" of the dead takes place. To be fair, there are a selection of New Testament passages that might appear to support his notion—but only if taken out of context in relation to the whole of the biblical teaching in the matter. Even though this chapter will wind up refuting that false teaching, it is not the purpose of this chapter to do a lengthy, verse-by-verse study of the topic.

311. The question has long been explored, "Where was Lazarus for those four days that his body was in the tomb?" The question is asked mainly for

two reasons: First, because Jesus said that Lazarus was only "asleep." (John 11:11). And second, because many cannot fathom how "cruel" it would have been of Jesus to have beckoned Lazarus back to this fallen earth, once having tasted of paradise—if that's where he truly was existing in a conscious state.

The term "asleep" as it refers to the death of a believer does not mean a literal, unconscious state of sleeping—in the natural sense. It is a euphemism for "death." It is the Christian understanding that for the death of a believer, the event is nothing more than "falling asleep" in your bed and waking up the next morning to a new day of life. In fact, in that same passage, in John 11:13–14, Jesus plainly tells His confused disciples that Lazarus is "dead." Jesus says the same thing of a little girl in Matthew 9:24 and Luke 8:55. Jesus clearly equates death for the believer with the analogy of "sleep."

Matthew Poole's Commentary

> There is such an analogy between death and sleep, that there is nothing more ordinary than to express death by sleep in Scripture, Deu 31:16 2 Samuel 7:12 1 Kings 1:21 2 Kings 20:21 Job 7:21 14:12 Daniel 12:2, and in a multitude of other texts, both in the Old Testament and in the New; so as it was evident **our Saviour meant he was dead, which he knew *as he was with God.*** (Emphasis added) https://biblehub.com/commentaries/john/11-11.htm.

Because Lazarus had tasted of the glory that was to come, he would serve as a powerful witness of Jesus' continual claims that there truly was life on the "other side" in "another realm" of physical reality. For Lazarus, this would have been no more "cruel" than it is for our Lord to call a mission-minded soul into ministry among the mud huts of Africa for the rest of their earthly life. The true servant of God would accept this task with gladness. And, so did Lazarus.

312. John 11:25, "Ellicott's Commentary for the English Reader," Biblehub. com, https://biblehub.com/commentaries/john/11-25.htm.
313. John 11:25, "Pulpit Commentary," Biblehub.com, https://biblehub.com/commentaries/john/11-25.htm.
314. John 11:25, "Meyer's New Testament Commentary," Biblehub.com, https://biblehub.com/commentaries/meyer/john/11.htm.

315. John 14. "Expositor's Greek Testament," Biblehub.com, https://biblehub.com/commentaries/egt/john/14.htm.
316. John 14. "Pulpit Commentary," Biblehub.com, https://biblehub.com/commentaries/pulpit/john/14.htm.
317. John 14. "Vincent's Word Studies," Biblehub.com, https://biblehub.com/commentaries/vws/john/14.htm.
318. John 14. "Jamieson-Fausset-Brown Bible Commentary," Biblehub.com, https://biblehub.com/commentaries/jfb/john/14.htm.
319. **Today you will be with me in paradise.** Those who are of the theological persuasion known as "soul sleep" have a tough time dealing with Jesus' promise given to the thief on the cross. The "soul sleep" teaching stands on the argument that Jesus' words really meant, "I tell you the truth today—you *will be* with me (one day in the future)—in paradise." They place the comma in Jesus' declaration after the word "today" rather than after the word "truth." Since most of the Greek text found in the New Testament does not contain punctuation marks, they feel justified in doing so. However, nowhere else in Scripture does Jesus speak like this—adding the word "today" after declaring "I tell you the truth." Not only does He never speak this way before going to the cross, but by doing so at the cross, it actually puts the meaning in Jesus' words that perhaps in times past Jesus has actually not been so truthful, but on *this* day, He finally speaks the truth. Of course, this idea, on its face, is an absurd notion. Of more than two dozen renowned and scholarly English translations of the Bible, every single one translates this promise of Jesus with the proper contextual punctuation, as indicating that *on this very day* you will be with me in paradise. (SEE: https://biblehub.com/luke/23-43.htm.).
320. **Paradise—*Gan Eden,* Bosom of Abraham:**
    During the time of Jesus—and to this very day—the Jews understood that death meant the soul departing to one of two places: The Hebrew designations are *Gehenna,* and *Gan Eden,* also known as "the Garden of Eden." Gehenna was the place of the "separated" or "damned"—the unbelievers. *Gan Eden* was the place of bliss, reserved for believers in Yahweh. The Talmud and Midrashim are also replete with these descriptions and their theological ramifications.
    Meyer's New Testament Commentary
        Hades corresponds to the Hebrew Sheol, which in the LXX. is

translated by ϛηδᾴ, and hence denotes the whole subterranean place of abode of departed souls until the resurrection, **divided into paradise (Luke 23:43) for the pious, and Gehenna for the godless.** https://biblehub.com/commentaries/luke/16-22.htm.

We derive the English word "paradise" in the various English translations of the New Testament from the Greek word παράδεισος. This word is translated into English as "paradise." This very same Greek word is used in the Septuagint (LXX) to translate the Hebrew phrase גַּן־עֵדֶן (gan eden) in the Tanakh. paradise is equivalent to "the Garden of Eden."

Thayer's Greek Lexicon:

Paradise—Universally, a garden, pleasure-ground; grove, park...thus, for that delightful region, **"the garden of Eden," in which our first parents dwelt** before the fall: **Genesis 2:8ff; 3:1ff.** https://biblehub.com/greek/3857.htm.

Bosom of Abraham (Thayer's)—In Abraham's bosom, to designate bliss in paradise. To obtain the seat next to Abraham, i.e., to be partaker of the same blessedness as Abraham in paradise, Luke 16:23. https://biblehub.com/str/greek/2859.htm.

321. Luke 23:43, "Benson's Commentary," Biblehub.com, https://biblehub.com/commentaries/luke/23-43.htm.

322. Luke 23:43, "Gill's Exposition of the Scripture," Biblehub.com, https://biblehub.com/commentaries/luke/23-43.htm.

323. Luke 23:43, "Expositor's Greek Testament," Biblehub.com, https://biblehub.com/commentaries/luke/23-43.htm.

324. Luke 23:43, "Jamieson-Fausset-Brown Bible Commentary," Biblehub.com, https://biblehub.com/commentaries/luke/23-43.htm.

325. Luke 23:43, "Parallel Bible Translations," Biblehub.com, https://biblehub.com/luke/23-43.htm.

326. Paul speaks of himself here—as practically every single scholarly commentary agrees. The terms "third heaven" and "paradise" are synonymous.

Gill's Exposition of the Entire Bible

The third heaven, the seat of the divine Majesty, and the residence of the holy angels; where the souls of departed saints go immediately upon their dissolution; and the bodies and souls of those who have been translated, caught up, and raised already, are; and where the glorified body of Christ is and will be, until his second coming. https://biblehub.com/commentaries/2_corinthians/12-2.htm.

Expositor's Green New Testament
Paradise is explicitly located in the "third heaven," which is the view recognized here by St. Paul. https://biblehub.com/commentaries/2_corinthians/12-2.htm.

327. 2 Corinthians 2:4, "Geneva Study Bible," Biblehumb.com, https://biblehub.com/commentaries/2_corinthians/12-4.htm.

328. 2 Corinthians 12:4, "Cambridge Bible for Schools and Colleges," Biblehub.com, https://biblehub.com/commentaries/2_corinthians/12-4.htm.

329. 2 Corinthians 12:4, "Barnes' Notes on the Bible," Biblehub.com, https://biblehub.com/commentaries/2_corinthians/12-4.htm.

330. Philippians 1:23, "Barnes' Notes on the Bible," Biblehub.com, https://biblehub.com/commentaries/philippians/1-23.htm.

331. Philippians 1:23, "Jamieson-Fausset-Brown Bible Commentary," Biblehub.com, https://biblehub.com/commentaries/philippians/1-23.htm.

332. Philippians 1:23, "Bengel's Gnomen," Biblehub.com, https://biblehub.com/commentaries/philippians/1-23.htm.

333. 2 Timothy 4:8. "Meyer's New Testament Commentary," Biblehub.com, https://biblehub.com/commentaries/2_timothy/4-8.htm.

334. 2 Timothy 4:6, "Expositor's Greek Commentary," Biblehub.com, https://biblehub.com/commentaries/2_timothy/4-6.htm.

335. 2 Timothy 4:6, "Gill's Exposition of the Entire Bible," Biblehub.com, https://biblehub.com/commentaries/2_timothy/4-6.htm.

336. **Subterranean**—Meyers uses that word here to describe the location of the "other world." The word can denote the literal—under the surface of the earth. But it also has the figurative meaning of: "existing or operating out of sight or secretly; hidden or secret." In context, this appears to be Meyers' use of the word. See Dictionary.com, Subterranean. https://www.dictionary.com/browse/subterranean.

337. Luke 16:22, "Meyer's New Testament Commentary," Biblehub.com, https://biblehub.com/commentaries/luke/16-22.htm.

338. Luke 16:22, "Expositor's Greek Testament," Biblehub.com, https://biblehub.com/commentaries/luke/16-22.htm.

339. Hades. NT #86. "Helps Word Studies," Biblehub.com, https://biblehub.com/greek/86.htm.

340. Gehenna. NT. 1067. "Concordances and Dictionaries" Biblehub.com, https://biblehub.com/greek/1067.htm.
341. For additional scholarly study of these truths see these excellent articles: a.) W. Edward Bedore, Th.D. "Hell, Sheol, Hades, Paradise, and the Grave," Accessed Dec. 31, 2018, https://www.bereanbiblesociety.org/hell-sheol-hades-paradise-and-the-grave.
b.) Got Questions? "What is the Difference between Sheol, Hades, Hell, the Lake of Fire, Paradise, and Abraham's bosom?" Accessed Dec. 21, 2018, https://www.gotquestions.org/sheol-hades-hell.html.
342. Basanos. NT #931. "Strong's Concordance," Biblehub.com, https://biblehub.com/greek/931.htm.
343. Basanos. Etymology. See: https://en.wikipedia.org/wiki/Touchstone_(assaying_tool). https://en.wikipedia.org/wiki/Basanite.
344. Basanizó. NT #928 (verb), "Concordances," Biblehub.com, https://biblehub.com/greek/928.htm.
345. Luke 16:24, "Pulpit Commentary," Biblehub.com, https://biblehub.com/commentaries/luke/16-24.htm.
346. Mark 9:48, "Barnes' Notes on the Bible," Biblehub.com, https://biblehub.com/commentaries/mark/9-48.htm.
347. Luke 16:23, "Ellicott's Commentary for English Readers," Biblehub.com, https://biblehub.com/commentaries/luke/16-24.htm.
348. Luke 16:23, "Pulpit Commentary," Biblehub.com, https://biblehub.com/commentaries/luke/16-24.htm.
349. Luke 16:24, "Gill's Exposition of the Entire Scripture," Biblehub.com, https://biblehub.com/commentaries/luke/16-24.htm.
350. Luke 15:24, "Whedon's Commentary on the Bible," Studylight.org, https://www.studylight.org/commentaries/whe/luke-16.html.
351. Mark 9:48, "Barnes' Notes on the Bible," Biblehub.com, https://biblehub.com/commentaries/mark/9-48.htm.
352. For an example of this fact, see the commentary entries at: https://biblehub.com/commentaries/luke/16-26.htm.
353. Luke 16:26, "Barnes' Notes on the Bible," Biblehub.com, https://biblehub.com/commentaries/luke/16-26.htm.
354. Luke 16:26, "Ellicott's Commentary for English Readers," Biblehub.com, https://biblehub.com/commentaries/luke/16-26.htm.
355. Christopher M. Date and Gregory G. Stump. "Rethinking Hell: Read-

ings in Evangelical Conditionalism," Lutterworth Press (November 27, 2014):31.

356. Genesis 3:15, "Jamieson-Fausset-Brown Bible Commentary," Biblehub. com, https://biblehub.com/commentaries/genesis/3-15.htm.

357. Genesis 3:15, "Richard T. Ritenbaugh—Forerunner Commentary," Bible-tools.org, https://www.bibletools.org/index.cfm/fuseaction/Bible.show/sVerseID/71/eVerseID/71/version/nasb.

358. Dr. Volkmer, Jeffrey. "Jesus in Genesis 3:15?" Biola University, 6-20-17, https://www.biola.edu/blogs/good-book-blog/2017/jesus-in-genesis-3-15.

359. Genesis 3, "Lange's Commentary on the Holy Scriptures: Critical, Doctrinal, and Homiletical," Studylight.org, https://www.studylight.org/commentaries/lcc/genesis-3.html.

360. Genesis 3, "Keil & Delitzsch Commentary on the Old Testament," Studylight.org, https://www.studylight.org/commentaries/kdo/genesis-3.html.

361. Dr. Lehman Strauss, Professor of Old Testament. "The Importance of Bible Prophecy" (The First Prophecy—Compound Prophecy), Bible.org, https://bible.org/article/bible-prophecy.

362. *Mashal*, Strong's OT # 4912. Biblehub.com, http://biblehub.com/hebrew/4912.htm.

363. Isaiah 14, "The Bible Exposition Commentary: Old Testament," (from The Bible Exposition Commentary: Old Testament © 2001-2004 by Warren W. Wiersbe. All rights reserved.), accessed January 19, 2019, https://books.google.com/books?id=Hg444gp41loC&pg=PA24&lpg=PA24&dq=The+Bible+Exposition+Commentary+This+highest+of+God%27s+angels+tried+to+usurp&source=bl&ots=Rvy9Q4Zhpx&sig=q4TRkgV4yB-bKac0gB0aZFR4EOg&hl=en&sa=X&ved=0ahUKEwjU4cii9vHSAhVBC2MKHYglAgoQ6AEIGjAA#v=onepage&q=The%20Bible%20Exposition%20Commentary%20This%20highest%20of%20God's%20angels%20tried%20to%20usurp&f=false.

364. Delitzsch, Franz, "Biblical Commentary on the Prophecies of Isaiah," accessed January 19, 2019, [Edinburgh: T. & T. Clark, 1875], 1:312.

365. Dr. Guzik, David. "Genesis 3—Man's Temptation and Fall," Enduring Word, https://enduringword.com/bible-commentary/genesis-3.

366. Isaiah 14:15, "Benson's Commentary," Biblehub.com, https://biblehub.com/commentaries/isaiah/14-15.htm.

367. Isaiah 14:15, "Keil and Delitzsch Biblical Commentary on the Old

CARL GALLUPS

Testament," Biblehub.com, https://biblehub.com/commentaries/
isaiah/14-15.htm.
368. Isaiah 14:15, "Barnes' Notes on the Bible," Biblehub.com, https://bible-
hub.com/commentaries/isaiah/14-15.htm.
369. Revelation 20:10, "Barnes' Notes on the Bible," Biblehub.com, https://
biblehub.com/commentaries/revelation/20-10.htm.
370. Revelation 20:10, "Jamieson-Fausset-Brown Bible Commentary," Bible-
hub.com, https://biblehub.com/commentaries/revelation/20-10.htm.
371. Revelation 20:3, "Jamieson-Fausset-Brown Bible Commentary," Biblehub.
com, https://biblehub.com/commentaries/revelation/20-3.htm.
372. Dr. Guzik, David. "Genesis 3—Man's Temptation and Fall," Enduring
Word, https://enduringword.com/bible-commentary/genesis-3.
373. Garland, Tony, "Q85: Is Satan in Isaiah and Ezekiel?" accessed March 11,
2017,http://www.spiritandtruth.org/questions/85.htm?x=x.
374. Ezekiel 28:13, "Verse by Verse Bible Commentary," Expository Notes of
Dr. Thomas Constable" accessed March 11, 2017, https://www.studylight.
org/commentary/ezekiel/28-13.html.
375. Ezekiel 28:13, "Verse by Verse Bible Commentary," E.W. Bullinger's Companion Bible Notes, accessed March 11, 2017, https://www.studylight.org/
commentary/ezekiel/28-13.html.
376. Robert Jamieson, A. R. Fausset and David Brown, "Commentary Critical
and Explanatory on the Whole Bible," (Ezekiel 28), 1871, http://www.
biblestudytools.com/commentaries/jamieson-fausset-brown/ezekiel/eze-
kiel-28.html.
377. Ezekiel 28:18, "Coffman's Commentaries on the Bible," Studylight.org,
https://www.studylight.org/commentary/ezekiel/28-18.html.
378. Ezekiel 31:8, "Jamieson-Fausset-Brown Bible Commentary," Biblehub.
com, http://biblehub.com/commentaries/ezekiel/31-8.htm.
379. Ezekiel 31:8, "Pulpit Commentary," Biblehub.com, http://biblehub.com/
commentaries/ezekiel/31-8.htm.
380. Jewish Virtual Library, "Encyclopedia Judaica: The Garden of Eden,"
accessed December 3, 2017, http://www.jewishvirtuallibrary.org/
garden-of-eden.
381. I engage in a several-chapter study of Ezekiel 31 in my previous book in
this series: *The God's of Ground Zero: The Truth of Eden's Iniquity*. More
than simply showing how Ezekiel 31 is directly linked to Ezekiel 28 and
Isaiah 14, I also show how it is meant to be a revelation concerning the

432

Garden of Eden itself—in several startling ways. I urge the reader to get that book and undertake that study as well.

382. Dr. Ritenbaugh, John W. "Bible Verses about Egypt as a Type of Sin," (Forerunner Commentary), Bibletools.org, https://www.bibletools.org/index.cfm/fuseaction/Topical.show/RTD/cgg/ID/16607/Egypt-as-Type-Sin.htm.

383. Revelation 1:18, "Ellicott's Commentary for the English Reader," Biblehub.com, https://biblehub.com/commentaries/revelation/1-18.htm.

384. Revelation 1:18, "Barnes' Notes on the Bible," Biblehub.com, https://biblehub.com/commentaries/revelation/1-18.htm.

385. Revelation 1:18, "Pulpit Commentary," Biblehub.com, https://biblehub.com/commentaries/revelation/1-18.htm.

386. 2 Thessalonians 1:9, "Ellicott's Commentary for English Readers," Biblehub.com, https://biblehub.com/commentaries/2_thessalonians/1-9.htm.

387. 2 Thessalonians 1:9, "Benson's Commentary," Biblehub.com, https://biblehub.com/commentaries/2_thessalonians/1-9.htm.

388. 2 Thessalonians 1:9, "Cambridge Bible for Schools and Colleges," Biblehub.com, https://biblehub.com/commentaries/2_thessalonians/1-9.htm.

389. 2 Thessalonians 1:9, "Barnes' Notes on the Bible," Biblehub.com, https://biblehub.com/commentaries/2_thessalonians/1-9.htm.

390. 2 Thessalonians 1:9, "Matthew Poole's Commentary," Biblehub.com, https://biblehub.com/commentaries/2_thessalonians/1-9.htm.

391. Aggelos. N.T. #32. "HELPS Word-studies," Biblehub.com, https://biblehub.com/greek/32.htm.

392. Matthew 25:41, "Pulpit Commentary," Biblehub.com, https://biblehub.com/commentaries/matthew/25-41.htm.

393. Matthew 25:41, "Benson's Commentary," Biblehub.com, https://biblehub.com/commentaries/matthew/25-41.htm.

394. Matthew 25:41, "Barnes' Notes on the Bible," Biblehub.com, https://biblehub.com/commentaries/matthew/25-41.htm.

395. Matthew 25:41, "Meyer's New Testament Commentary," Biblehub.com, https://biblehub.com/commentaries/matthew/25-41.htm.

396. Villines, Zawn. "Hematidrosis (sweating blood): Causes and treatments," Medical News Today, 8-26-17, https://www.medicalnewstoday.com/articles/319110.php.
Also see: Web MD. "What Is Hematidrosis?" Accessed January 12, 2019, https://www.webmd.com/a-to-z-guides/hematidrosis-hematohidrosis#1.

397. The Scriptures do not directly identify that Satan was literally in the Garden of Gethsemane. However, it has long been held, because of indirect scriptural evidence, that Satan did show up there—gin person. We know he was there when Judas showed up with the Temple guard. Jesus had already declared at the Last Supper that Satan had entered Judas. For a scholarly example of this assumption see: Chambers, Oswald, "His Agony and Our Access," Accessed January 24, 2019, https://utmost.org/his-agony-and-our-access.
398. Luke 22:3.
399. Dr. Stewart, Don, "Did Jesus Receive a Fair Trial?" Blue Letter Bible, https://www.blueletterbible.org/faq/don_stewart/don_stewart_250.cfm.
400. Isaiah 53:7.
401. John 10:18.
402. Revelation 13:8.
403. *Pulpit Commentary*
    This is a strong affirmative asseveration, and on Christ's lips carries with it the full meaning of the words used by Caiaphas, "I am the Messiah, the Son of the Blessed One, God of God, of one substance with the Father." From this moment, beginning from now, from my Passion, my triumph and my reign are inaugurated.... Shall ye shall see the events about to be consummated, the preludes of the great assize, and the coming of Messiah's kingdom. This was the plainest and most specific declaration of his real nature, power, and attributes, made with calm majesty, though he knew it was to seal his condemnation, and open the immediate way to his death. https://biblehub.com/commentaries/matthew/26-64.htm.
404. See Psalm 22. Especially verse 6 and following.
405. Regarding the word "pierced" in Psalm 22, please see the following scholarly commentary:
    [The] confusion is that the two Hebrew words for "pierced" and "lion" are remarkably similar. All that separates the two Hebrew words is the length of an upright vowel stroke. A majority of Hebrew manuscripts, from the Masoretic text, of Psalm 22 have the "lion" reading, while a minority of manuscripts contain the "pierced" reading. Even though the Hebrew manuscripts that say "lion" outnumber the manuscripts that

say "pierced," **the older Hebrew manuscripts, and manu-scripts in other languages that predate most of the Hebrew manuscripts, strongly argue for "pierced" being the correct reading.** The Dead Sea Scrolls, which predate most other Hebrew texts by over a thousand years, note that the term is unmistakably "pierced." In addition, the oldest Syriac, Vulgate, Ethiopic, and Arabic versions also go with "pierced." The same is true in the Septuagint, the first Greek translation of the Hebrew Scriptures, which was completed approximately 200 years before the birth of Christ. Those who argue for "lion" typically claim that "pierced" is a corruption, inserted by Christians, in an attempt to create a prophecy about Jesus. However, the fact that there are many manuscripts that predate Christianity that have the "pierced" reading disproves this concept. In fact, it is more likely that the "lion" reading in the Masoretic Hebrew text is the corruption, as the Masoretic ma5nuscripts predominantly date to the 3rd and 4th centuries AD, after Christianity was established, giving the Jews a reason to conceal what the Hebrew Scriptures predict regarding Jesus Christ. Two things about all this solidify for us that "pierced" is the correct translation: 1) within its context, this word makes sense of the whole passage and agrees with the rest of Scripture, and 2) the mere fact that the Dead Sea Scrolls support this rendering and none other, especially that of "lion," leaves no doubt that our modern versions have it right. https://www.gotquestions.org/Psalm-22-16-lion-pierced.html.

Also see https://www.oneforisrael.org/bible-based-teaching-from-israel/psalm-22-a-prophecy-about-jesus-crucifixion.

406. Psalm 22:8.
407. Bar, Eitan. "Psalm 22 A Prophecy About Jesus' Crucifixion," One For Israel, Accessed January 12, 2019, https://www.oneforisrael.org/bible-based-teaching-from-israel/psalm-22-a-prophecy-about-jesus-crucifixion.
408. Matthew 27:54.
409. See my book, *Gods and Thrones* (Defender Publishing, October 2017)255–264 for a detailed biblical examination of why Jesus was on the earth for exactly forty days after His resurrection.

410. Thomas Alfred Gurney. "The Church of the First Three Centuries," (Sagwan Press, February 9, 2018) 40.

411. John. "Fox's Book of Martyrs," Bible Study Tools, https://www.biblestudytools.com/history/foxs-book-of-martyrs/john.html.

412. The region of the seven churches to which the book of Revelation was addressed was a province of the Roman Empire called Asia Minor. Today it is called Turkey. Turkey is where the headwaters of the Euphrates River form. It is also the place where Noah's ark finally came to rest, and from where the world began again. It later became the central starting point of the Ottoman Empire, an Islamic controlled empire that was spread over three continents and two million square miles. Today Turkey is a vital part of the OIC (Organization of Islamic Cooperation). The OIC was founded in 1969, consisting of fifty-seven member states, with a collective population of over 1.8 billion. A number of biblical scholars and prophecy watchers consider modern Turkey to be a central player in end-time prophecy culmination. They see it as a resurrecting Ottoman Empire and a direct threat to the prophetically returned nation of Israel, as well as the overall stability of the Middle East. In 2018, after the return of Jerusalem as the official and legal capital of Israel—the OIC immediately breathed out threats of war against Israel. Turkey's capitol, Ankara, is exactly due north of Jerusalem. The prophecies of Ezekiel 38 speak of the end-times coalition attack against Jerusalem originating from the "north." This is the area to whom the book of Revelation was originally addressed.
Edroos, Faisal. "Erdogan Calls on Muslim Countries to Unite and Confront Israel," Al Jazeera, May 18, 2018, https://www.aljazeera.com/news/2018/05/erdogan-calls-muslim-countries-unite-confront-israel-180518185258629.html.
YeniSafak, Editor. "What if a Muslim army was established against Israel? If the member states of the OIC unite militarily, they will form the world's largest and most comprehensive army" 12-12-17, https://www.yenisafak.com/en/world/what-if-a-muslim-army-was-established-against-israel-2890448. (Yeni Şafak is a conservative Turkish daily newspaper. The newspaper is known for its hardline support of President Recep Tayyip Erdoğan and the AK Parti).

413. Ezekiel 28:18–19; Isaiah 14:12–17; Revelation 20:10–15.

414. For example: Daniel 10:8–12.

415. John 21:22.

416. See: Isaiah 65:17; Isaiah 66:22; Revelation 21:1–2.

    Barnes' Notes on the Bible

    There are plans and purposes of God which are yet made known to none of his creatures. https://biblehub.com/commentaries/1_peter/1-12.htm.

    Barnes' Notes on the Bible

    If an inhabitant of the earth should dwell after death in any other of the worlds now existing, it would be to him a "new" abode, and everything would appear new.... The same thing would occur if he were to dwell on any other of the heavenly bodies, or if he were to pass from world to world.... No one can prove that this may not be.... there is no evidence that [planet earth] will be their permanent and eternal home or that even all the redeemed will at any one time find a home on this globe. https://biblehub.com/commentaries/2_peter/3-13.htm.

417. See: 1 John 3:2, Matthew 22:30, Romans 8:17.

OTHER BOOKS BY CARL GALLUPS
AND DEFENDER PUBLISHING

Gods and Thrones

Gods of Ground Zero

The Rabbi, the Secret Message, and the Identity of Messiah